THE CLUMSY CHILD

A program of motor therapy

THE CLUMSY CHILD

A program of motor therapy

DANIEL D. ARNHEIM, D.P.E., F.A.C.S.M., F.A.C.T.A.

Professor of Physical Education and former
Director of the Institute for Sensory Motor
Development, California State University,
Long Beach; Director of Sensorimotor Therapy,
Infant-Child Development, Inc.,
Irvine, California

WILLIAM A. SINCLAIR, Ph.D.

Associate Professor of Physical Education and
Director of the Institute for Sensory Motor
Development, California State University,
Long Beach, California

with 205 *illustrations*

The C. V. Mosby Company

Saint Louis   1975

Library of Congress Cataloging in Publication Data

Arnheim, Daniel D
    The clumsy child.

    Bibliography: p.
    Includes index.
    1. Psychomotor disorders. 2. Movement disorders.
3. Gymnastics, medical. I. Sinclair, William Andrew,
1938-   joint author. II. Title. [DNLM: 1. Motor
skills—In infancy and childhood. 2. Physical education and training—In infancy and childhood. WE103
A748c]
RJ506.P68A76   618.9′27′40624   75-4890
ISBN 0-8016-0314-5

GW/M/M 9 8 7 6 5 4 3 2 1

*To the professional
who is concerned with physical awkwardness
and its effect on the child's total development*

PREFACE

This book is designed to be used by the classroom teacher and the special educator as well as the physical education specialist. In every classroom or physical education program there is one child or several children who are "play failures" and perform most typical motor skills ineffectively. In the past these children were relegated to the lowest social position in their group. Unable to participate satisfactorily in physical activities, these children are often devastated by a sense of worthlessness and defeat. It is to assist these children that this book has been developed.

Approaches and methodologies presented are based on our many years of experience in working with children who were referred to us because of their physical clumsiness.

This book represents a foundation for the burgeoning field of motor therapy and is presented as a practical and working model for the professional person concerned with movement efficiency in children. *The Clumsy Child* is designed to be used as a basic text in the area of motor therapy and as an adjunct to current elementary and adapted physical education texts.

The purpose of this book is to enable the teacher to assist the child who, because of physical, mental, or emotional factors, is clumsy in his motor behavior. This clumsiness inhibits the effective learning of motor skills. We are staggered by the number of individuals who are limited in experiencing a fulfilling life because of their inefficient motor performance.

The physically awkward or clumsy individual may also have further impairing learning disabilities, mental deficiencies, or minimal physical handicaps as well as emotional problems. Clumsiness may also be associated with minimal cerebral dysfunctions, dyslexia, perceptual disorders, aphasia, visual or hearing defects, mental retardation, emotional disturbances, or cultural deprivation. Excluded from this list would be obvious physical handicaps resulting from serious brain injury or orthopedic impairment. The problems of cerebral palsy and crippling conditions requiring locomotion by crutch or other conveyances should obviously be excluded from the category of physical clumsiness. We seek to help that child who initially might be considered physically, mentally, and emotionally normal, yet who is unable to effectively carry out some typical motor tasks required in play, home, or classroom.

The portion of movement education that is concerned with the clumsy person is described in this book as motor therapy. The primary purpose of this therapy is to modify an individual's movement behavior. Motor therapy provides a prescriptive program of selected developmental motor activities that are specifically designed to be employed for a particular movement ability level. Movement efficiency is progressively gained by the participant accomplishing one task at a time and then building a more difficult task on the completed task until a specific skill is acquired. Motor therapy assists the child in integrating specific tasks into efficient patterns of motor behavior that are essential for carrying out more complicated coordinated acts. The participant in the motor therapy program is provided with a positive nonfailure atmosphere. Tasks are selected on the basis of what can be achieved by the participant without failure. If failure is imminent, then activity difficulties are reduced to the extent that success is possible. Confidence in the ability of the body to do the mind's will and a positive self-concept and body image are the most important outcomes of the motor development program for the clumsy child.

This book is structured to implement the foregoing objectives. Part I, The Focus, is concerned with providing a basis for understanding the many major ramifications inherent in the problems of physical clumsiness. Discussed are some selected factors in motor development, reasons for clumsiness, approaches that are directly or indirectly concerned with movement efficiency, a review of selected tests designed to assess the clumsy child, a description of learning in the psychomotor domain emphasizing motor learning characteristics of the clumsy child, and successful teaching or therapy approaches. Part II, The Motor Therapy Program, presents step-by-step procedures that can be easily followed by an instructor or therapist interested in establishing and carrying out a successful remedial program. It includes organizational and administrative suggestions, diagnostic procedures, and additional content necessary for an effective program. Part III, Motor Therapy Task Categories, presents prescriptive techniques using motor tasks that are sequenced in the order of their complexity. Each category is presented in such a manner that the remediation specialist can make activity selections based on a particular child's maturation and developmental level. To increase the usefulness of this book, a glossary of important and unique terms is included as well as a bibliography.

Sincere appreciation is extended to students, colleagues, and friends who gave their time to read and evaluate the contents of this book, especially to Mrs. Jane Beck, Mrs. Helene Arnheim, Mrs. Marilyn Sinclair, and Mrs. Robyn Mack for their assistance in preparing the manuscript.

Daniel D. Arnheim
William A. Sinclair

CONTENTS

PART I

THE FOCUS

Part I is designed to give the reader pertinent information on motor development and a definition of physical clumsiness. It also reviews current fields of understanding in the area of inefficient motor behavior and sets the stage for developing an effective program of remediation.

1

MOTOR BEHAVIOR

The unborn infant becomes a unique entity through orderly cell division, differentiation, and tissue integration. The fetus undergoes a progressive differentiation of cells, tissues, and organs until outward features and limbs are developed that are eventually controlled by a highly complex nervous system.

The first diffusion of undifferentiated cells becomes organized and interrelated into highly complex organs and systems. Physical development and maturational direction occur from head to foot and from the center of the body outward. Movement control follows this same line of developmental direction. The unborn infant first displays movement of the head followed by movement of the back, the arms, and then the legs. This same pattern of developmental direction and integration continues after birth until full movement maturity is finally acquired. Ideally, from gross, undifferentiated, and uncoordinated movement emerge efficient and highly coordinated movement patterns. Along with the head-to-feet and middle-to-outward body control development, the individual gains control first of the large muscles of the body and then of the smaller muscles.

Early motor behavior of the newborn infant is primarily controlled by reflexes. Conscious control of motor acts has a direct relationship to physical maturation. The newborn is dominated by reflex behavior, out of which gradually emerges conscious body control. The highly coordinated movement patterns necessary for locomotion initially emerge from immature reflex patterns (Cratty, 1970). Each movement milestone that the child accomplishes is dependent on physical maturation as well as the opportunity to experience a specific act. Many of the reflexes found in the neonate are based in survival, for example, breathing, yawning, coughing, sneezing, rooting, and sucking; according to evolutionists, others appear to be remnants of lower primate life. Still other reflexes in the very young infant provide a basis for eventually achieving the upright posture. The infant is dominated by its primitive reflexes, movement being determined by the spinal and brain stem levels of the central nervous system. Gradually, however, midbrain and cortical control take over as the child gains in postural control and changes from a completely grounded organism to one that is able to effectively transport itself in the upright position (Fiorentino, 1963).

The infant ultimately seeks movement independence with the ability to move about the environment freely, but he is initially almost completely dominated by

Fig. 1-1. Sensory stimulation through a variety of movement experiences.

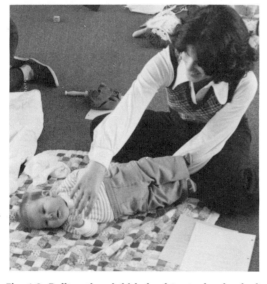

Fig. 1-2. Rolling the child helps him to develop body control.

the force of gravity. To reach and enjoy full motor maturity, the infant must receive constant stimulation that comes from experiencing a rich variety of stimuli (Figs. 1-1 and 1-2). From a relatively uncontrolled, purposeless physical attitude the newborn slowly gains control of its limbs and from unintentional squirming develops the ability to purposefully roll over. From the ability to lift the head and move the arms in a purposeful manner comes skill in transporting the body about the terrain. By pushing with the legs while pulling and reaching with the arms, the infant is able to propel himself in an unsophisticated manner about the crib or floor.

Each new skill develops from a less organized skill. This is true of every learned motor task that the infant or child will attempt to accomplish. From the rudimentary locomotor technique of crawling the child eventually acquires the ability to maintain a balanced position on his hands and knees, a considerably less stable attitude than that of reclining. Maturation then allows the infant to precariously move from the quadrupedal position (Fig. 1-3) to a bipedal posture. Pulling himself up against the pressures of gravity, the infant is gradually able to maintain balance, first on the knees and then finally standing unsteadily on the two small surface areas of the feet. In all, 9 to 12 months of practice and maturation may be necessary before the infant is able to perform the transition from the confined reclining posture to that of standing and moving about in the upright posture, one of man's greatest achievements. The infant is then free to explore with the hands and fully experience the delights of the environment. (See Fig. 1-4.)

The ability to effectively manipulate objects is also extremely important to an individual's eventual movement sophistication. Grasping and releasing objects at will is the beginning of efficient object management. Before 2 months of life the infant reflexively grasps an object when pressure

Fig. 1-3. Locomotion in the quadrupedal position.

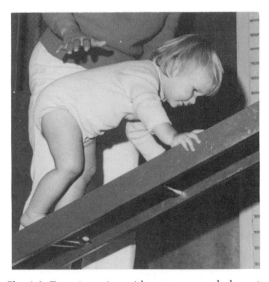

Fig. 1-4. Experimenting with new ways and places to transport the body.

is applied to the palm of the hand. Later the infant can grasp an object with just the fingers. The thumb does not begin to oppose or become actively involved in the grasping act until about 16 months and is not really proficient until 2 years of age. The ability to effectively deal with objects or projectiles in space requires a highly complex interweaving of visual, tactile, manipulative, and large-muscle control.

The senses of smelling, tasting, seeing, hearing, feeling, and moving must be intact if the human organism is to adequately select and process information provided by the body and its environment. Seeing, hearing, touching, and possibly smelling and tasting act individually or in combination to alert the organism to danger as well as serve to guide the organism in carrying out a purposeful motor act. The most important sense organs to the acquisition of skilled movement are the organs of vision, touch, and *kinesthesis,* or the sense of movement. Hearing, or audition, is important but not as important as the aforementioned three sense organs.

The ocular-motor system consists of six coordinated pairs of eye muscles that function together in allowing the organism to accurately view and respond to the environment. The teaming of the two eyes in a coordinated manner allows them to accommodate incoming light and to properly guide the body, especially the limbs, in executing coordinated movements. Besides ocular-motor coordination, the eyes assist the individual in the balance process, working closely with the righting reflexes initiated by the inner ear and the muscle receptors located within the neck in providing the organism with spatial and postural awareness.

Touch, or tactile sense, provides the organism with valuable information through the skin surfaces of the body. Discrimination through touch is known as *stereognosis;* it is accomplished by identification of familiar objects through manipulation by the fingers and hands. The combination of the senses of tactility and kinesthesis, or movement, is known as the *haptic sense* and is essential to the activities of play and work.

The kinesthetic sense provides the organism with the awareness of body movement and its relative position in space. Organs called *proprioceptors,* located in muscles, tendons, joints, and the *semicircular canals* of the inner ear, provide the organism with a constant stream of information about movement. Without proprioceptors the body would lose its postural orientation and muscle tone. Without the sense of body orientation and muscle tone the individual would be unable to maintain equilibrium.

Hearing, or audition, provides the organism with a means to localize and discriminate sound. Auditory development is closely associated with language development. Without an intact hearing organ the individual finds difficulty in socializing and in following directions. The hearing-impaired person encounters difficulty in game situations or in social interaction situations that require the following of rules and discrete procedures.

The *perceptual-motor process* is the accurate processing of information that comes to the individual through his sense organs. Response to perceptual-motor processing is based on the individual's past experience. Information coming to the organism through the sense organs must be recognized, identified, and discriminated before it can be specifically utilized by the central nervous system. The information that is processed becomes integrated and compared with previously stored information; then it becomes available for immediate or future use, depending on the needs of the organism. Perception is continually being modified with a constant flow or feedback of information to meet these needs. "Perception is the integer between a child and its environment. It enables him to interpret objects and events and assists him in his learning capabilities" (Arnheim et al., 1973).

Essential to the development of motor behavior is the stimulus that comes from socialization. Humans are by nature gregarious, a trait that is apparent in a range of activities from the first smile that is expressed to a familiar face to the ability to interact in highly complicated social situations. Play is necessary for motor development as well as essential to the weaving of the psychosocial milieu so important to a positive self-concept and emotional stability. From the egocentricity of the infant and the side-by-side play of the toddler gradually emerges the ability to interact, to give and take graciously, to follow, to lead, and to compete under rigid rules of conduct.

2

WHY CLUMSINESS?

Why clumsiness? There is no simple answer to this question; skilled movement involves an intricate weaving of physiological and psychological components and must be judged by the factors of culture, age, sex, maturation, and past experience plus expectations stemming from the environment. A great deal of study and careful thought must be given before an individual is judged to have a motor impairment. A person's movement ability may be compared against standards that are not typical for the specific population in which he may normally function.

"The problem of motor impairment is one that has been created by the demands made upon the individual to learn certain skills that are regarded as important, or at least desirable from a normal developmental viewpoint" (Morris and Whiting, 1971).

Before discussing the primary causes of physical clumsiness, the terms "impairment," "disability," and "handicap" should be defined and clarified. An impairment is considered a disruption in the normal functioning of the organism; on the other hand, disability refers to a physical deviation that

can be described clinically. The restrictions imposed by a disability that may prevent the individual from achieving his full potential result in a handicap. Often the handicap is self-imposed; that is, the individual's personal feelings about his problem keep him from achieving a particular goal. Therefore, in essence, physical clumsiness may or may not be a handicap.

Many of the factors that result in mental retardation, organic behavioral disorders, epilepsy, and cerebral palsy can produce physical clumsiness. There are many causes of dysfunctions within the nervous system and developmental and maturational lags resulting in clumsiness. Countless factors can adversely alter the integrity of the infant's nervous system and result in motor impairment.

In general, fetal growth can be divided into three basic phases: hyperplasia (cell proliferation), decline of hyperplasia, and increase of cell size, or hypertrophy (Hughes, 1971). An increase in the number of cells occurs predominantly within the first 12 weeks of life, commonly known as the embryonic stage, while the last 6 months, or fetal period, are concerned with cellular size.

Although it is not the intent of this book to detail all the disease factors related to the unborn and newly delivered infant, it is necessary to give the reader some of the major factors that may eventually lead to physical clumsiness.

MATERNAL FACTORS

Maternal abnormalities and disorders that can adversely affect the unborn child are numerous. Mothers with a past history of abnormal deliveries have a higher incidence of defective children than those with a history of normal deliveries. Haynes (1967) points out that mothers under the age of 16 or over the age of 36 having their first child or those over 40 who have had several children run a higher risk of having a neurologically defective child. Also, statistics show that height and weight of the mother can adversely affect pregnancy and birth; for example, taller mothers gaining less pregnancy weight offer less hazards to their infant than shorter mothers who gain relatively more weight. Chronic organic disorders such as diabetes mellitus or various endocrine disorders in the mother can result in high-risk pregnancies and developmental defects. Viral infections, particularly rubella (German measles) and influenza, play an important role by increasing the risk of abnormal pregnancies. The spirochete of syphilis is also devastating to fetal development. The wide variety of legal and illegal drugs consumed plays an increasing role in causing fetal defects. A mother who is addicted to morphine or heroin will probably have an infant dependent on that drug, while barbiturates may depress the unborn infant's central nervous system, causing respiratory distress and anoxia. Overuse of an antibiotic such as streptomycin can produce such sensory disorders in the newborn as deafness, whereas excessive use of vitamin D by the mother may produce cardiac defects, mental retardation, and various sensory abnormalities in the fetus.

Large doses of aspirin or cigarette smoking may be a primary cause of low birth weight infants.

Toxemia, or poisoning due to pregnancy, is characterized in the mother by hypertension, an increase of fluid in the tissues, and protein in the urine with occasional convulsions and even coma. These conditions may adversely affect not only her health but also that of the fetus. Constant vomiting on the part of the mother followed by an upset in metabolism may eventually lead to weight loss, dehydration, liver impairment, and subsequent retardation in the growth and development of the fetus.

Multiple births also increase the chances of developmental disabilities as well as organ disorders (McLennan and Sandburg, 1974). In twin pregnancies, for example, premature labor often occurs, and an excess of amniotic fluid leads to an overstretching of the uterus, increasing the probability of malpresentations of one or both babies. In most cases a multiple pregnancy compounds the risk to both the mother and children; however, the risk to both fetuses is not the same because one is usually in a better position for birth than is the other.

An excessive amount of amniotic fluid is often an indication that there is a fetal defect, or it may produce abnormalities in the normal fetus. For normal fetal growth to occur there must be good metabolism stemming from a normally functioning placenta. Fetal respiration is dependent on the integrity of the placental vessels that provide a good exchange of oxygen and carbon dioxide between mother and child. Impairment in the ability to maintain good circulation between mother and fetus may result in serious developmental problems.

The Rh blood factor can result in incompatibility of the mother and her fetus, resulting in tissue death and giving rise to stillbirth or the condition known as erythroblastosis fetalis. Approximately 85% of humans are Rh positive, while 15% are considered Rh negative. An Rh-negative pregnant woman may become sensitized by the blood of an Rh-positive fetus and in each additional pregnancy develop more sensitivity until there is a rejection of the fetus by the mother. In extreme cases the baby is born dead; however, in less severe conditions the baby may be born alive but become severely jaundiced, or yellow colored, within the first 24 hours after birth (*kernicterus*), a condition that can lead to death or the development of varying degrees of neurological dysfunctions.

As indicated, the probability of an unborn child having developmental disorders is very high. When one considers that over 10 million children and adults in the United States are afflicted by some major central nervous system disorder, it is not difficult to imagine that there are many more who have less obvious, subtle problems resulting in minimal nervous system dysfunctions.

FACTORS RELATING TO LABOR AND DELIVERY

Labor is the process by which the infant and placenta are expelled from the mother's body. Before the actual labor begins, there occurs a lightening or settling process by which the head of the infant moves into the brim of the pelvis. The labor process itself is divided into three stages. The first stage is a period during which the infant, in putting pressure on the lower end of the uterus, begins to stretch its way outward. As it does so the uterus walls become thinner and the external opening begins to dilate. The pressure becomes so great that the sac membrane, which is compressed with liquid, eventually ruptures. Downward movement of the infant is directed by contractions of the uterus muscles that increase in frequency from one every 15 to 30 minutes in the early labor period to one or more per minute in the later stage of the process. As labor proceeds the contractions increase in length from 30 to 90 seconds. The second stage of labor is the actual

expulsion of the infant. Following the rupture of the fluid membrane there is a temporary cessation of pain, and then the contractions recur with greater force and frequency. The infant is carried through the birth canal by the force of each uterine contraction in combination with a voluntary abdominal and diaphragm muscle contraction. As the infant makes its torturous way through the birth canal, the primary force of the contraction is at first on the spinal column and then on the head. The curve of the infant's spine straightens until its head impinges on the mother's pelvic floor. After about an hour in this position, additional contractions make the scalp visible. The head of the infant emerges from the mother in an extended position, face down. As birth takes place, the infant's neck turns, bringing the head to one side, followed by an internal rotation of both shoulders and the emergence of one shoulder, and then the other. The third and last stage brings forth the placenta about 5 to 30 minutes following the birth of the infant.

The length of labor varies according to each mother's unique characteristics; however, the average for the woman having her first child (*primigravida*) is 13 hours. For the woman who already has at least one child (*multigravida*) the average time ranges from 4 to 8 hours. Labor that lasts longer than 18 hours in the primigravida or 8 hours in the multigravida increases the health risk to the child.

Precipitate labor is the result of an excessively forceful contraction during labor. Labor that is too rapid or contractions that are too vigorous can result in lacerations to the soft tissues of the infant's skull. This head trauma may also lead to permanent brain injury. In contrast, labor that is too slow indicates uterine inertia, a condition in which there is an inadequate amount of muscular force for the proper expulsion of the infant. The birth canal may also be blocked by an abnormally narrow bony pelvis or soft tissue that provides unusual resistance. If the infant is not expelled in a reasonable time, special means might have to be taken by the physician.

It is commonly accepted that the use of forceps in delivery increases the risk to the infant. The primary function of the forceps is to assist the delivery process when the infant or mother is in danger as a result of labor that lasts too long. The use of forceps has increased with the widespread use of spinal or caudal anesthesia, which often causes the mother to be unable to exert normal voluntary muscular contractions needed to complete the second stage of labor. The forceps may be used without proper indications, more as a matter of convenience than need. The use of such an instrument may cause the infant to have cerebral hemorrhage or skull lacerations, thereby increasing the probability of central nervous system injuries, fracture of the skull or neck, or permanent injury to the growth areas of the long bones. It may also permanently injure nerves and cause paralysis.

In obstetric situations care must be taken in the use of anesthetics. The unborn infant is particularly sensitive to sedating drugs given to the mother and reacts by developing respiratory depression. In certain cases an anesthetic may even inhibit or completely stop uterine contractions. Most physicians agree that the use of anesthetics in obstetrics must be held to a minimum.

Of all the abnormal presentations occurring in human births, the breech type has the highest incidence, between 2.5% and 4% of all deliveries. There are many types of breech presentations; however, the most common are feet presentation, buttocks presentation, one-foot presentation, and knee presentation. Because of the abnormal position of the infant within the mother, a breech birth can present many dangers to the mother as well as the child. Fetal mortality is three times as great in breech births as in the normal frontal position and is caused most often by pressure on the umbilical cord that produces a depression of the fetal heart rate and increases the probability of cerebral hemorrhage.

It has been determined that a cesarean delivery, or the removal of the baby through an incision in the uterus and abdominal wall, produces more of a risk to the infant than a normal delivery. The choice of this procedure is usually made when there is a danger to the mother or infant. In this procedure, risk to the infant is greatly increased by the circumstances that led the physician to select surgery.

Another common cause of injury to the infant is premature expulsion or prolapse of the umbilical cord through the birth canal. The cause of this prolapse is variable; abnormalities in fetal presentation, an increased amount of amniotic fluid, or perhaps a deformed pelvis may be the cause. Such an occurrence can endanger circulation, result in a decrease in the amount of oxygen and cause permanent nervous tissue destruction.

Prematurity is a major risk to the unborn infant. A birth weight of 4½ pounds or less indicates prematurity. An infant is considered premature if it is born before the thirty-seventh gestational week. The premature infant may suffer chronic asphyxia in the mother and sustain severe respiratory depression at birth. It has been determined that smaller undergrown infants also have a higher incidence of congenital anomalies. Some of the more common causes of lower birth weight are fetal anoxia and placental abnormalities that prevent the adequate exchange of nutriments through the placenta. Hughes (1971) reports that growth retardation has been demonstrated in infants of mothers who consume 20 or more cigarettes daily; smoking apparently causes a restriction of blood vessels and diminution of the adequate transfer of the nutriments from the mother to the infant via the placenta.

A common practice in many hospitals is to use the Apgar scoring system to aid in appraising the condition of the newborn infant (Apgar, 1953). The Apgar system provides an index based on the newborn's

Table 1. Apgar scoring chart to identify high-risk babies

Sign	Score 0	Score 1	Score 2
Heart rate	Absent	Slow (below 100)	Over 100
Respiratory effort	Absent	Slow, irregular; hypoventilation	Good; crying lustily
Muscle tone	Flaccid	Some flexion of extremities	Active motion, well flexed
Reflex irritability	No response	Cry; some motion	Vigorous cry
Color	Blue, pale	Body pink, hands and feet blue	Completely pink

heart rate, respiratory effort, muscle, reflex response, and color. The evaluation is made 1 minute after delivery. A score from 0 to 2 is given for each sign; a total score of 10 indicates that the newborn is in optimal condition, while a score of 4 or lower indicates the probability of the baby having physical problems. (See Table 1.) Haynes (1967) points out that 10% of newborn infants have an Apgar rating of 7 or better. On the other hand, infants with a very low Apgar score are often found to have neurological abnormalities and are therefore considered to be high-risk infants.

The signs of central nervous system dysfunction in the newborn often are reflected early by the presence of either poor muscle tone or an increase or unevenness of muscle tone throughout the body. Other more overt signs of neurological dysfunction are such characteristics as back arching, muscle twitching, convulsions, a weak or shrill cry, a staring gaze, excess irritability or lethargy, and the presence of abnormal reflex responses that may be present singly or in combination.

PSYCHOSOCIAL FACTORS IN DEVELOPMENT

Besides the actual physical risk to the unborn and newborn in terms of developmental disabilities and neurological dysfunctions, one cannot dismiss emotional and social influences. If a mother is in a lower socioeconomic class, is unmarried, has an unwanted pregnancy, has emotional or psychiatric disorders, or has a problem with alcoholism or drug addiction, the chances of an infant being defective are increased. Although research is not conclusive as to the exact effects of continued adverse emotional stress on the unborn infant, there are indications that the incidence of in utero problems as well as birth difficulties is increased. It can be speculated that emotional stress over a long period of time can disturb the intricate physiological balance between the mother and fetus, disrupting normal growth and increasing the possibility of permanent impairment (Morris and Whiting, 1971). Unfortunately a child who has had a stressful 9 months within the mother often comes into the world as a new human being in distress, both physically and emotionally.

The psychosocial milestones of the individual can be considered to be dependence, autonomy, sexual adjustment, and the adjustment to agression. The first 6 months of the infant's life is a period of almost complete dependence. During this period the baby is primarily concerned with satisfying the biological needs of hunger, warmth, and comfort. At this time the new person learns to trust or mistrust his surroundings. If the infant is in some way deprived or unable to satisfy his basic needs, he begins to question and mistrust the environment.

Gradually the infant seeks independence as a person. As self-awareness occurs within the child, he gradually strives for control of the immediate surroundings. This is a time when there should be an encouraging and accepting environment plus one that guides and assists in helping the young child to accept discipline. During this time complete freedom of expression and egocentricity is abnormal and unreasonable; conversely, complete thwarting of attempts at independence produces abnormal fears and rigidity of personality. "The right amount of discipline and freedom becomes a subtle matter of creating or establishing a firm but loving and accepting environment" (Arnheim et al., 1973).

The period of becoming autonomous and learning discipline continues throughout life but is most obvious from childhood to the puberty period, at which time the important psychological stage of sexual development becomes paramount in the life of the individual. During puberty the individual views himself in a new way, stimulated by the powerful physiological changes taking place within the body. During this period feelings about the body become exaggerated.

The last of the major psychological growth stages to be considered is the development of the ability to successfully manage aggression. Aggression is defined as an emotional feeling of anger and hostility stemming from frustration. From the earliest days of life every individual must deal with frustration. Ideally the individual will learn to cope with aggressive behavior in a socially acceptable way. For this to be accomplished anger must be understood as to its exact cause and directed toward positive rather than negative expressions; therefore, in order for the child to function in a physically efficient manner and without undue emotional tensions stemming from frustrations, his basic needs must be satisfied.

One of the most important needs of the growing child is to know and feel *love* and *affection* from the persons who are most close to him. Love means being fully accepted as an individual and having the basic needs of food, shelter, and clothing satisfied. It also means being listened to, played with, and provided with a sense of warmth and security.

Children must feel that they are *accepted,* no matter what their capabilities or disabilities. It is important that a child feel he is not being put into a mold made by his parents and that he has the opportunity to solve problems utilizing his own individual strengths and weaknesses. A child must not feel that he is being forced into the image of the parent, but be allowed to develop enough ego strength so that he is able to accept failure and either try again or go in a different direction without a sense of guilt. Unreasonable expectations in academics or sports can only create abnormal tensions and emotional problems within the child. Encouragement and opportunities should be provided and standards for levels of attainment established, but the child should become self-motivated, setting and striving to attain his own goals without the external prodding of overly eager parents. Above all, the child needs to feel worthy and important in the eyes of those that are closest to him. Having *self-respect* means having a positive self-concept in which he can accept himself for what he is and not be plagued by feelings of inferiority, timidity, or overaggressiveness. The child with self-respect has enough ego strength so that he is willing to take a chance on failing.

Basic to the child's development is the *need to achieve.* Life is based on milestones and periods of achievements. From the time of birth, individuals are goal seekers, and every child should have the opportunity to set and accomplish personal goals without continual guiding influences from some outside force. Overprotection by the parents can thwart a child's natural inclination for adventure and new learning experiences. All human beings need to be *recognized for their achievements.* The neglected child, not recognized for any achievements, often lives in a void without either approval or disapproval. Hughes (1971), in discussing the emotional development of children, states "the child is his parent's most important business. If this business is neglected, there is bound to be a bankruptcy of affection."

PSYCHOSOCIAL FACTORS AND PHYSICAL CLUMSINESS

How a person feels and thinks about himself is reflected in his movement behavior, such as an emotion resulting in a minor increase in muscle tension, a flick of an eyelid, or a gesture. Physical clumsiness can also be caused by adverse emotional stress. It is often very difficult to ascertain whether or not a child's clumsiness stems from some neurological dysfunction or whether it is a reflection of how he feels about himself. Quite frequently clumsiness stems from both neurophysiological dysfunctions and the psychological response to having these dysfunctions. A whole system of psychotherapeutics has been developed to deal with the physical expression of psychological problems manifested in body structure and movement of the patient. This system is termed bioenergetic therapy (Lowen, 1958).

Expectations of the child

Parents who set unreasonable expectations for their children often become disappointed when they fail. Parental disappointment does not go undetected by sensitive children. Knowing that they have displeased their parents or that they will not achieve at the level expected, children may become anxious and tense and reflect these feelings by clumsy, asynchronous motor behavior. The "klutz" in our society is characterized as a person who, no matter what he physically attempts to do, muffs it up in some way. He lacks confidence in his actions and displays unpredictable motor responses in tense situations, especially when being observed or in some way trying to make a good impression. Typically, the "klutz" has a very poor self-concept accompanied by feelings of belittlement, particu-

larly when in the presence of a superiorly skilled person.

The abused child

Hughes (1971) estimates that 10% or more of the children under 5 years of age who are seen in pediatric emergency rooms fall into the category of having been battered or physically mistreated. This type of child has been called "the battered child" or is said to suffer from the "maltreatment syndrome." Among the maltreatment areas are deprivation of food and/or shelter and physical abuse by an adult. Prolonged abuse often causes permanent physical and psychological damage. Besides physical trauma that may include bruises, fractures, or severe dislocations as well as permanent brain injury, the emotional and psychological trauma is incalculable. The abused child often reflects his neglect in severe anxiety, muscular tension, a rigidity of posture, and/or a clumsiness in his motor behavior. The hostility he feels from the environment may cause him to thrash out in bursts of anger or, conversely, to withdraw into a protective shell.

CEREBRAL DYSFUNCTIONS

Although "cerebral palsy" has been used as a blanket term since it was first suggested by William Little, an English surgeon, before the turn of the century, it has gradually come into disuse. Literally, cerebral palsy means "paralysis of the cerebrum." In the last few years a movement spearheaded by Denhoff (1967) has brought the more descriptive term "cerebral dysfunction" into greater use; it encompasses cerebral palsy, mental deficiency, epilepsy, hyperkinetic behavior disorders, and visual, auditory, and perceptual problems.

Neuromotor disorders

Neuromotor disorders are commonly caused by injuries that occur during pregnancy, labor, delivery, or the early childhood period. Neuromotor disorders vary in intensity according to the degree of trauma. Identifying characteristics range from very "hard" signs such as muscle spasticity or uncontrolled movement to the subtle disorders or "soft" signs that may be found in learning problems or clumsiness. Dysfunctions may lie in different brain centers such as the *motor cortex, basal ganglia,* or *cerebellum,* and they may stem from a brain lesion or a lag in neurological development. Individuals with a neuromotor disorder can have a variety of symptoms such as an increase or decrease in muscle tone, inability to effectively move one or more of the body segments, or associated problems of limb rigidity and hand tremors. Hughes (1971) indicates that about one to five major neuromotor disorders occur in every 1,000 live births; the causes were enumerated in the discussion of the high-risk baby.

The severely brain-damaged child is in most cases multiply disabled, with two or more identifiable impairments. Accompanying brain damage may cause mental deficiency, convulsions, perceptual disabilities, and learning disabilities as well as behavioral problems.

Convulsive disorders

When discussing the syndromes of cerebral dysfunction resulting in movement problems, one has to consider the area of convulsive disorders, generally termed in the past as epilepsy. The primary reason for including convulsive disorders in this book is the affects that some types have on learning and motor behavior. Convulsions, or seizures, are caused by an imbalance in the brain's electrical potential that produces excessive neuronal discharge and various other clinical ramifications. The cause of these disorders is often unknown.

Impulse disorders

Commonly associated with cerebral dysfunction is the group of behavioral characteristics that come under the heading of hyperkinetic impulse disorders. These may originate from an organic cerebral dysfunction or may have genetic antecedents. Often associated with hyperkinetic impulse disorders is a lag in the child's physical growth and development. It is also interesting to note that boys demonstrate by far the highest incidence of hyperkinesis. Characteristically, there is short attention span, difficulty in concentration, impulsiveness with an inability to delay gratification, irritability, explosiveness, and associated neuromotor disturbances that may affect performance in school and at play.

The child displaying extremely immature emotional behavior with constant overactivity that appears to be compelled or involuntary may be considered to be *hyperactive.* Parents of this type of child commonly state that his motor development was quite advanced when compared to the norm, particularly in the locomotor skills of standing and walking, and usually occurred well before the child was 1 year of age. The child's behavior is typified by constant motion that is seemingly without purpose. He dashes here and there, picks up objects, drops them, and moves on to the next activity without attending to any one goal for more than a second or two.

Because the child is easily distracted and unable to focus attention on one object for any length of time, his power of concentration is minimal. The problem is due to the child's inability to filter out and select specific stimuli from the environment, making attention negligible and success in school almost impossible.

The hyperkinetic child is usually impulsive and has little inhibition, responding to stimulation without considering the consequence of his actions. It is almost impossible to delay gratifying his immediate wants. Typically, the hyperkinetic child has a very low toleration to frustration; he often has fits of anger without obvious provocation, the degree of reaction far exceeding the original stimulus.

Another problem that is associated with hyperkinetic behavior is that of preservation. This behavior is manifested by the child being unable to shift his attention from one stimulus to the next, becoming "locked into" one activity. Usually it is a motor task, especially one that is evenly sequenced and rhythmical such as ball bouncing. Schoolwork may be very difficult for the hyperkinetic child, particularly when it consists of visual-motor or auditory-motor perception tasks that ultimately cause problems in communication skills such as reading and writing. Clumsiness, while not always associated with the hyperkinetic impulse disorder, is commonly related to the child's inability to control his emotional behavior and inattention, which causes him to drop objects, trip over obstacles, or bump into things.

In contrast to the hyperkinetic child is the individual who is hypokinetic. The hypokinetic child is characteristically lacking in muscle tone, apathetic, and lethargic in behavior. In both problems there is an inability to effectively modulate energy output.

Minimal nervous system dysfunction

The term "minimal nervous system dysfunction" is an all-inclusive description of a wide range of conditions. Describing many characteristics included in the category "minimal brain dysfunction syndrome," Chalfant and Scheffelin (1969) list disorders in the processes of thought, conception, learning, memory, speech, language, attention, perception, emotional behavior, neuromuscular coordination, reading, writing, and arithmetic; discrepancy between intellectual achievement levels; developmental disparity; and physiological processes related to education. The term "minimal brain dysfunction syndrome" implies that there is a problem with information processing stemming from the child's functioning and not from specific neurological lesions or from environmental experiences. However, it must be noted that nervous system lesions are often difficult to pinpoint by current scientific methods. Therefore alterations within the nervous system could be

caused by scattered nerve cell damage rather than by a specific local destruction of the nerve sheath covering.

Before a child is designated as having minimal nervous system dysfunction, a careful neurological examination must be undertaken. Ideally, a pediatrician specializing in neurology should administer this examination, since only a highly trained eye can pick up the subtle signs that are characteristic of minimal nervous system dysfunction and differentiate them from developmental lags or mild mental retardation. Touwen and Prechtl (1970) have identified seven primary factors of minimal nervous system dysfunction.

Hemisyndrome or lateralization syndrome. A child with hemisyndrome reflects a group of signs that are displayed predominantly on one side of the body and may be identified by an increase or decrease in tendon reflexes as well as unilateral weakness in one limb. The greatest motor problems appear in large-muscle activities and, in some cases, difficulty in executing fine coordinated acts.

Dyskinesia. Defined as a deficiency in voluntary movement, dyskinesia is obviously present in many types of cerebral palsy and often occurs in minimal nervous system dysfunctions reflected in such aspects as variations in muscle tonicity and involuntary movements. The child with minimal nervous system dysfunction may have jerky or slow irregular movements of the fingers and wrist. Large muscles may also be affected, causing movements that are arrhythmical, writhing, irregular, or of the tremor type.

Synkinetic movement. Synkinetic or associated movement accompanies purposeful activity with a mirroring of these movements on the opposite side of the body. Synkinetic movement is particularly apparent when the child is asked to do fast repeated movements. It can also be seen when the child attempts a difficult balancing activity or a complex movement. Because synkinetic movements decrease with age, they are considered by many to be indications of nervous system immaturity. Therefore the presence of obvious mirroring in the execution of rapid movements may be considered an indication of developmental retardation. Occurrence of synkinetic movements on one side of the body and few or none on the other side may indicate the presence of obvious cerebral dominance or the presence of some cerebral dysfunction on one side of the body as compared to the other. Also related to synkinesis and maturational lag is the inability to effectively execute gross or fine motor tasks that would be expected for a specific age. On the other hand, defects in parts of the cerebellum and parietal lobes of the brain can also produce varying degrees of balance difficulties and clumsiness.

In general, the ability to execute static and dynamic balance activities, to make postural changes rapidly, and to execute fast sequential or rhythmical movements together with the use of small muscles required in manipulation indicate whether a child falls into the category of being clumsy. This is particularly obvious to parents when their child is unable to perform motor tasks such as tying shoelaces and undoing buttons at a certain age.

Auditory and visual perceptual disturbances affecting the child's ability to adequately process information and resulting in learning problems both in the cognitive and psychomotor domains are commonly associated with minimal nervous system dysfunction. These defects may originate at the point of sensory input or in perceptual processes of analysis, synthesis, and storage of selected data or in their expression in a motor act.

It is not uncommon that a child with minimal nervous system dysfunction often exhibits some inappropriate behavior as characterized by impulse disorders. Dysfunctions in the cerebral cortex can produce hyperkinesis; however, minimal nervous system dysfunction may produce emotional overlays not expected or directly related to a neurological lesion or cerebral disorder. This situation stems from society not recognizing the child's problem, which is much less visible than an obvious physical or mental disability. A child with an easily recognized impairment receives some tolerance, while the child with minimal nervous system dysfunction seems always to be judged on normal standards and is often belittled (Touwen and Prechtl, 1973). Mistrusting the seemingly hostile environment, the child soon builds up barriers for protection and as a result often develops overt patterns of behavior that are not socially acceptable. Failure at play and the inability to succeed at school may serve to compound the child's feelings of worthlessness, increasing his inappropriate responses to the demands of society.

ORTHOPEDIC PROBLEMS AND SKELETAL DYSPLASIA

Closely associated with the problem of movement inefficiency is how the body is structured and whether or not disorders of the locomotor system are present. Dysplasia refers to disharmony between different regions of the body as they relate to one another (Sheldon, 1940). Of particular importance to the professional interested in clumsiness are those children having a history of leg or foot problems early in life. Children restricted in playing experiences because of orthopedic problems may lag developmentally behind normal peers or, when disorders cannot be satisfactorily ameliorated, can never compete on a par.

The proportions of the body segments to one another must be given consideration in the problem of physical awkwardness. For example, a person having a disproportionate amount of weight in the upper body as compared to the lower may find balance activities difficult as compared to a well-proportioned individual. The same may be true when looking at skeletal dysplasia, relationships of joint such as ankles, knees, and hips, and the incidence of bodily injury due to sports participation (Arnheim, 1966).

THE CLUMSY CHILD SYNDROME

The minimal brain dysfunction syndrome has been used synonymously with other descriptive titles. Such terms as "minimal birth injury," "motorial infantilism," "congenital maladroitness," and "minimal cerebral palsy" all refer to the same syndrome. Less descriptive, although commonly used in the past, was the designation of clumsy persons as "motor morons." One can deduce from these many different expressions for clumsiness that it is very difficult to define. Critchley (1968) points out that clumsiness is an inadequate and imperfect term without definite meaning to a neurologist. Physical clumsiness often is equated erroneously with mental deficiencies or learning disabilities. Critchley also states that "clumsiness may entail a number of physical deficits . . . and no non-medical observer should stumble into this trap and make the diagnosis of a clumsy child without obtaining the opinion of an expert as to the cause and the nature of the clumsiness."

In general, the clumsy child is usually subjectively identified as one who falls a lot, is continually knocking into things and has bruises to show for it, drops things, and cannot keep up with the other children in physically active games. He is also described as an individual with whom other children will not play because he is "no fun," who has difficulty in climbing, throwing, and jumping, who plays with children younger than himself, or who, if he is a boy, prefers to play less strenuous "feminine" activities. He may have difficulty in writing, drawing, or copying; he has a self-defeating attitude; he constantly gets into fights, often losing, or beats up on younger children; and he may have trouble buttoning a coat or tying shoes.

One must conclude that the clumsy child is commonly a person with minimal nervous system dysfunction combined with emotional problems that are reflected in his inability to perform typical motor skills. The clumsy child is one who has motor re-tardation, performing as would a much younger child. Fully realizing that clumsiness is a difficult, if not sometimes impossible, problem to adequately define, the following working definition is presented to the reader. *The clumsy child is one who has motor learning difficulties and displays asynchronous and inefficient motor behavior when attempting to carry out movement tasks that he would commonly be expected to accomplish under reasonable circumstances.*

Preventing clumsiness

Because of the variety of causes of the clumsy child syndrome, it is difficult to speculate as to how it might be prevented or lessened in intensity. One factor of prevention that does stand out is that of early detection of those individuals who present overt signs of movement problems. For example, highly suspected are babies with low Apgar scores or the aforementioned "high-risk" infants with a history of conditions that might affect their motor system. Parents usually know from their own background whether they or some close relative had movement problems, inferring a possible genetic relationship to clumsiness. Obvious early sensory deprivation and disruptive environments such as occur in divorce or unhappy family situations can cause children to reflect patterns of movement that mirror their unstable and tense beginnings.

Prevention of the syndrome of clumsiness should start as early as infancy by providing a planned program of developmental movements and sensory stimulation. Professional programs of this type are beginning to be organized throughout the country. They are designed to instruct parents on how to most effectively provide motor development activities and sensory stimulation for their child. In such a setting an infant is provided with the opportunity to reach full potential as dictated by his maturity level. Through such a program of developmental play the child begins to

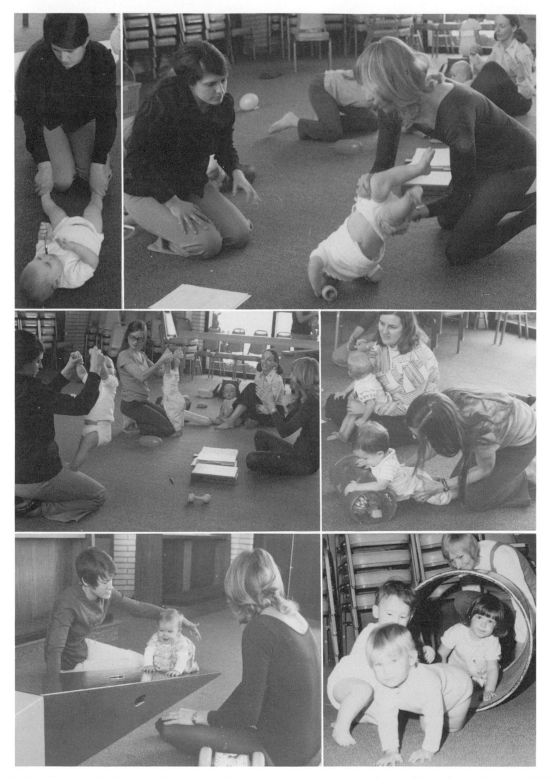

Fig. 2-1. Programs dedicated to developmental movement and sensory stimulation of the infant and young child are a means to the early prevention of the problem of cluminess. (Photos provided by Infant-Child Development, Inc., Irvine, Calif.)

enjoy a positive relationship with his parents and gains control over his body. Many of the physical and emotional problems arising out of minimal nervous system dysfunction can be held to a minimum or even eliminated by an early intervention program. (See Fig. 2-1.)

A discussion on the prevention of clumsiness must not exclude educational programs at the childhood, preschool, primary grade, and secondary grade levels. Daycare centers and preschool programs conducted by public and private agencies should be vitally concerned with children's motor and social competencies. Programs that are totally dedicated to helping the child become a better classroom participator and are solely interested in cognitive development to the exclusion of motor development will ultimately cause serious problems for the developing child. We hold that a rich environment of movement and sensory opportunities is much more important to the young child than is the gaining of early mental discipline leading to skills in reading, writing, and arithmetic. In fact, there is an inherent danger in denying a child the basic right to move. Producing an unnatural atmosphere with emphasis on small-muscle control under highly structured, restrictive conditions often creates within the child an early dislike of teachers and school.

3

THEORIES, SYSTEMS, AND SPECIAL TECHNIQUES

No specific approach dealing with the remediation of clumsiness would be complete without first discussing some of the influences that have gone into developing that approach. *The Clumsy Child* has drawn its content from many sources: education, physical education, perceptual-motor training, and therapeutic exercises. Theories, systems, and special techniques have been combined to formulate an eclectic approach to working with clumsy children.

In general, classroom teachers are not particularly concerned with children who display physical clumsiness; rather they are concerned mainly with academic success. If a child is able to conduct sit-down activities necessary in the classroom environment, little note is taken that he might be a failure at play. Only when a child displays some abnormal overt behavior such as aggression or withdrawal from social situations do teachers tend to become concerned. However, they readily become concerned when a child has difficulty in writ-

ing, filling in between lines, or performing other classroom motor tasks.

EDUCATIONAL APPROACHES
Maria Montessori

Montessori was born in 1870 and at the age of 26 became the first woman physician in Italy. Through her association with mental institutions Montessori became interested in educating the mentally deficient and as the result of this interest developed her philosophy based on multisensory stimulation and concrete experiences rather than education through abstraction. The Montessori approach is one that is based on self-development and self-teaching in an environment that is specially prepared by the teacher for the optimum growth of the child. Besides the prepared environment, which includes bright, colorful, and happy surroundings, there is structural learning in which specially constructed learning aids assist the child in mastering concrete concepts and, hopefully, eventually lead to the understanding of abstractions. Inner discipline and social responsibility are learned when there are opportunities provided to the child for ordering his own environment.

A multisensory approach to learning, called cosmic curriculum, provides a choice of a great variety of activities. Self-education is often encouraged; the child learns at his own rate, his own level, and in his own way without being compared to other children. Standin (1967), in discussing the Montessori method, explains that a child gains in both physical and intellectual independence at his own pace. Comparison of one child to another is a primary cause of discouragement and feeling of failure, particularly in those children who are developmentally slow in some aspects of their growth. The Montessori approach cannot be considered a method that is completely dedicated to movement as a way to maximize maturation; however, it does provide children with sensory stimulation and a positive self-concept.

In general, the Montessori method may be divided into the practical life curriculum, sensory education curriculum, and curricula that are concerned with language skills and mathematical concepts. The practical life curriculum is concerned with self-care activities. Such practical motor activities as snapping, hooking, buttoning, and tying are practiced as well as such tasks as pouring different materials (for example, water or grain) accurately into containers. A sensory education curriculum provides the opportunities to learn the discrimination of sizes, sounds, shapes, textures, and colors. Learning therefore is approached through all of the child's senses.

Jean Piaget

Piaget is currently one of the most quoted and discussed educational theorists. His early background was mainly in biology until interest led him to the study of child behavior, learning, and the underlying bases for logical thought. To fully understand the development of mature intelligence, Piaget undertook a systematic program of observing his own three children. Based on these observations, Piaget concluded that logical thought goes through five stages: reflex stage, sensory-motor stage, preoperational stage, concrete operational stage, and final formal operational stage. Piaget considers operational intelligence as unique to humans and the sensory-motor stage as underlying all operational intelligence (Furth, 1970).

Preschool and elementary schoolteachers of today, influenced indirectly by both Montessori and Piaget, are usually concerned with the child's motor behavior. A teacher who realizes that a child has had inadequate experience at the sensory-motor level may suspect that he will have some difficulties in making adaptations to the demands of the immediate environment.

B. F. Skinner

The work of Skinner has had widely sweeping effects on education as it is practiced today. Belonging to the stimulus-response connectivist group of learning theorists such as Guthrie and Thorndike, Skinner has developed the concept of operant conditioning. The operant factor refers to what occurs within the organism after the stimulus has been initiated but before the response is initiated. According to Skinner, the operant period and particular reaction of the organism are dependent on past experiences. Other common names given to operant conditioning are positive and negative reinforcement and behavior shaping. From Skinner's experiments it was discovered that behavior can be altered and undesirable behavior characteristics extinguished by suitable rewards. Skinner's work has particular importance to the teacher and therapist who desire to make changes in movement behavior.

Of particular value to the teacher and therapist desiring to modify inappropriate motor behavior is the use of positive reinforcement techniques. Various types of reinforcers should be selected based on the child's maturity, mentality, needs, and interests. Concrete rewards such as food, money, or objects and planned verbal praise are commonly used to modify behavior.

PHYSICAL EDUCATION

Most educators would concede that physical education is an integral part of the total educational process. Ideally, if physical education was carried out effectively in all schools, special programs to remedy clumsiness in children would not be needed. However, like other education ideals, physical education has not made the impact on the total educational process that it should have. Because children are being formally educated at increasingly younger ages, as exemplified by the current proliferation in early childhood programs, it is even more important that children be given extensive opportunities for developmental movement. The time up to and including the early childhood period is the most advantageous time to identify children who have movement problems and to remedy the problems.

The physical educator or the classroom teacher who conducts the physical education program is in the best possible position for detecting clumsy children. When a child is observed to move with difficulty or inefficiently, immediate provisions should be made for diagnosis and remediation. Diagnostic testing should follow initial identification, and a prescriptive program should be developed for the child. Because of current confusions as to what is the best physical education program for each child, those needing special attention are often overlooked; the typical schoolteacher is concerned with making better academicians or highly skilled athletes.

There appear to be four threads interwoven into the fabric of today's elementary physical education. These threads represent movement education, perceptual-motor training, the traditional program, and a mixture of approaches, or the eclectic program.

Rudolf Laban and movement education

Laban was born on December 15, 1879, in Bratislava, then part of the Austro-Hungarian Empire. His primary interest was in stage design, dancing, and all the crafts that had to do with the theater (Thorton, 1971). In Laban's early career he sought to create a dance form for all people, rather than the widely accepted classical ballet. Until 1935 Laban had a successful career as a choreographer, teacher, and writer of dance in Germany; at that time he was declared undesirable by the Nazi government and sent to Staffelberg. While in Staffelberg, Laban increased his interests in how children utilize space, in their drawings, and in their movement. After moving to England in 1938 he carried on research in the psychology of movement. Through the war years he continued to develop his theories on movement, particularly in educational dance, which was later to become known as movement exploration and subsequently movement education.

Thorton (1971) describes the philosophy of Laban under seven headings: (1) the significance of movement in the life of man, (2) harmony in nature and in man, (3) natural rhythm, (4) the creative influence in the universe and in man, (5) art as a creative force, (6) movement, effort, and communications, and (7) conflict. To Laban, movement is the way a person gains knowledge about the world and himself. There is a natural harmony in life, with all things having a relationship to another. Through movement man can become closer to the creative forces that underlie all of the universe. Movement, particularly dance, is the most basic of human endeavors. The inner impulse causing movement Laban called *effort,* which he divided into four basic factors: *space, weight, time, and flow.*

Laban's theory of movement education has evolved into a highly accepted educational approach throughout the world. It stresses free and individualized movement, de-emphasizing highly structured movement that is commonly associated with traditional physical education. In movement education the teacher becomes the initiator of movement problems that are to be solved by the child. The primary intent is to help develop a keen awareness of the human body's full potential. Contrasted to the traditional method of physical education in which the teacher explains and demonstrates, the participator executes a skill, and then the teacher evaluates how well it was executed, movement education challenges the person with movement questions to which an individual response is made in the best way possible. An example of a movement question would be "How many ways can you move across the floor?" or "How slow or how fast can you move?" Besides verbal questions, problems can be set by the use of flash cards or other visual cues. Movement education is an effective approach to assisting motor development; however, there are times when a skill should be demonstrated and taught in a formal manner, particularly the more difficult sport skills. Critically speaking, some teachers use movement education as a way of remaining uninvolved in the movement experience.

In terms of working with the clumsy child who has experienced nothing but failure from attempts at efficient movement, the movement education approach may be totally inadequate in the initial stages of the problem. Rather, it should be used with the clumsy child only when confidence has been gained and there is a willingness on his part to chance failure.

Muska Mosston—from command to discovery

Mosston (1966) proposes an approach to physical education that is based on *becoming* rather than on the rigidity that is often associated with physical education. Using many of the concepts of Maslow, Skinner, and Brunner, the teacher gradually relinquishes command, eventually becoming an equal participator with the student. Mosston's approach helps the teacher relinquish decision making to the student through logical strategy, until movement skills can be effectively learned without the teacher's direct intervention. Mosston encourages the student to make decisions in program organization or choose the time to have a particular activity. Other decisions given over to the student are the teacher's role, the student's role in the class, and aspects of the actual execution of the class such as what is to be taught and how it is to be taught. To accomplish the purpose of making the student self-motivating and able to make mature decisions, Mosston describes five stages through which the student must go: command, task, reciprocal, small group, and individual.

Teaching by command is the most prevalent method used by physical educators today. It is almost totally teacher centered, similar to what one might expect in the military services. Skills taught by this method normally begin by teacher demonstration followed by an explanation of what was accomplished, execution by the class, and finally evaluation by the instructor as to how effective the class was in their skill execution. As can easily be seen, the command method of skill instruction allows for little decision making on the part of the individual student.

The *task method* of teaching is a gradual shift away from the teacher. The task method refers to a particular set of activities or movement tasks that are given to the student, who independently carries them out. The task method frees the teacher to move around the class, assisting each student individually.

Reciprocal teaching, known otherwise as the buddy system method of teaching, is contrasted to both the command and task style by shifting the decision making to another student. In this method the peer acts as a spotter in a tumbling skill or acts as an aide as the teacher makes suggestions on how the performer may improve his skill. From students working in pairs, decision making is then given over to a small group consisting of three students assuming the roles of doer, observer, and recorder. The doer performs the skill, the observer provides teaching hints, and the recorder writes down key factors of the performance for future review.

The *individual method,* unlike the reciprocal and group methods, totally shifts the evaluation of the activity to the performer himself. The individual method implies that the student works independently on a given activity without direction or immediate intervention by the instructor. In this method the role of the teacher is one of devising a challenging task, observing the performance, and suggesting corrections at the appropriate time. The student initiates the task and then evaluates how effectively it was performed. Additionally, following the individual stage of relinquishing decisions to the student, Mosston adds the stages of guiding, discovery, and problem solving, finally bringing the student through the cognitive barrier and into the intellectual and creative realm.

The traditional physical education program

Ideally, the primary objectives of the traditional physical education program are physical development, gaining knowledge and understanding, acquisition of specific game and sport skills, and development of attitudes and appreciation. In physical development the child is assisted in his general motor control, which includes muscular strength, stamina, flexibility, and postural efficiency. Besides general motor control, physical education attempts to provide the child with those basic skills that will make him successful in play: locomotion, object management such as throwing, catching, kicking, and striking, and skill in the areas of rhythm and aquatics. In developing knowledge and understanding the instructor attempts to give the child

a "good" feeling for physical activity and the fact that time is well spent in the learning of games and sports. The child learns that physical activity can be an effective means of self-expression as well as a means of relaxation and reduction of muscular tension. The child also learns the value of getting along with other children and adults and at the same time learns that physical activity is necessary for maintaining physical and emotional effectiveness. In a good program of physical education a child learns to play games and sports and how to regulate his actions through rules, strategies, and self-analysis. Two attitudes that may be built into physical education activities are sportsmanship and cooperation in group situations in which there are opportunities to express self-control, fairness, and personal integrity. In general, standard physical education at the elementary level attempts to satisfy these objectives by dividing its curricular offerings into four major areas: games and sports, self-testing, dance, and physical fitness (Arnheim and Pestolesi, 1973).

Kindergarten and first-grade children are taught lead-up activities and basic movement activities. Second- and third-grade children are given simple games and activities along with the opportunity to learn basic movement skills that are necessary for future success in the more complicated games common to the fourth and fifth grades. It is expected that by the time the child has reached the fifth and sixth grades he should be able to effectively participate in a wide variety of complicated skills including sports, stunts, and rhythmics (De Santis and Smith, 1969; Anderson et al., 1966; Kirchner, 1970).

One common criticism of the standard physical education program is that it is primarily group centered rather than individualized, allowing children with movement problems to be easily overlooked by the teacher. Another criticism is that rather than gearing its offerings to children's needs, the traditional approach is usually program centered, making the child adapt to the requirements of the program.

Perceptual-motor training programs in physical education

Perception is the most important factor in a child's understanding of himself and the environment. It enables the interpretation of objects and events and is involved in all learning (Arnheim et al., 1973). Recently there has been an increasing awareness of the importance of perception in the development of motor skills in physical education. In the past 10 years many physical educators have ceased using a typical physical education curriculum and started conducting a perceptual-motor training program. Like the movement education approach, perceptual-motor training programs provide multisensory experiences. However, unlike the movement education concept in which emphasis is placed on personal freedom and exploration, the perceptual-motor training program is sequentially structured as to task difficulty in order for the performer to gain a progressively higher order of experiences.

Critics of perceptual-motor training programs as a replacement for physical education say that in reality all physical education is perceptually based. Efficient movement would be impossible without accurate processing of perceptual information. We must concur that all physical education does affect perception; however, perceptual-motor training programs are specifically designed to assist the child in accurately processing information through the senses.

The balanced approach to physical education

All current approaches to physical education of children have merit when professionally taught. We believe, however, that a balanced approach to elementary physical education includes movement education, perceptual-motor training, and the tradi-

tional approach (Arnheim and Pestolesi, 1973). Children from 3 to 5 years of age at level I would benefit most from 35% movement education and perceptual-motor training type of activities, 45% self-testing, 15% rhythms, and 5% game type of activities. The emphasis of level I is on motor development in which a child develops spatial relationships and body awareness. Level II involves ages 6 through 8 and constitutes 25% movement education and perceptual-motor training, 30% self-testing, 20% rhythm, and 25% games and sports activities. Having experienced level I activities successfully, the child is now ready, both physiologically and emotionally, to experience more sophisticated and difficult movement experiences. Level II provides sequential movement problem-solving activities, both individual and group, that are of intermediate difficulty. Creative rhythm is introduced to assist the child in spontaneous response. In the area of games and sports, emphasis is placed on locomotor type of activities with a gradual introduction to the more specific skills of running, throwing, catching, and striking. Level III includes children who are ages 9 through 12 and should consist of 15% movement education, 25% self-testing, 15% rhythm activities, and 45% games and sports. Level III builds on what has been gained by the child in levels I and II. Movement education and perceptual-motor training are still important during this period; however, they are less important than the activities of self-testing, gymnastics, and sport skills. Level I offers participants opportunities to learn stunts, pyramid building, and those activities that require strength, flexibility, and muscle and cardiovascular stamina. Specific dance activities such as square and social dancing are introduced at this time. Individual and team sports become very important to the child during this period. In-season sports are taught from both the participant's and the spectator's point of view.

In the balanced physical education program the clumsy child is identified early in level I activities and immediate individualized remediation provided. For example, when a child is having difficulty in one category of the physical education program, remediation can be accomplished by increasing the percentage of experiences in that specific category. Also, using the level concept, an older clumsy child can be provided remediation by participating in activities representative of a lower level; in this way the lower category becomes prescriptive and remedial. If there is a well-balanced physical education program for all children, the need for a special remedial program may become unnecessary.

PERCEPTUAL-MOTOR TRAINING CONCEPTS

As discussed earlier, the influence of perceptual motor training on current physical education practices has been considerable. Although the main thrust of these approaches is to make the participants better learners, they have had a great stimulating effect on all professionals concerned with movement, including physical educators, special educators, educational psychologists, and communicative disorders specialists. Whether one is an advocate of the precepts of perceptual-motor training, is neutral, or opposes these approaches, one must concur that they have changed education in America.

Newell C. Kephart

Kephart is one of the pioneers of perceptual-motor training as a means to increasing a child's academic potential and remediation of learning disorders. Kephart is a developmentalist, considering that child behavior is based in early motor responses and that more complex behavior evolves out of less complex behavior. Kephart's basic concepts are discussed in detail in his now classic book *The Slow Learner in the Classroom* (1960). Kephart's learning and memory concepts stem mainly from the theories of Hebb (1949). Hebb considers that in-

dividual neurons are, for the most part, randomly connected. Under some circumstances excitation of these neurons can establish a reverberatory activity that may continue for minutes or even days after the stimulus has diminished. Excitation may be facilitated by synaptic junctions joining two or more systems. Impulses originating from a neuron can cause a temporary facilitation, which in turn produces a weak circuit that becomes increasingly more facilitated as the reverberatory activity is repeated. Hebb calls this reverberating circuit "cell assembly," which eventually causes anatomical changes and a permanent memory trace to be laid down (Sage, 1971). Kephart therefore considers that if learning is to take place effectively, perception and movement must be matched, a process that occurs through a wide variety of sensory experiences and movement opportunities. As a result, movement and perception are joined and function as one. Also important to the Kephart theory is the ability of the child to discern a figure from a background. Without this, the child would have great difficulty in classroom activities such as reading and writing. He would also have difficulty in discerning flying objects on the playground or in attempting to coordinate and handle objects in space. Interestingly, both the hyperkinetic and hypokinetic child often have difficulties in determining figure-ground relationships (Gearheart, 1973). The slow learner is often one who has a developmental lag or breakdown in the way he is able to process information coming into the various sense channels. Kephart considers posture as the primary pattern of movement on which all other motor patterns are based. He conceives of learning as being dependent on four basic movement generalizations: balance and posture, locomotion, contacting and receiving objects, and propelling objects. According to Kephart, laterality, or the recognition of right and left sides of the body, is necessary for movement efficiency and the ability to recognize symbols. The expression of laterality is directionality, in which objects can be accurately located outside the body. An accurate body image is also necessary before learning can effectively take place because it gives a sense of relationship to the surrounding space. Kephart stresses ocular training for gaining eye control, particularly through ball tracking, chalkboard training, and other activities in which the eye is required to pursue and fixate on specific objects. To carry out the perceptual-motor training program of Kephart, tools such as walking boards, balance boards, and trampoline, dance games, and rhythmical activities are necessary.

Gerald N. Getman

Like Kephart, Getman, an optometrist, believes that perception, primarily visual perception, can be developed through motor training. As a developmentalist who has worked closely with Gessell, Getman indicates that an individual acquires learning in stages, first from general through specific motor patterns that are primarily guided by the eyes. The acquisition of special movement patterns through eye-hand coordination and integration of sensory-motor skills comes second. Third are eye movement patterns in which the vision replaces the hands as a means for exploring the environment, and finally visual language patterns develop in which the auditory and motor systems are combined. According to Getman, therefore, visual perception is learned on a developmental sequence base. Agreeing with Hebb, Getman considers that "mental life is motor life." Vision, then, is derived from a number of sensory-motor systems. This is in accordance with the work of Skeffington (Getman, 1965), who developed a theory of vision including these components: the *antigravity process* by which the individual is able to transport himself in the environment; the *centering process* in which the individual develops an awareness of *me*, or self; the identification process in which the individual develops a *whatness to objects;*

and finally, the *speech-auditory process,* which is developed as postural, transport, and manipulative movement patterns, spatial orientation, and assigning labels to things in space become changed to visual and then speech communication. These four interwoven visual processes form the complex function of vision. Building on Skeffington's model, Getman developed the theory of a visual-motor complex in which visual perception is developed from the infant's earliest reflex behavior, progressing through locomotion and upward through the more sophisticated human responses of eye coordination, ocular-motor systems, and speech systems until, finally, cognition and intelligence are developed.

Getman implies that visual perception can be developed by special exercises and activities. However, his approach is primarily concerned with training the eye and, unlike Kephart, Getman is less concerned with movement for total development than with its specific effect on visual perception. Basic components of Getman's program consist of general coordination activities, balance, eye-hand coordination, eye movement, form recognition, and visual memory (Gearheart, 1973). Use of the walking beam, chalkboard, and templates together with specific exercises for developing eye control and hand-eye coordination are characteristic of the Getman approach and the Kephart approach.

Raymond H. Barsch

In the area of perceptual-motor systems, Barsch would be considered an eclectic, drawing on the works of many theorists, particularly Getman, Skeffington, and Kephart. Barsch (1967) has developed a movement theory known as movigenics, a learning system based on the efficiency of movement. Barsch, like other perceptual-motor theorists, is a developmentalist and considers movement as basic to learning. Motor skills should be sequentially learned, with one motor skill developed on a lesser skill until a desired level of motor functioning has been acquired. Vision, as in the theories of Kephart and Getman, takes precedence over the other sensory channels. Barsch considers movigenics as basic to thinking and movement acting as basic to promote efficient cognitive processing. He proposes movigenics as a precise system for assisting the child in his spatial orientation, which in turn assists him as a learner. Barsch defines movement efficiency as a person who "can manage his body weight so as to maintain stability at rest or in motion and can produce and control force in a comfortable and economic pattern of movement so as to successfully resolve the demands which confront him with the least possible strain and minimal expenditure of energy appropriate to the task" (Barsch, 1968). Movigenics utilizes many different activities to help the child reach his goals. Activities such as rolling, crawling, walking, jumping, moving to the pace of the metronome, chalkboard activities, and the planned inclusion of various stressors are specifically included.

Carl H. Delacato

The work of Delacato and other contributors to the concept of neurological organization as a basis of learning is conducted mainly at the Institute for the Achievement of Human Potential in Philadelphia. From the Institute, of which Delacato is co-director, has evolved this neurophysiological system. Neurological organization has been used for children with severe brain damage and/or behavioral disorders as well as those with severe learning disabilities. This highly controversial system contends that man's development recapitulates phylogeny during the first trimester of gestation and continues until the child is about 6½ years of age. It is eclectic, steming from the work of such researchers as Orton, Gesell, Getman, and Fay.

Delacato contends that man possesses the highest level of nervous system organization, having evolved over millions of years. Delacato considers that the higher the neurological organization, the higher the physical and intellectual functioning of the individual; conversely, the more neurological disorganization, the more difficulties in movement and in learning. Within the mother the developing fetus is considered to go through all the possible evolutionary stages of life—ontogeny recapitulates phylogeny. For example, the fish stage is controlled by what would be equal to the brain stem of man, the medulla oblongata; the amphibian stage by a slightly more complex nervous system, the pons; the reptilian stage by the midbrain; and the mammalian stage by the cerebral cortex. Man goes through these various stages, according to Delacato, in his embryonic and fetal development, and organization continues up until the age of 7 or 8 (LeWinn et al., 1966).

The neurological organization system is concerned with three basic types of movement: homologous movement controlled by the cord, homolateral movement controlled by the pons, and highly sophisticated movement patterns controlled primarily by the midbrain and cortex. Before and just after birth, motor control is primarily initiated by the spinal reflex centers; the infant is controlled initially by the medulla oblongata, in 4 to 5 months by the pons, and at 10 months by the midbrain; finally, the cortex assumes control with the emergence of the upright posture. The advocates of the neurological organization system go a step beyond the cross-pattern movement as the most sophisticated of human coordinated activity, adding that cerebral dominance is necessary for the highest level of human functioning.

The central theme of neurological organization is establishing normal patterns of motor behavior by a system of passive or active movements based on normal reflex behavior. A multisensory approach is used to reestablish normal integrative responses within the brain by programming it to respond in a normal manner. Delacato indicates that the vast majority of learning and behavioral disorders in children are the result of brain lesions and should be remedied by a program of organizing the nervous system through basic movement patterns and sensory stimulation.

Of late, the concept of neurological organization has come under some sharp criticism by many professionals concerned with the neurologically impaired child. In summarizing the Delacato system, Gearheart (1973) has suggested some areas of controversy that have been voiced: that patterning effects the brain directly, excluding the child from normal activities, making parents therapists, lack of research to back up claims, and the validity of the Doman-Delacato neurological developmental profile.

A. Jean Ayres

Ayres proposes a neural behavior theory to assist the child with learning deficits: a therapy of sensory integration that can be carried out by educators and psychologists as well as related professionals. Ayres draws heavily from neuropsychological research, particularly that of Rood. She indicates that disordered sensory integration is the primary cause of learning disorders and that by improving this area learning can be facilitated. Ayres (1973) states that sensory integration is "the ability to organize sensory information for use which can be improved through controlling its input to active brain mechanisms." Specifically, Ayres contends that integrated processing results in perception, and the ability to synthesize sensory data helps the individual to interact efficiently with the environment. The sensory integrative approach differs from other perceptual motor systems in that it does not instruct the child in specific skills as does Kephart's matching of visual and motor stimuli. Ayres' primary concern is to assist the brain in functioning optimally by modifying any neurological dysfunction that may be interfering with a child's ability to learn. Unlike the Delacato system, sensory integrative therapy does not attempt to eliminate the cause of inadequate neurological organization but rather to eliminate some of the neurological conditions that interfere with learning. Ayres is a developmentalist and accepts that early neurological development may be related to ontogenetic processes; however, she contends that it cannot be assumed that an individual recapitulates his own evolutionary history of brain levels discretely separated one from another. In each evolutionary stage the brain retains some of the older organization and incorporates it into the next higher level until the organism is complete. Sensory integration therapy is mainly concerned with the lower brain, particularly the brain stem, which ultimately affects the competence of the higher, more complex brain levels. According to Ayres (1973), "Cognitive function has its tap root in a spinal cord, most of the rest of its roots in the brain stem and other subcortical structures and the cortex assumes a mediating role over all."

Sensory integration therapy draws to a great extent on the work of Kabot and Knott (1948), Fay (1954), and Rood (1954). Therapy includes tactile stimulation through rubbing the skin with different textured materials, vestibular stimulation, and the normalizing of the postural reactions through a combination of tactile and vestibular stimulation.

Activities designed to bring about vestibular stimulation are spinning in a swing or net hammock. Additional proprioceptor stimulation is obtained by the child performing different positions and unique tasks on a scooter board. Scooter board riding in different positions stimulates labyrinth reflexes and tonic neck reflexes, depending on the specific needs of the child. Ayres also has the child roll on a large therapy ball to assist in the development of normal reflex behavior as well as other rolling activities such as rolling on a rug and rolling in several inner tubes tied together.

Bryant J. Cratty

Cratty is the director of the Perceptual-Motor Learning Laboratory at the University of California at Los Angeles and is considered to be one of the most prolific writers in the area of motor learning. Every professional field needs its critics in order to ensure that overzealous creators of closed systems do not predominate. Cratty fills this role for education, specifically physical education. Criticizing to a great extent the many claims that have been made by the devotees of perceptual-motor systems, Cratty is particularly critical of the idea that reading or learning improvements made through the use of perceptual systems are panaceas for enhancing the cognitive domain of the child. However, Cratty does agree that an inability to play games can lower self-esteem as well as acceptance by peers, which in turn may adversely affect motor and cognitive functioning. Game and sports participation as a reinforcement for the acquisition of basic learning concepts helps a child to gain personal control, increases arousal level, and can lengthen attention span. Movement can provide opportunities for problem solving; however, Cratty does not place movement as the primary basis for mental, social, and emotional development but considers it one facet in the child's total development.

The perceptual-motor systems discussed in this section express mainly the developmentalist point of view of assisting children in reaching their maximum cognitive development. We think that these perceptual-motor systems, especially at the preacademic level, may help some children reach their full motor development, particularly if they have some minimal motor dysfunction. The question arises as to whether or not one perceptual system is preferable over another or whether any well-planned program of physical education activities would have the same benefits. Although this book is not concerned specifically with cognitive development or with an individual's ability to excel in the classroom, it is difficult to separate motor learning disorders from disorders that effect the child at the cognitive level.

THERAPEUTIC EXERCISE TECHNIQUES AND MOTOR DYSFUNCTION

When discussing theories, systems, and methods that could be used to assist the clumsy child, one would be remiss in overlooking the extensive work that has been done in the field of physical medicine and the care of neurological disorders. This section is divided into two major categories: neurophysiological and standard approaches to overcoming serious movement disorders.

Neurophysiological techniques

Bobath neurodevelopmental approach. K. Bobath and B. Bobath have added considerably to the field of knowledge having to do with treatment of neurological disorders. Their primary work has been in developing techniques to assist persons with a central nervous system lesion that causes muscle incoordination. They are mainly concerned with disorders of movement and restoring postural tone and normal postural reflex behavior. Their work has dealt chiefly with cerebral palsy; however, they consider it suitable for a number of other disorders involving the motor system (Semans, 1967). Therapy is designed to work with abnormal reflex activity and to increase or decrease muscle tone, depending on individual requirements. The major postural reflexes with which the Bobaths work are the tonic, Landau, placing, labyrinthine, neck righting, and Moro reflexes. By inhibiting the tonic reflex, which originates from the spinal cord and brain stem, righting and balance reactions are facilitated (Denhoff, 1967). The Bobath approach is not specifically concerned with developing muscular strength, but it does employ tactile stimulation by muscle tapping and encourages perceptual-motor activities through experiencing as many normal patterns of behavior as possible within the limitations of the individual.

Temple Fay approach. Fay, a neurosurgeon, began his work in the early 1940's and developed a neurophysiological concept known as neuromuscular reflex therapy. Page (1967), in describing Fay's basic premise, states, "Essential to subsequent thinking is the basic concept that primitive or rudimentary movements, for the purpose of maintenance and protection of the species, result from reflexes, spinal automatisms and tonic responses appropriately reacting to stimuli, with such movements being possible without a highly developed or integrated cerebral cortex." Fay's approach is phylogenetically based and considers that lower forms of life such as amphibian and reptilian must normally be experienced before human bipedal movement can be accomplished. Neuromuscular reflex therapy holds that ontogeny recapitulates phylogeny and for man to be fully functioning he must successfully accomplish the movements of the fish, amphibian, and reptile; the quadruped position; and finally the primate upright bipedal position. Fay's method also incorporates the establishment of cerebral dominance and laterality as a means of improving intellectual functioning. Therapy is carried out by active and passive movements that are executed both precisely and smoothly for up to 100 repetitions (Keats, 1965). In general, the primary aim of Fay's technique is to decrease muscle and postural disturbances.

Proprioceptive neuromuscular facilitation. The proprioceptive neuromuscular facilitation (PNF) method developed by Kabot and Knott is one of the most common neurophysiological techniques used in physical medicine today. Denhoff (1967) describes its main feature as "a system of exercises, involving all parts of the body which are performed in a manner to take advantage of the diagonal spiral patterns of muscles." PNF uses the entire limb rather than single joint movements to bring about a desired voluntary action. It also employs maximum resistance, initiating a stimulus to dormant neurons. Kabot and Knott are developmentalists in theory, contending that normal motor development proceeds in a cephalocaudal and proximal distal direction and that early reflex motor behavior becomes sequenced in an orderly fashion into movement patterns and finally into mature motor behavior. Voss (1967) indicates that the PNF approach is based on the works of Sherrington (1940), Gellhorn (1949), Coghill (1929), McGraw (1943), Gesell and Amatruda (1945), Hellabrandt et al. (1951), and Pavlov (1928). She summarizes the PNF approach by stating that "as many influences as possible are brought to bear on the patient including: recapitulation of total patterns for developing motor behavior, the use of spiral and diagonal patterns, coupling of voluntary movement, the use of postural and righting reflexes, selection of appropriate sensory cues, techniques for facilitation of movement and postural responses, using maximal resistance and excitation or inhibition, and the use of repetitive activity for coordination training."

Rood approach. Stockmeyer (1967), in describing the philosophy of Rood, states that it "is concerned with the inner action of somatic, autonomic and psychic factors and their role in the regulation of motor behavior." In keeping with the Bobath concept, Rood considers that it is possible to stimulate the higher cortex through peripheral stimulation. In contrast to the Bobath technique, however, Rood facilitates the stimulatory nerve centers instead of the inhibitory nervous centers. Through skin stimulation such as brushing, pressure, and temperature alteration, the proprioceptors are stimulated, resulting in an integration of the body's involuntary responses that normally occur below the cerebral cortex. Rood considers motor functions to be inseparable from sensory responses. The primary basis of the neuromuscular system, according to Rood, is to assist the organism's survival through protection, movement, and adaptation to the environment. By stroking the skin, muscles are stimulated through nonspecific pathways, with impulses being carried to the sensory-motor cortical region. Ascending pathways flowing via the reticular formation within the brain stem can either inhibit or facilitate muscle tone. Rood stimulates the pale muscle fibers or light work muscles by brushing them for about 10 seconds, followed by stroking the skin surface with an ice cube and then blotting it to initiate movement. Also, large muscles are stimulated by the application of pressure to the bone and muscle insertions (Keats, 1965).

Summary. In summary, neurophysiological approaches are used mainly for the treatment of cerebral disorders. In discussing the basis for neurophysiological approaches, Denhoff (1967) describes them as being dependent on two concepts—first, ontogeny recapitulates philogeny, and second, Sherrington's principles, which place emphasis on the relationship between proprioception and voluntary movement. The main theme is the inhibition of atypical neuromotor responses and the acquisition of normal patterns of motor development; therefore, through the selected application of sensory and motor stimulation techniques, more orderly patterns of neuromuscular behavior are obtained.

Standard therapeutic approaches to overcoming motor dysfunction

Generally, the standard approach to remedying motor dysfunctions is through formalized exercise programs that include categories of activity such as relaxation, physical conditioning, posture, and movement education. Like the neurophysiological approaches, standard therapeutic exercise programs are designed to assist in developing effective muscular control where there is dysfunction. Unlike the neurophysiological approach, the standard approach is devoted to establishing or reestablishing voluntary control of the skeletal muscles and the treating of specific deficits through prescribed routines (Bennett, 1965).

Relaxation. Relaxation training is often given to individuals with motor dysfunctions, particularly those who, in addition to their movement problems, are anxious and tense. The most common goal is the learning of conscious control of muscle tonus and the ability to reduce it at will. Through practice the participant gradually becomes highly sensitive to the body's tensions and gains the ability to consciously reduce them.

Physical conditioning. Physical conditioning includes strength, flexibility, muscular endurance, cardiorespiratory endurance, and coordination. When compared to normal peers, individuals with motor dysfunctions are usually below par in many areas of physical conditioning.

Strength. Strength is one of the most important factors in skilled movement because without it a certain level of coordinated movement is impossible to accomplish. Strength gain is based on overloading the musculature in a progressive manner known as progressive resistance exercises (PRE). PRE provides increased motor learning and increased innervation of nerve pathways and postural reflexes as well as stimulation of proprioceptors.

Joint flexibility. Working in conjunction with strength development, flexibility is a necessary component of optimal motor functioning. Inflexibility may accompany motor problems, particularly in situations of hypertonus and faulty habit patterns; imbalance between a muscle and its opposing set of muscles can result in joint restrictions.

Muscle endurance. Muscle endurance, or the ability to sustain specific movement, is dependent on how many muscle contractions can take place before the onset of fatigue. Muscle endurance is part of the strength continuum, beginning after one muscle contraction has taken place. However, it is usually considered as beginning when 10 repetitions of a particular resistance have been executed.

Cardiorespiratory endurance. Essential to good physical conditioning is the efficiency of the heart and lungs in order that oxygen be delivered effectively to the body. Without an efficient cardiorespiratory system, the level of motor performance is held to a minimum. To adequately deliver oxygen to the body's tissues, the heart and lungs must be stressed by a progressive program of overloading.

Coordination. Coordination and efficient patterns of skilled motor behavior become increasingly more important to the participant as strength, flexibility, and endurance are increased. Coordination is then developed by constant practice until normal habit patterns are well established.

Posture. Last but not considered least in importance is the component of posture. It is the proper segmental alignment of various parts of the body to one another. Generally speaking, good posture is body alignment that requires the smallest amount of effort to maintain it, either in a static or dynamic position.

The primary aim of therapeutic exercise is the enhancement of body balance and muscle coordination. Therapeutic exercise attempts to correct body imbalances and malfunctioning through specific exercises and by engaging in normal patterns of movement. The ultimate objective of posture training is the maintenance of energy in order to accomplish a particular motor act.

●　　●　　●

In Chapter 3 we have attempted to provide the reader with major areas that are concerned with the child as a mover. It is obvious that each area, because of its complexity, could not be presented in its entirety; however, factors were discussed that have a direct bearing on remediation of the clumsy child. *The Clumsy Child* is an eclectic endeavor, combining many different ideas and approaches that are concerned with the child as an efficient mover. Education, perceptual-motor training, physical education, and the complex therapeutic approaches dealing with the individual with a motor disorder blend to create a program for helping the clumsy child.

4

ASSESSING FACTORS
IN CLUMSINESS

There are currently many tests used in education and therapy designed to assess children's development. Unfortunately, in many cases the interpretation of quantitative test scores is left primarily to the subjective judgment of the tester. Accompanying the profusion of tests have been numerous attempts to determine the relationship between physical, mental, and emotional factors in children. In developing a program for the clumsy child the professional must concern himself with determining the causes of poor motor ability in each child, estimating to what extent he would be able to obtain satisfactory improvement, and molding an individualized program. For this to occur it is absolutely necessary that each child thought to be clumsy be pretested in an effort to judge specific developmental performance levels.

This chapter presents a brief historiographical development and critical review of selected tests currently being used to measure motor performance abilities and perceptual-motor, psychological, and emotional factors in children.

TESTS OF BODY COORDINATION AND MOTOR IMPAIRMENT

One of the first tests based on an interrelationship between motor ability and intelligence was reported in 1923 by Garfield. The data obtained from her test as well as the data from subsequent tests developed by Johnson, Brace, Lensch, Harris, Parker, and McCloy are not definitive enough to be used as diagnostic tools in categorizing the clumsy child. For example, in 1927 Brace published his motor ability test. The test is composed of 20 stunts, each of which is scored in terms of success or failure. The individual test scores are not categorized into specific areas such as eye-hand coordination, flexibility, and gross motor coordination. All points are tabulated and a final composite score is given; consequently, specific weaknesses can go undetected by the tester. This may be due in part to the fact that the individual tests are primarily concerned with large-muscle activity involving strength. Thus the Brace test is designed to measure only one facet of clumsiness.

In 1923 Oseretsky, who was then at the Psychoneurological Children's Clinic in Moscow, published the Oseretsky Test of Motor Proficiency. This test was an attempt to measure the severity of awkwardness in children. The original test resembled the Binet test in construction and gave a motor age in the same manner that the Binet test provides a mental age. From the results of the Oseretsky test a deficiency grade could be calculated for each age level. A performance score from 1 to 1½ years below normal indicated slight motor retardation, 1½ to 3 years below normal indicated moderate retardation, 3 to 5 years below normal indicated marked retardation, and a child 5 years or more below normal was considered a "motor idiot." Advanced motor development and motor retardation were judged by the difference between motor age and chronological age. Oseretsky's original general categories, each of which was composed of six groups for each age, were as follows: general static coordination, dynamic coordination of the hands, general dynamic coordination, motor speed, and simultaneous voluntary movements. However, in order to extend the test range these items were added: rhythmic ability, motor strength, formulation of motor formulas, speed of mental set, automatized motor action, orientation in space, regulation of innervation and denervation, and automatic defense reactions.

Borovikov used the Oseretsky test in his study involving children with speech defects and deaf-mutes. He found that they had less motor proficiency than normal children of the same age and that proficiency increased as they became older.

Kemal's (1948) study revealed that until age 8 there were no significant differences between motor performance scores of boys and girls. After that age two separate scales

became necessary. The study also revealed that in normal children no correlation existed between mental development as measured by the Terman test and motor development as measured by Oseretsky's test. In mentally retarded children, however, a correlation of 0.70 was found to exist between motor ability and intelligence quotients.

Using the Oseretsky test, Kopp (1943) found marked motor disturbance in 50% of stuttering children tested. Only 2% of the subjects tested were found to be superior, 6% were found to be normal, 20% showed motor deficiency, 26% showed severe retardation, and 46% were rated as motor idiots. She concluded that the motor deficiency was part of the same condition responsible for stuttering and possibly responsible for other related speech disorders.

Doll (1946) sponsored a translation of Da Costa's port adaptation of the Oseretsky test and hoped to promote interest in the United States in the Oseretsky scale. He indicated that the Oseretsky scale could facilitate development of a better understanding of the limitations of mentally deficient children and adults in respect to motor coordination and the practical aspects of motor proficiency. According to Doll (1946), the Oseretsky scale was used primarily as a means for clinical research, but it has since been used increasingly in education. The examiner tries to classify and measure the inadequacies of the child's motor ability in order to adapt a program that will be most beneficial and remedial. It is in this aspect that the Oseretsky test best serves the child.

In spite of the extensive use of the Oseretsky test throughout the world there is some doubt as to its validity and reliability because of a lack of experimental evidence. There seems to be a consensus of opinion that the entire test, which originally consisted of 85 items, is too time consuming to administer. Also, since the scoring is basically dichotomous, it is not sufficiently definitive to offer a high level of diagnostic significance. In administering and scoring the Oseretsky test the following methodological difficulties are apparent: assisting the child's responses by supplementing the verbal direction of the examiner with demonstration, ambiguity of the directions as to the number of trials, lack of uniformity in scoring the different test items, and no allowance for sex differences. In spite of these weaknesses the Oseretsky test was one of the first relevant endeavors designed for diagnosing motor impairments.

Sloan (1955) published the Lincoln adaptation of the Oseretsky test, which was designed to test the motor ability of children between the ages of 6 and 14 years. It is an individually administered scale consisting of 36 items involving a wide variety of motor skills such as finger dexterity, eye-hand coordination, and gross activities of the hands, arms, legs, and trunk. Both unilateral and bilateral motor tasks are involved in the scale. The length of the test and the training required to administer it make its use prohibitive in most public schools.

In 1966 Stott published a test of motor impairment based on Gollnitz's revision of the Oseretsky test. Stott's main objective was to develop a research instrument with the potential to assess motor deficiencies that result from neural dysfunction. In selecting the items for the test Stott tried to minimize as many of the interfering variables as possible, such as previous learning, perceptual acuity, cognitive ability, and cultural influences. With these considerations in mind, Stott selected five tasks for each age group, from younger than 5 years to older than 13 years. Norms were established by testing 854 children from 6 to 15 years of age divided into four socioeconomic groups from 31 schools. In order to establish a realistic degree of difficulty for the tasks involved in the test a 15% failure rate was chosen. All the subjects were tested at their own age level and 1 year above and 1 year below their age level. The testing continued until the sub-

jects passed all five items on one level. The reliability of the test was checked by Keogh (1968), who conducted a test and retest of 20 of the tasks over a period of 2 weeks. He found an overall coefficient of correlation of 0.71. A validating study was carried out by Moyes (1969), who tested 39 children from 6 to 8 years of age after asking teachers to select 60 children ages 6 to 8 years old who they thought showed some motor impairment. The test was administered to the group with motor impairment and a control group that was matched for age, sex, and social class. Once the children had been nominated, the same teachers were asked to rate the motor ability of all the children. A tetrachoric correlation of 0.85 was obtained from the teachers' rating and the test scores. This represents a total disagreement of only 17.5%, establishing that the test scores and the assessments made by the teachers were mutually confirmatory.

Frostig Movement Skills Test Battery

The Frostig Movement Skills Test Battery was developed (by Orpet) in 1972. Its purpose is to provide an evaluative instrument for assessing strengths and weaknesses in the sensory-motor development of children 6 to 12 years of age with norms for each age group. The experimental sensory-motor test battery consists of the following 12 subtests.

1. Bead stringing: bilateral eye-hand coordination and dexterity
2. Fist-edge-palm: unilateral coordination involving motor sequencing
3. Block transfer: eye-hand and fine motor coordination involving crossing the midline of the body
4. Beanbag target throw: visual-motor coordination involving aiming and accuracy
5. Sitting, bending, and reaching: ability to bend forward while sitting to flex the spine, back muscles, and hamstring ligaments
6. Standing broad jump: ability to jump horizontally from a standing position (primarily a measure of leg strength)

7. Shuttle run: ability to run rapidly between two given marks and to make quick stops, changes of direction, and changes of body position
8. Lying on the floor to standing position: speed and agility in changing body position from a lying to a standing position
9. Sit-ups: abdominal muscle strength
10. Walking board: ability to maintain dynamic balance while walking a rail in heel-to-toe fashion
11. One-foot balance: ability to maintain static balance with eyes open and with eyes closed
12. Chair push-ups: strength of arm and shoulder girdle muscles

The subtests are relatively easy to administer and require very little special training. An individual child can be tested in approximately 20 to 25 minutes and a group of four children in about 45 minutes. The sample used in establishing the norms was composed of 744 white elementary school students in southern California. The selection provided a sample that is restricted in geographical location, racial origin, and socioeconomic level. Testers must be cautioned not to use data from any sample that is generalized beyond the population from which it was taken unless correlation has been established between the obtained norm and the sample in question. Validity was established by means of a factor analysis of the intercorrelations for each of the seven age groups. The reliability scores obtained ranged from 0.44 to 0.88. Means, standard deviations, and scaled equivalents for raw scores have been derived for both males and females of ages 6 to 12 years. The study revealed the following five interpretable and psychologically meaningful factors: balance, hand-eye coordination, strength, visually guided movement, and flexibility. From these factors, composite mean scores can be tabulated for each individual and provide an assessment of the individual's ability to perform in the areas tested.

With the exception of the obvious limitation in establishing the norms caused by the restricted sample used, the Frostig test can be used to categorize perceptual-motor problems in children. The test was constructed on the premise that sensory-motor competence is highly differentiated, and therefore it was designed to test such attributes of movement as coordination, agility, flexibility, strength, and balance.

Hamm-Marburg Body Coordination Test for Children (Der Körper-koordinationstest für Kinder)

The Hamm-Marburg test was developed by Schilling and Kiphard (1967) to detect developmental retardations of total body coordination in children from 5 to 14 years of age. Schilling, in a revised edition, reduced the six original tests to the four that follow.

1. Balancing backwards: This test is concerned with dynamic balance; the child attempts to maintain his balance while walking backwards on three balance beams. The dimensions of the beams are as follows: length, 300 cm; height, 3 cm; and widths, 3 cm, 4.5 cm, and 6 cm. The child is given three trials and is awarded 1 point for every step he takes without losing his balance, up to a maximum of 8 points per board.

2. One-foot hopping over: Involving leg strength, agility, and balance, this test measures the child's ability to hop over one or more stacked foam rubber pads on one foot and maintain his balance for at least two hops after landing. After each successful attempt another pad is added to gradually increase the difficulty of the task. Twelve rectangular foam rubber pads, 50 by 20 by 5 cm, are used. Three attempts are given at each height; if the task is completed successfully on the first attempt, 3 points are awarded, 2 points are awarded on the second attempt, and 1 point is given on the third attempt.

3. Jumping sideways: This task involves gross body coordination and agility. It consists of jumping as fast as possible, jumping sideways with feet together, and jumping over a wooden board for 15 seconds. A

wooden board, 65 cm long, 4 cm wide, and 2 cm high, is used. Two trials are given and the number of successful jumps from both trials is the final total.

4. Shifting platforms, sideways: This task involves balance, coordination, and crossing over the midline of the body. Two platforms are placed on the floor 25 cm apart. While standing with both feet on one platform, the child attempts to move himself sideways as fast as possible by stepping from the first platform to the second, lifting up and setting the first platform ahead of the second one, and continuing this sequence for a total of 20 seconds. The child must maintain balance at all times and not let his feet touch the ground. One point is scored for moving the vacant platform and another point is given for shifting the body to the next platform. Three trials of 20 seconds each are given and the points from the trials are summed for the final score.

The four-test battery was administered to 800 children between the ages of 3 and 14 years from various socioeconomic levels. From the analysis of the data the following points for application can be given. (1) The results of factor analysis point to a marked homogeneity of the tasks, which mainly test total body coordination and control. (2) Using various random samples, the retest reliability for the separate tasks was 0.80, whereas the reliability of the entire test was 0.93. (3) The test could be used as a developmental test of body coordination because of the high age dependency as well as the low intelligence dependency. (4) It can be used as a diagnostic tool because groups of handicapped and clumsy children have shown significantly different total scores and subtest scores than normal children.

SELECTED PSYCHOMETRIC TESTS
Goodenough Draw-A-Man Test

The Draw-A-Man Test was originally published in 1926 by Goodenough. Since its conception the test has become enormously popular; 20 years after its introduc-

tion Louttit and Browne determined it to be the third most used test in clinical psychology. In 1961 Sundberg and Ballinger (1968) found it still in the top 10 most used tests. Originally the test was used as a measure of intelligence only, but in 1963 Harris published the results of an extensive revision of the Draw-A-Man Test. Harris extensively revised the scoring criteria, emphasizing the developmental aspect by regarding the drawing as a measure of intellectual maturity. After working to obtain a new standardization for the test, Harris converted the IQ computation from a mental age/chronological age ratio to a deviation IQ. Finally, Harris developed a companion to the Draw-A-Man Test, the Draw-A-Woman Test, and added a drawing quality score. The number of scorable items was increased from 51 to 73 but, like the original test, the new revision focuses on the child's accuracy of observation and on the development of conceptual thinking rather than on artistic skill. The scoring is on an all-or-none basis; raw scores are converted to standard scores with a mean of 100 and a standard deviation of 15. Attempts to utilize the drawings as a projective technique for the assessment of the personality characteristics of children have been, for the most part, unsuccessful. After extensive research Harris concluded that "consistent and reliable patterns having diagnostic significance for personality probably cannot be found in children's drawings" and that such drawings "primarily express cognitive processes." Norms were established by testing 2,975 children between the ages of 5 and 15 years from four major geographical areas and various socioeconomic levels. Reliabilities of 0.80 to 0.96 have been established and correlations with the Stanford-Binet test range from 0.36 to 0.65. Harris proposed that the drawings reveal the child's conceptual maturity but fail to show discrimination when progressing from concrete to a higher order of cognitive functioning. The Goodenough-Harris Draw-A-Man Test could easily be integrated with other screening tests into a battery to be used to select children who should receive more detailed attention. Scoring time averages 10 minutes and the test may be administered either individually or to groups. If it is administered individually, it should be the first test given in the battery because it is nonthreatening and quick, and it often elicits interesting comments on the part of the subject.

Minnesota Rate of Manipulation Test

The Minnesota Rate of Manipulation Test (MRORT) has established itself as a standard instrument for use in selecting applicants for jobs requiring gross arm-hand manipulatory movements. In addition, it is concerned with simple reaction time and initiated movement time in response to visual stimuli, with the most important aspects being the movement speed of the arm and fingers in grasping, placing, and releasing small objects. The basic apparatus of the MRORT consists of two rectangular boards, each with 60 wells arranged in four rows of 15, and 60 cylindrical blocks that fit into the wells. The test battery consists of five tasks: placing, turning, displacing, one-hand turning, and one-hand placing. Scoring is based on the total time in seconds required to complete a sequence of four trials. Norms for the MRORT were established in 1946, with no new technical data added or revisions made since 1957. We consider this unfortunate because with establishment of adequate norms and validity this test could be a valuable source of information for screening in the area of motor performance.

Gibson spiral maze test

A psychomotor test of speed and accuracy, the spiral maze test developed by Gibson (1964) requires only a pencil and paper and was designed to explore the association between a standardized psychomotor performance and certain limited personality characteristics, primarily delinquency. The test can be administered quickly with instructions that are concise and simple to follow. The test consists of a card on which is printed a spiral 9 inches in diameter, presenting a track rather than a maze. Printed O's about half the width of the track form obstructions along the track. The subject is instructed to start at the center and to get out as quickly as possible without touching the sidelines or any of the 56 obstacles.

Two variables are considered in test scoring: the time taken to draw a pencil line along the path and the number of errors made by touching the bordering lines of the path. Validity was originally established by Gibson when he compared the scores derived on the test with the degree of "naughtiness in school" as rated by classroom teachers. Gibson stated that "good" boys clearly score well in both quickness and accuracy, whereas the scores of "naughty" boys indicate quickness and carelessness.

Although some modifications could make the Gibson spiral maze test useful for detecting motor impairments, in its present form the test has inadequate norms and shows little evidence of reliability or validity.

Developmental Test of Visual Perception

In 1963 Frostig devised a test to determine visual perception. Although it is primarily designed to assess visual perception, it does determine hand-eye coordination as well as overall motor skills as they relate to visual configuration. Frostig's test battery is subdivided into the following five subtests.

1. Eye-motor coordination, involving eye-hand coordination as measured by the drawing of continuous straight, curved, or angular lines within boundaries of various widths or from point to point without guidelines

2. Figure-ground perception, measuring the ability to perceive specified figures that are placed against increasingly complex backgrounds (In general this subtest is considered by many to cor-

relate highly with reading readiness because the discrimination of shapes and context of configurations is comparable to the recognition of letters and numbers.)

3. Shape recognition, designed to measure ability to recognize a variety of geometric figures of different sizes, shadings, textures, and positions in space and the ability to discriminate and compare similar geometric figures

4. Position in space perception, which measures the discrimination of figures as they appear in different spatial positions (Ability to comprehend the meaning of the concepts "same" and "different" and following specific directions are also included in this subtest.)

5. Spatial relations perception, which measures the ability to analyze simple forms and patterns consisting of lines of various lengths and angles, the child reproducing the patterns using dots as reference points (Essentially, subtest 5 requires both motor coordination and short-term memory for visual designs.)

Generally speaking, the Frostig battery measures overall perceptual levels as well as the ability to recall and transform visual configurations. It also gives an indication of the child's motor development as reflected by his eye-hand coordination.

Norms on the Frostig test battery were established by testing 2,116 nursery school and public school participants who lived in southern California and were 3 through 9 years of age, primarily middle class, and white. Reliability was first established in 1960 by a test-retest study involving 50 children with learning difficulties. The Pearson product-moment coefficient of retest reliability was 0.98 using the full range in ages, with a 3-week average interval between test administrations. In a study conducted in 1961 and based on separate testers a correlation of 0.80 was obtained. Validity was established by comparing Frostig test scores of 374 kindergarten children with their teachers' rating of "classroom adjustment," "motor coordination," and "intellectual functioning." Scores on all three variables proved to be significant at the 0.001 level of confidence when compared to the Frostig test by means of chi-square comparisons. The statistical data obtained from the reliability and validity studies would certainly support further study and use of the test for both its screening and diagnostic values.

The test is an excellent tool in dealing with clumsiness in children not only because it is statistically definitive but because it is subdivided into five basic areas, thus allowing the therapist to be more specific in determining where the emphasis should be placed in remedying the child's movement problems.

Purdue Perceptual-Motor Survey

The Purdue Perceptual-Motor Survey was developed in 1966 for the express purpose of identifying children 6 through 10 years of age who may be lacking in the perceptual-motor abilities necessary for academic success. Validity was established by correlating scores on the survey with the teachers' subjective ratings. A correlation of 0.65 was obtained using a sample of 297 children. On the other hand, a reliability coefficient of 0.95 was obtained by a test-retest method in which different examiners tested 30 subjects at an interval of 1 week. This would seem to indicate that the coefficient of stability is quite good. The item means show expected variation according to age, and the item variances remain constant for all practical purposes. Statistically these findings make the test a usable tool in research and evaluation programs.

The Purdue Perceptual-Motor Survey is easy to administer, requiring very little special training or sophisticated equipment. A major problem arises in the interpretation of the data, however, and in exactly what a particular score or series of scores means in terms of perceptual-motor function or a child's classroom performance. Therefore results from this instrument must be used with caution.

Southern California sensory integration tests

From 1962 through 1966 Ayres developed four tests dealing with specific perceptual problems in children: (1) the Ayres Space Test, designed to evaluate perceptual speed and space visualization; (2) the Southern California Motor Accuracy Test (SCMAT), designed as an objective tool for measuring fine movement discrimination and hand-eye accuracy; (3) the Southern California Kinesthesic and Tactile Perception Test (SCKT), consisting of a battery of six tests developed for evaluating dysfunction in somesthetic perception in children; and (4) the Southern California Figure-Ground Visual Perception Test (SCFG), devised to assist in the determination of deficits in visual perception that requires selection of a foreground figure from a contrasting background.

The norms and other statistical information were derived from data obtained in testing children from various socioeconomic levels in the metropolitan area of Los Angeles. In all cases the statistical treatment of the data in dealing with the factors of reliability and validity is quite explicit and well done.

The tests for the most part are easy to administer because of well-defined instructions, short duration, and ease of scoring. Although there has been some criticism of the degree of reliability and lack of discrimination in the range of scores, these tests are basically well constructed, statistically sound, and specific enough to aid teachers in detecting certain perceptual problems in children.

Eye-movement photography with the reading eye camera

Eye-movement photography provides the examiner with a record of a performance

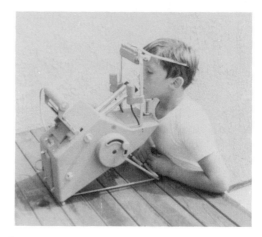

Fig. 4-1. Diagnosing reading problems with the aid of the reading eye camera.

skill in reading (Fig. 4-1). As the reader moves his eyes along lines of print in a left-to-right fashion, a photograph is made. Reading material is selected according to the age and level of understanding of the individual. While reading takes place, a small ray of light is reflected into both eyes and eye movement is recorded on movie film. From the film record the following variables are analyzed.

1. Fixation, or eye stops, during which the eyeball is held stationary for a short period of time while perception takes place (A more efficient reader requires fewer fixations in reading a given line than a poor reader.)
2. Duration of fixations, or length of time the reader's eyes pause during a fixation
3. Regressions, right-to-left eye movements instead of normal left-to-right movements (Regressions usually indicate problems in visual acuity, perceptual inadequacies, and a lack of sufficient interpretive or organizational ability.)
4. Span of recognition, the amount of words or word parts perceived during a fixation or eye pause
5. Comprehension time, the time required by a reader to read a given

selection with adequate comprehension

Arnheim and Sinclair (1973), in a 1-year study involving elementary schoolchildren, found a high correlation between motor ability as measured by the Frostig Movement Skills Test Battery and fixations, regressions, and reading comprehension as measured by the reading eye camera. More research should be done in this area before any definite conclusions can be drawn as to the potential secondary use of the reading eye camera as a diagnostic tool in the area of clumsiness.

●   ●   ●

In this chapter we have made no attempt to be all-inclusive or to present a complete historical development of the testing field. Many of the early tests are inferior to those published recently; when such tests add little or nothing to resources for testing clumsiness in children, they have been omitted. Many tests currently available were designed to assess perceptual-motor inadequacy and clumsiness in children, and the reader has the option of screening out or selecting the tests that would be most appropriate for his particular situation. Regardless of which test is used, pretesting at the beginning of any program is most essential.

Needless to say, human beings are such complex organisms that at this time it is virtually impossible to devise a test battery that can precisely assess all of the numerous variables that are involved in movement patterns. However, some of the tests that are currently being used are sufficiently definitive to provide a logical starting point in a developmental program for the remediation of clumsiness.

5

LEARNING IN THE PSYCHOMOTOR DOMAIN

As discussed earlier, children interact with their environment in three domains: cognitive, affective, and psychomotor. Learning in the psychomotor domain is the process by which movement skills are acquired. In essence, psychomotor learning is concerned with the learner's change of behavior stemming from movement. In the past several years the entire field of motor learning has become increasingly more important to movement specialists (Oxendine, 1968). The ultimate goal in psychomotor learning is to bring about the most skillful motor performance possible. A movement skill is defined as "the ability to bring about predetermined results with maximum certainty, often with the minimum outlay of time or energy or both" (Knapp, 1964). This chapter discusses the most pertinent aspects of psychomotor learning relevant to the physically awkward or clumsy individual. The information presented here is designed to assist the teacher or therapist in developing a motor

therapy plan that is both diagnostic and individualized.

SOME LEARNING CHARACTERISTICS OF THE CLUMSY CHILD

Three major factors stand out as most important in the psychomotor learning of the clumsy child. These are the factors of readiness, motivation, and specific learning conditions.

Readiness

The subject of readiness is extremely complex and has been a major topic of discussion among educators for centuries. It becomes even more complex when the variables of physical, mental, or emotional problems are added. Most authorities agree that a learner must be sufficiently mature to profit from a learning situation. An adequate maturity level may be obscured and discouraged by a history of defeat. A poor self-image combined with a lack of confidence may hinder a child from attempting a new movement challenge.

The movement problems of the clumsy child are seldom obvious but lead to a negative sequence of developmental events. For example, the individual with a history of movement failures or of having been constantly belittled by either parent or peers as to his lack of motor abilities will most likely not want to explore and reach out into new movement vistas. As a result his acquisition of movement skills is inhibited and his motor retardation compounded. Also, from a growth and development standpoint the child may be ready to learn a certain skill, but he may have failed to acquire the level of motor fitness necessary to achieve the desired motor task. A severe defeatist attitude may prevent the clumsy child from taking a chance, and he will not utilize his full capacities in order to try a new physical activity.

Readiness of the clumsy child to learn movement tasks is determined less by his observed behavior than by other factors. For example, diagnostic testing, a medical history, and information provided by other professionals can be compiled to give a good idea of what to expect from the child. The child must be considered the best indicator of what type of skills he can learn best, the amount of learning that can take place at one time, and the speed with which it can be integrated into his total behavioral system. As discussed in Chapter 7, the behavioral objectives technique provides an excellent indication of the child's readiness to learn.

Motivation

Motivation can generally be defined as the state of activity that results in some overt motor behavior. Two very important facets of motivation are *need* and *drive*. Need refers to a deficiency within the organism, while drive is the ingredient within the organism that propels it to activity (Cratty, 1973). The areas that stand out in specifically relating the complex subject of motivation to the clumsy child are increas-ing the aspiration level and positively altering motives.

Raising aspirations. The clumsy individual who has had a succession of past failures says inwardly, if not overtly, to the therapist, "I don't believe I can succeed, but prove me wrong." The individual who constantly fails when attempting a motor task will usually develop a *failure syndrome* and as a result set his movement goals either too low or unrealistically high. Setting lower goals than one can achieve tends to protect the individual against the possibility of additional painful failures. On the other hand, a child who sets goals that are too high after many failures is outwardly expressing a fantasy in which he has equal or better physical ability than his peers.

The teacher or therapist must assist the clumsy person in setting realistic goals by looking objectively at both his abilities and disabilities. A motor therapy program that is based on success will in most cases raise the aspiration level of the participant, while failure will only serve to lower the aspiration level.

Altering motives. The motor therapist must have a great deal of skill in motivating the clumsy child. Motivational techniques should be based on the specific needs and characteristics of the clumsy child. For example, an individual who is hyperkinetic will not usually respond to motivational techniques that increase arousal. On the contrary, the best approach is one that reduces tension and calms agitated behavior. Conversely, a child who is hypokinetic and phlegmatic in his motor behavior needs to be aroused to excitement. Soothing techniques for the hypokinetic child may hamper motor development; increasing the level of muscular tension will often produce better conditions for learning.

Positive versus negative reinforcement. The problem of whether to use positive or negative reinforcement, reward or punishment, must be seriously considered by the instructor who is seeking maximum motivation. In general, a child with low self-esteem will respond more positively to reward situations than to punishment; however, both can be used to some advantage if skillfully applied. Both reward and punishment can be either extrinsic or intrinsic. Extrinsic rewards are external factors such as points, money, and candy, while intrinsic rewards come from within the child as a sense of adequacy and acceptance because something was done well.

Ideally, the child should be assisted to develop internal acknowledgment of self-improvement rather than seeking external rewards. Positive reinforcement commonly is preferred to negative reinforcement because it engenders a feeling of worth. On the other hand, negative reinforcement such as punishment serves only to compound the feeling of defeat. Also, negative reinforcement, particularly in group situations, raises muscular tension levels, increases self-doubt, and often deters from a learning goal. This should not, however, completely rule out the use of punishment because completely unacceptable behavior cannot be tolerated. Such behavior often negates prior achievements; therefore verbal reprimands and the taking away of privileges may assist the child to return to a teachable condition.

LEARNING CONDITIONS

In order for clumsiness to be remedied most effectively the proper conditions for learning must be present. These conditions can be internal or external to the learner.

Anxiety and tension

Anxiety has been defined as an abnormal amount of undefined fear. Chronic, unexplained fears are often present in individuals lacking in self-confidence and are reflected in serious neuroses. Such personality disturbances are common among individuals who are clumsy or physically awkward. Anxiety can raise the general muscular tension level, produce asynchrony, and make skill learning difficult. Tension-release methods have been found

to make the anxious child more amenable to learning movement skills (Chapter 12).

Stress

Stress is the disruption of internal equilibrium, known as homeostasis, and stems from emotional and physiological origins. Life in general can be described in terms of losing and gaining homeostatic balance. Stress, however, is a more extreme state of imbalance than usually occurs and if continued over a long period it can lead to disease. Stress as described here will, if not controlled, deter motor learning. Cratty (1973) concurs with this point, indicating that stress adversely affects highly anxious subjects, disrupting both their mental and motor performances.

Characteristically the clumsy child is overly anxious, has a defeatist attitude about his abilities, and has a low tolerance to the many stressors that commonly affect his daily life. One important therapeutic goal is to assist the child in tolerating stress through a carefully planned and gradually administered program of intervention. Toleration of such stressors as energy output, fatigue, noise, an unstructured environment, or relating to other individuals in a cooperative manner can be selectively introduced into the motor therapy program.

Length of motor therapy sessions

In considering optimum learning conditions it seems appropriate to discuss the length of time that a motor therapy session should last. The most important considerations are the total length of time for a single session and the minimum number of sessions per week that are necessary for maximum learning to occur. Through trial and error we have found that the most advantageous length of time for a motor therapy session is between 20 and 40 minutes for individual therapy and between 40 and 60 minutes for small-group (two to four children) therapy sessions. This length of time was arrived at when considering the variables of fatigue, retention of learned material, motivation, and the span of time in which a skilled instructor can be effective.

The number of times a motor therapy session should be offered during the week is difficult to determine because of the many factors involved in carrying out such a program. If motivation could be maintained at a maximum level, a 6 day per week program with 2 or 3 sessions per day would be considered ideal. For example, Kiphard, in his motor therapy program at the Institute for Child Psychology in Hamm, Germany, offers a program every day for 6 weeks with great success. However, unless such a program is carried out in an institutional setting under highly controlled conditions it may be impractical. Although a daily multisession exposure to motor therapy is desirable, effective learning can still occur in a twice-a-week program. To supplement a minimum program exposure, a home routine can be initiated if appropriate conditions are present in the home; the most important factor is understanding and patient parents. Parents acting as therapists will be discussed more fully in Chapter 9.

The learning environment

In recent years the term "engineering the environment" has crept into educational jargon and is very descriptive of what a motor therapist attempts to do. Even though the clumsy child requires a personal type of environment in which to best express his own particular needs, experience has taught that in the initial stages of the program a highly structured environment is preferred. In the beginning of the program the child should feel a predictability and consistency in the physical setting and people associated with the therapy environment. For example, the therapy room is always arranged in the same way and the instructor is always on time or, if that is impossible, the child is prepared beforehand.

Another very important factor is that whoever works with the child responds consistently and in the same manner under similar circumstances. It is also desirable that in the initial stages of instruction a room with as few distractions as possible be utilized. Ideally the child should engage in one activity at a time without the distraction of play equipment and objects strewn about the room. As the child gains confidence in himself and the environment, less structure is necessary and more stress can be tolerated.

BASIC INSTRUCTIONS FOR MOTOR THERAPY

The purpose of this section is to provide a basis for giving instruction. Because this is an extremely theoretical and complex area, only those aspects of instruction that are specifically relevant to clumsiness will be discussed.

Instructional approaches

Because the physically awkward child is not usually gifted in psychomotor learning, the therapist must be aware of which senses should be utilized most in the delivery of instruction. The senses of hearing, sight, touch, and movement are of relative importance when instructing the child; therefore an effective therapist must know when to use and when not to use these senses individually or in combination.

Visual guidance

Vision far surpasses the other senses as a learning mode for the normal population. This may or may not be true for the clumsy person, particularly if the individual has perceptual-motor problems, and instructing through this mode may serve only to frustrate. If vision is chosen as a learning avenue, learning cues must be carefully selected to assist the child in successfully completing the specific task.

Teaching through the means of visual guidance consists of the teacher demonstrating the skill to be learned and the learner mimicking the performance of the teacher. It is important that the instructor be able to demonstrate the task accurately if visual guidance is to be used effectively. However, when the instructor is unable to adequately demonstrate a skill, visual aids such as film loops, slides, or pictures should be used. A *cue* provides guidance or a hint that leads to a course of action. It is important that a teacher or therapist be able to provide the most appropriate cues for learning. It should be noted that the more skilled the learner becomes, the more he is able to ignore irrelevant cues and attend to subtle cues.

Manual guidance

It is commonly accepted that proper kinesthetic feedback is a primary factor in effective motor performance. This factor is especially important to the clumsy individual for whom motor learning is often difficult and inappropriate motor responses are typical. In our experience manual guidance in the early stages of learning a skill is as important or even more important than visual guidance. At times when information processing through the visual mode may only confuse the learner, concentrating on how the action should feel provides a better vehicle to gaining skill in movement.

At first the instructor takes the child through the correct movements passively; then he encourages active movement with verbal guidance. Many techniques can be used to increase awareness of the correct feel of a motor skill, such as wearing weights on the body part that is being moved, application of manual resistance by the instructor, or pulling against the resistance of heavy rubber bands while performing the movement pattern.

Verbal guidance

Generally verbal guidance is less effective than visual and manual guidance in directing the acquistion of a motor skill. As mentioned earlier, some children learn better through one sense mode than another. This is true for the auditory as well as the visual

and kinesthetic senses. Children with perceptual handicaps may have difficulty in processing information effectively from verbal instructions or cues. Therefore we suggest that when verbalization is used terms and phrases should be kept to a minimum and only concrete words should be used for initiating directions. A common error made by both instructors and therapists is that of talking too much; it often confuses the performer by injecting too many action possibilities into the instructions. Rather than confusing the clumsy child with lengthy instructions, the therapist should use concrete terms like "stop," "go," and "move" to assist in discrimination of right from wrong motor responses. Verbalization must also be considered as a form of feedback of cues while the child performs a particular motor activity.

Multisensory instruction

For the child with psychomotor learning difficulties, skill development is best attained through a multisensory approach. In other words, all the senses should be used in a variety of ways to assist the child in fully ingraining and retaining a motor skill on a long-term basis.

Knowing performance results

It is commonly accepted that the learner improves best when there is immediate knowledge of whether or not the movement is correct. Immediate feedback eliminates trial-and-error learning to a great extent and provides a basis for future actions as well as for modifying and refining motor responses.

Distribution and massing

How to distribute the time allotted for learning a specific skill has long been a problem for teachers and therapists in the movement professions. Massed practice is practice that is conducted continuously without pause, while distributed practice provides some intervals of rest between practice periods. In most cases short, frequent practices are more favorable to learning motor skills than are long, continuous sessions. The length of each practice and rest period varies according to individual needs and makeup. In our experience practice sessions can effectively range from 2 to 10 minutes, while rest periods should vary from less than 30 seconds to 5 minutes or longer depending on such factors as the attention span, motivation, and skill level at which the child is performing.

Whole versus part learning

A skill has been previously defined as an organized pattern of motor responses. Whole and part learning refers to practicing a movement skill in its entirety and in parts. The extent to which whole or part learning is practiced depends on the complexity of the task and the particular abilities of the learner. If the instructor thinks that the task should be broken into units for ease of learning, division should be such that each part can logically be built on another until an entire skill has been learned. However, it is important that the learner have the whole skill in mind before a portion of it is practiced. To facilitate this the instructor demonstrates the entire skill to the child, highlighting the various units to be practiced later. It also must be remembered that "the focus of attention should be on the task as a whole and the perceptual cues rather than on the specific motions involved" (McGraw, 1943). For the clumsy child who is easily distracted by extraneous stimuli and who is lacking in confidence, the accomplishment of a whole task may be confusing and discouraging. Concentrating on units of a skill is more logical than bewildering the child with the complexity of the whole. On the successful completion of part of a task, positive reinforcement provides the deficient child with enough confidence to try the next part until, to his surprise, the whole skill has been learned.

Mental practice

Mental or image practice refers to rehearsing a motor task by thinking it through without an actual overt movement taking place. Although it is not as effective as the physical practice of a skill, going through the complete movement routine in the "mind's eye" is better than no practice at all. Mental practice is particularly advantageous to the below-average mover because it is one more means to learning a skill. Mental practice is an excellent technique for children who are impulsive and move without thinking about their actions. Oxendine (1968) feels that mental rehearsal should be used just prior to performing a skill, between practice sessions, or in places that are different from where the skill will actually be performed.

Intrapersonal communication

Intrapersonal communication refers to verbalization by the performer of how a specific task is to be performed. Intrapersonal communication can be in the form of talking out loud to one's self or subverbal rehearsal more commonly known as "verbal mediation." Verbal mediation or mental practice, as discussed earlier, is the process of changing concrete stimuli into symbols that are later translated into overt behavior. In essence, intrapersonal communication consists of talking to one's self before and during the execution of a particular motor task. This is an excellent teaching technique for children having difficulty in motor planning. Encouraging the clumsy child to verbalize what he is about to do and to continue this verbalization throughout the execution of the skill also serves to reinforce retention.

Overlearning

Overlearning has been suggested by most authorities in the area of psychomotor learning as a means to best retain a particular skill. This factor is particularly important when working with the physically awkward individual. Often the person who has motor learning difficulties finds problems in retaining efficient movement patterns unless they have been overlearned. Therefore, once the child has seemingly mastered a desired skill, drills and practice sessions should be provided to more firmly establish the specific patterns of movement as a permanent addition to his motor repertoire.

6

ASSUMPTIONS, PRINCIPLES, AND STRATEGIES FOR REMEDIATION

It is a commonly accepted premise that physical clumsiness is an extremely complex problem that should not be taken lightly by those charged with the responsibility of remediation. Because of the inconspicuousness of symptoms and the difficulties inherent in diagnosing clumsiness, delay in remediation has in the past been the rule rather than the exception. Obscured by personal indifferences and the emotional consequences of a relatively hostile and unaccepting environment, the problems of clumsy children are compounded as they become older.

In general, movement specialists should accept the awkward individual as he appears and base the program not on chronological expectations but on the participant's developmental level. Although imperfect in many ways, remediation of clumsiness in children has been successfully accomplished in programs such as those conducted at the Early Achievement Center of Santa Ana, California, and the Institute for Sensory Motor Development conducted at California State University at Long Beach; the stimulus and direction of these programs are to assist in developing movement efficiency.

A PROGRAM BASED ON DEVELOPMENTAL PRINCIPLES

In our experience the most effective remedial program for the clumsy individual is one founded on the principles of psychomotor development. These principles in general stipulate that the individual gains movement control starting at the head and progressing to the feet and from the center of the body outward. Remediation begins from a generally diffused motor behavior. Large-muscle control is gained first and is followed by a gradual acquisition of small-muscle control. Also, as maturation and motor development occur, there is the gaining of countless specific movement skills. After the child has accumulated a bank of motor skills, then he develops the ability to *motor plan* and solve unique movement problems utilizing the backlog of movement skills that have been acquired earlier. Remediation is best determined by the point of view that the body functions first as a whole, then as individual parts.

SEQUENCING OF TASKS

In the early stages of the remediation program for clumsy children, experience has shown that sequencing of motor tasks with a gradual increase in complexity provides the greatest chance for success. The sequenced task method employs movement units designed for a particular child's level of maturation and development. Selection of motor tasks is based on the challenge they offer and on the particular category of movement development that the child needs. More specifically, 12 task categories are employed: (1) tension release, (2) locomotion, (3) balance, (4) body and space perception, (5) rhythm and temporal awareness, (6) rebound and airborne activities, (7) projectile management, (8) management of daily motor activities, (9) selected play skills, (10) motor fitness, (11) aggression management, and (12) water submersion. These categories are the most important movement channels through which a child can gain skill competence, efficiency, and development of a catalyst to movement exploration and spontaneous self-expression.

DIAGNOSING AND PRESCRIBING

Ideally, effective programming is based on an accurate diagnosis identifying specific motor areas in which the individual is having difficulty. When the primary movement and/or psychoemotional factors that are producing motor inefficiencies have been determined, an appropriate prescriptive program can be designed and initiated. However, remediation must be considered as both an inexact science and an art, much as most other existing educational and therapeutic approaches. It is commonly agreed that diagnosis relating to prescriptive movement activities is at best approximate and inconcise as well as fallible. As in most of the helping professions, including medicine, past experiences and intuition are in many cases as important to the delivery of assistance as relying totally on the tools of assessment. One must consider that the remediation program in itself is an ongoing program of assessment; the child's successes and failures are continually observed and allowed for by increasing or decreasing the difficulty of specific activities. The program incorporates the no-failure concept whereby no child is allowed to flounder at activities that are too difficult but given only those activities that the instructor has predetermined that he can successfully accomplish.

MOVEMENT FREEDOM AND CREATIVITY

As previously described, a clumsy child displays a variety of atypical behaviors. Such a child often requires an orderly and highly structured environment to bring meaning and predictability into his life. We contend that the clumsy child will respond best to a task-oriented program that gradually increases in complexity and allows freedom to explore after the child has successfully achieved a backlog of specifically prescribed individual skills in a setting almost completely dominated by the teacher or therapist. As the child gains in self-confidence and movement efficiency, decision making is gradually turned over to him and he is given freedom of movement self-expression. The introduction of permissive teaching techniques such as movement education should be delayed until a good foundation of successful movement experiences and a positive self-concept have been established. Armed with good feelings about himself plus a storehouse of motor abilities, the child can respond without fear of failing in comparison to others and can be allowed to explore freely without the imposition of external constraints.

MOVEMENT PROBLEM SOLVING

For a child to be considered coordinated he must have the ability to solve unique movement problems using appropriate motor responses. One of the most important ingredients necessary to accomplish movement problem solving is the ability to motor plan, in other words, to retrieve information from the backlog of experiences to solve a particular movement problem (Fig. 6-1). Children unable to execute motor planning are unable to solve the simplest movement problems or copy the movements of another person. Barsch (1967) describes apraxia as "one form of difficulty on the negative side between the polar opposites of planning and nonplanning." Children with an extreme problem in motor planning who lack the ability to set goals and to determine their behavior may act impulsively and in confusion. Barsch describes such an individual as lacking in the ability to identify himself as part of a spatial surrounding; he becomes lost in space. To be purposeful and self-directing, a child must be able to plan and then order his actions. Motor planning begins at birth and continues throughout life. The typical person who engages in new and unaccustomed movements is at first inefficient but is usually able to assess his responses and make changes based on past movement experiences. He is also able to develop strategies for future actions and has the ability to make immediate alternative movement decisions when confronted with various obstacles. Therefore a remediation program designed to overcome clumsiness should provide the child with a backlog of successful movement experiences that will enable him to solve novel movement problems.

PLANNED STRESS

The term "stress" has many definitions, depending on the professional discipline using it. From a mechanical point of view it is the physical pressure, pull, or other force exerted on one thing by another; in other words, it refers to the strain applied to a particular unit or system. In *Movement Behavior and Motor Learning* (1973),

Fig. 6-1. Solving unique movement problems. **A,** Hula-Hoop activities. **B,** Using scooter board.

Cratty discusses the recently developed medical concept of stress, indicating that it is an intervening variable located between the situational input and the movement output. Abnormal amounts of muscular tension traditionally have been thought to be directly associated with stress and become the emotional manifestation of anxiety and fear. Selye (1956), one of the pioneers of psychosomatic medicine, suggests that stress produces a general adaptation syndrome (GAS) in all animals, including man. The first stage of the GAS theory is *alarm reaction,* the normal reaction that occurs when the body experiences emotion. In the second stage, *resistance to stress,* the body utilizes a great deal of physiological resources in its attempt to resist the stress that is being imposed. The final stage, *exhaustion,* occurs when the organism has used up its defenses and comes to the stresses with a subsequent breakdown in cells, organs, or organ systems; the breakdown is manifested in disease processes. The anxious person, one who has a preponderance of undefinable fears, is likely to have physical problems caused by a variety of external and internal stresses.

It is highly important that the physically clumsy child learn to tolerate stress by having it gradually interjected into the remediation program (Fig. 6-2). A poor self-image, a rigid nonyielding personality, and anxiety are traits common to the clumsy child, decreasing his ability to withstand sudden or, in many cases, sustained stress. The planned stress program gradually introduces stresses that can be tolerated through movement or cognitive activities. The introduction of stress is subtle and directed toward a specific target behavioral response. Through a well-planned program, the child can gradually become desensitized to stress, learning to rule out nonessential stimuli and develop a more flexible and resilient personality.

THE NO-FAILURE CONCEPT

A child who is physically awkward usually is considered emotionally fragile. Helping the child to gain self-confidence should have the highest priority. Success must be built on success. Consequently, if a child hesitates or questions his ability to accomplish a given motor act, the instructor must decide whether to decrease, maintain, or increase the difficulty of the task. Convincing a child that a particular hurdle can be overcome requires excitement, confi-

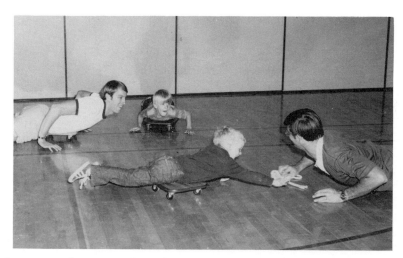

Fig. 6-2. Increasing toleration to physical and emotional stress through a scooter board game of "keep away."

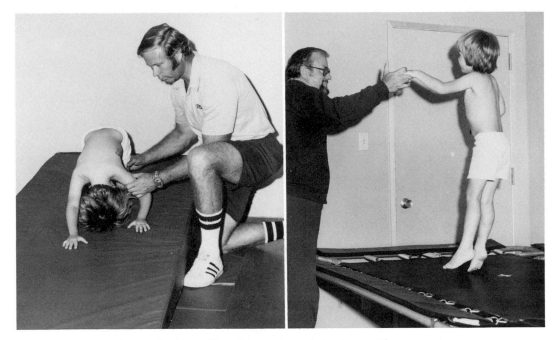

Fig. 6-3. Gaining self-confidence through developmental movements.

dence, and intimate involvement by the therapist with each accomplishment that is made. As a positive self-concept is built, ego strength develops to a point at which the child can risk failure. Risking failure requires courage; therefore one of the important goals of a remediation program is confidence building (Fig. 6-3). In the therapy setting the child is encouraged to develop security and trust in the environment. If the child begins to have trust, confidence increases rapidly and is followed by a desire to learn more and to engage in a wide variety of motor activities.

SENSORY INTEGRATION

As discussed in Chapter 1, one of the primary functions of the brain is to organize stimuli that come from the environment and process them into usable information. Ayres (1973) defines integration as "being able to put data together, but not inexorably so, into a kind of directed flexibility." She further indicates that integrative processing occurs in all aspects of brain functioning, but the areas that are concerned with sensory-motor integration are most significant in learning disorders. Therapeutic programs concerned with sensory integration, such as those of Kabot and Knott (1948), Fay (1958), Rood (1954), Bobath (1957), and Ayres (1967), are designed to remedy sensory and motor functions by integrative processes. Ayres proposes rubbing the body with different textures to provide tactile stimulation. She also proposes vestibular stimulation for remediation of sensory integrative dysfunctions by such activities as scooter board riding and spinning in a hammock as well as other tasks designed to stimulate the brain stem and vestibular apparatus (Fig. 6-4). The effective processing of information emanating from the environment is one of the primary goals to be accomplished by the clumsy child. Although the remediation program is basically nonacademic, provisions should be made for experiences employing integration of the senses.

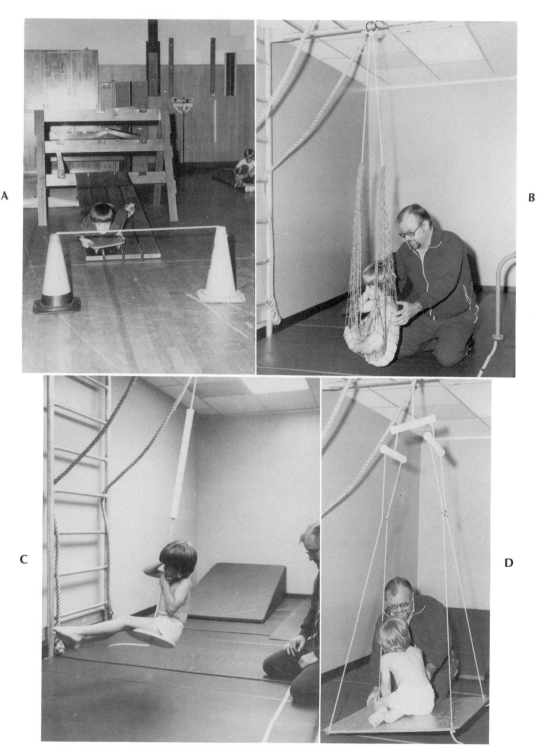

Fig. 6-4. Activities proposed by Ayres for vestibular stimulation and sensory integration. **A,** Riding a scooter board in the prone position. **B,** Spinning and swinging in a hammock. **C,** Bouncing, turning, and swinging. **D,** Swinging and turning on a platform.

THE FUN PRINCIPLE

One of the motor therapist's greatest tools is that "moving can be fun." Enjoyment should be built into every aspect of the therapeutic program. Joy of movement is natural for children; distaste for movement is unnatural. Therefore every effort should be put forth to motivate the clumsy person toward a positive feeling for physical activity. Through positive reinforcement, the no-failure concept, and providing activities within each child's ability level, the child acquires a feeling of enjoyment of movement. Also, a therapeutic session should not be totally dedicated to what is not done well but should offer definite opportunities for success in activities that involve the child's greatest strength.

When considering the fun principle one should not discount the effect of the instructor's personality on the child. A person who displays a positive personality, who is genuinely interested in the child's accomplishments, and who is highly sensitive to his feelings is the type of person who can best apply the fun principle in remediation. The child should not be considered as a medical entity or as a scientific specimen but looked at from a developmental point of view. When there is honest excitement about progress and accomplishments rather than concentration on specific dysfunctions, a positive bond usually occurs between instructor and child. The important test of the fun principle is whether the child looks forward to returning for another session.

PART II

THE MOTOR THERAPY PROGRAM

Part II is concerned with the important aspects of organizing and administering the motor therapy program. Because we believe that motor therapy should not be restricted only to the professional movement therapists but should be an integral part of education, this part is designed for a wide variety of professionals interested in developing and carrying out a remediation program.

7

ORGANIZING AND ADMINISTERING THE PROGRAM

Programs exclusively dedicated to assisting the clumsy person are relatively scarce in the United States. Because in the past the clumsy child has not been accurately identified or labeled as having clearly definable traits, schools and other institutions have been reluctant to offer special programs.

However, it should be noted that programs of motor therapy can be offered by almost any institutions dedicated to serving people, such as schools, recreational facilities, YMCA's and YWCA's, churches, community centers, state hospitals, and universities. Motor therapy can also be a small part of a regular ongoing program such as physical education or recreation or a program entity in itself. Of primary importance is that the clumsy child be identified as early as possible and given opportunities for remediation.

FACILITIES AND EQUIPMENT

The facilities and equipment necessary to carry out a successful motor therapy program can be quite simple or elaborate, depending on the emphasis, the number of children served, and, of course, the funds available. (See Fig. 7-1.) It must be remembered that a successful program is primarily determined by the enthusiasm of the therapist and not by how elaborate the facilities or equipment are. The following is a partial list of equipment for specific motor therapy categories.

1. Relaxation
    a. Quiet room
    b. Individual mats
    c. Metronome or record player for soothing rhythm
2. Locomotion
    a. Large mats for rolling, crawling, and creeping

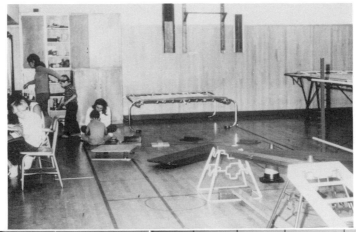

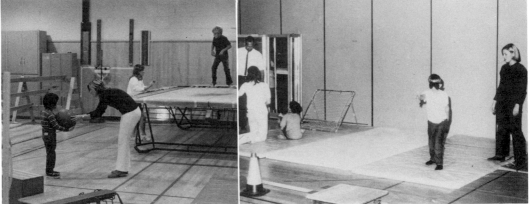

Fig. 7-1. Motor therapy laboratory.

b. Space to run
c. Steps
d. Objects to jump from, for example, tires, rocks, logs
e. Objects to climb, for example, ladders, ropes, cargo nets
f. Hurdles to jump, for example, lines, sticks, string
3. Balance
   a. Balance beams
   b. Balance boards
   c. Sticks
   d. Lines
   e. Gymnastic apparatus
4. Body perception and spatial awareness
   a. Mirrors
   b. Hula-Hoops
   c. Ropes
   d. Mimic cards

5. Dexterity and hand-eye control
   a. Assorted balls, for example, Nerf ball, Whiffle ball
   b. Clothespins
   c. Blocks
   d. Pegs
   e. Marbles
   f. String beads
6. Rhythm and temporal awareness
   a. Metronome
   b. Record player and records
   c. Percussion instruments
   d. Space to move
7. Rebound and airborne activities
   a. Inner tubes
   b. Trampoletes
   c. Trampoline
   d. Springboards
   e. Jumping boards

8. Mechanical efficiency
   a. Mirror
   b. Objects to push, pull, lift, and carry
   c. Posture screen
9. Projectile management
   a. Assorted sizes and kinds of balls, for example, Fleese, baseballs, Whiffle balls
   b. Beanbags
   c. Balloons
10. Classroom motor skills
    a. Blackboard, chalk, and eraser
    b. Large roll of wrapping paper, pencil, and crayons
    c. Assorted surfaces to work, for example, clay, wet paint
    d. Scissors
11. Common play skills
    a. Things to throw, for example, balls, beanbags
    b. Things with which to catch, for example, gloves, boxes, cutaway bleach bottles
    c. Things with which to strike, for example, batting tees, bats, paddles, rackets, tether balls
    d. Things to kick, for example, balls, balloons
12. Motor fitness
    a. Opportunities for sustained large-muscle activity
    b. Gymnastic apparatus or special equipment for hanging and swinging
    c. Overhead ladder
    d. Chinning bars
    e. Resistance equipment, for example, sandbags, ankle and wrist weights, dumbbells, barbells

PROGRAM LOCATION

Ideally the motor remediation program should have access to several locations, depending on the child's individual needs. It is desirable to have a location for individualized or small-group instruction including a motor therapy room with enough space for each child to run and jump freely without fear of running into a wall or other obstruction. In the early stages of therapy, equipment or supplies should not be located directly on the floor; rather, it should be stored and only brought out when needed. Solid walls are desirable for bouncing balls and for target-throwing activities. We also suggest that one wall contain a blackboard and mirrors. A large storage room immediately adjacent to the activity room is desirable. The primary purpose of the motor therapy room is to allow for a structured environment, particularly in the early stages of remediation. A room that is clear of clutter and extraneous equipment affords less confusion and distraction from the primary program objective. If the ideal motor therapy room is not available, any indoor space that allows the child to move freely can be utilized. In fact, almost any indoor or outdoor area can be set aside for motor training by the use of lines, ropes, or even natural indicators such as trees, shrubs, and the like.

PERSONNEL

Persons who effectively carry out a motor therapy program may have any of a variety of backgrounds. Probably the most logical professionals to perform motor therapy would be members of the moving professions—physical education, recreation, physical therapy, occupational therapy, and dance therapy. Professionals in the areas of communicative disorders, learning disabilities, and special education also could effectively conduct such a program with proper training. Subprofessionals or lay persons must not undertake the entire responsibility for motor therapy but could be used as assistants or aides to qualified therapists. There are many sources for therapists seeking program assistance, for example, parents, peers, older children (who perhaps themselves have some movement difficulties), future high school teachers, college or university volunteers who are majoring in the helping sciences, and even volunteers from the retirement community. However, ensuring the effectiveness of an

MOTOR DEVELOPMENT PROGRAM MEDICAL CLEARANCE FORM

The motor development program is designed for children
having motor coordination difficulties. There are
opportunities for individual improvement in the following
areas: (1) basic developmental movement patterns;
(2) perceptual-motor activities; (3) visual-motor
activities; (4) auditory-motor activities; (5) classroom
motor activities; (6) special exercise and posture training;
(7) swimming pool motor activities; (8) basic play skills;
(9) rhythmic control activities; (10) physical fitness
activities; (11) self-awareness and body image activities;
and (12) common children's activities.

The degree of emphasis in each area is individualized
to meet the specific needs of the child.

- -

TO WHOM IT MAY CONCERN:

_____ was given a routine physical

examination for the purpose of participation in a motor development

program. All findings at this time are negative and within normal

limits with the exception of:_____

_____

I further certify that this individual has no medical problems that

will interfere with his (her) participation in an active motor

development program as described.

_____   _____, M.D.
Physician's name (Please type)   Physician's signature

_____
Address

_____
Phone

Fig. 7-2. Form for medical clearance to engage in physical activity.

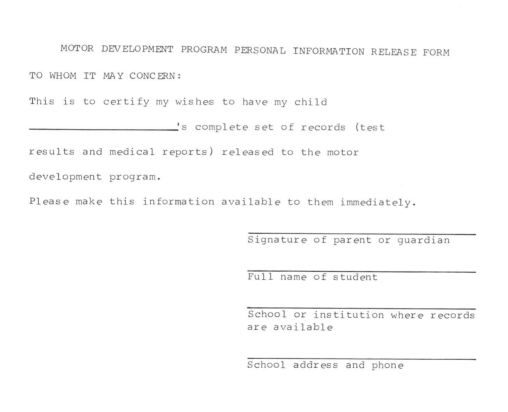

MOTOR DEVELOPMENT PROGRAM PERSONAL INFORMATION RELEASE FORM

TO WHOM IT MAY CONCERN:

This is to certify my wishes to have my child

_____'s complete set of records (test

results and medical reports) released to the motor

development program.

Please make this information available to them immediately.

_____
Signature of parent or guardian

_____
Full name of student

_____
School or institution where records
are available

_____
School address and phone

Fig. 7-3. Release form to obtain school test results and medical reports.

aide program includes a careful in-service training program incorporating all the safety factors to be practiced and the important "do's and dont's" necessary to working with the clumsy child.

LEGAL RESPONSIBILITIES

Inherent in any movement activity is the possibility of physical injury. This is particularly true for the clumsy individual. In our experience, injuries seem to occur less often in the well-supervised motor therapy program than in regular physical education or recreation programs. However, the possibility of injury is always present and to avoid such problems the instructor must thoroughly know each student's abilities, disabilities, and idiosyncrasies that might provoke or be associated with an injury situation.

The motor therapy environment must be one that reflects confidence in the child's abilities but, on the other hand, provides a solid underlying safety base that takes into account the unexpected occurrence. In other words, there must not be an overprotective climate that stifles self-expression but rather a reasonable and prudent approach to all activities attempted by the child. For example, mats must be provided where falls may occur, children must not be encouraged to exceed their ability limitations, and at all times the participant must be spotted to protect against harm to himself and to others.

INTAKE AND PLACEMENT PROCEDURES

In our experience, four steps are successful in admitting children to a motor therapy program. They are (1) initial participant contact, (2) parent-child-therapist interview, (3) individual motor behavior survey, and (4) child placement.

Initial participant contact

The initial participant contact is usually made through a referral by a parent or a teacher, psychologist, physician, or other professional in human services. If there has been no professional referral, we suggest that the parent receive expert advice on whether or not the child is indeed in need of a specialized program. Often the parent is confused as to the exact reason for the child's referral to such a program. To ensure that the professionals in the community are apprised of what the program is all about, brochures, speeches to community groups, telephone conversations, and letters should be employed to clarify the children best served by this type of program. When it appears that a particular child might find success in a motor remediation program, official forms are sent by mail to the parent. The forms include a clearance form for physical activity to be signed by the child's physician (Fig. 7-2), an application for admission to the program specifying a particular date, a release form to obtain school test results and medical reports (Fig. 7-3), and a record of the child's medical and developmental history (see Appendix). All of these forms must be completed and returned before the intake interview is made.

Parent-child-therapist interview

An initial interview involving both parent and child is highly desirable before a decision is made as to admission into the program (Fig. 7-4). The purpose of the inter-

Text continued on p. 73.

Fig. 7-4. Initial parent-child-therapist interview.

```
                    INDIVIDUALIZED MOTOR BEHAVIOR SURVEY

   CHILD'S NAME _____ AGE _____ DATE _____

   OBSERVER _____

      The Individualized Motor Behavior Survey (IMBS) is designed to be
   used by professional personnel to determine obvious problems in
   movement behavior of children from 4 to 12 years of age. The IMBS
   can normally be conducted in 15 minutes. Motor behavior problems
   determined by the IMBS must only be considered indicators for more
   definitive testing.
      Starting with category C, imposed muscle tension, each motor task
   that the child is requested to perform should be first demonstrated
   once by the observer.

   A.  GENERAL BEHAVIOR
       1. Cooperation
          Procedure: The child is observed while he is waiting to be
             tested. To better assess cooperation, the observer may request
             the child to carry out specific instructions such as to
             sit or to stand.

          0  Cooperates fully
          1  Hesitates but still cooperates
          2  Is reluctant and needs a great deal of encouragement
          3  Is withdrawn or sullen, expresses anger, or refuses
             to be observed

       2. Nongoal directed responses
          Procedure: The child is observed when sitting or standing
             quietly for 3 minutes. Nonessential or purposeless
             movements such as sudden turns of the head and movement
             of the hands or trunk without specific intent are noted.

          Gross movements

          0  No nonessential movements involving the head, trunk, arms,
             or legs
          1  One or two nonessential movements
          2  Three to five nonessential movements
          3  Six or more nonessential movements

          Fine movements

          0  No nonessential movements of the fingers, face, or feet
          1  One or two nonessential movements
          2  Three to five nonessential movements
          3  Six or more nonessential movements
```

Fig. 7-5. Individualized Motor Behavior Survey and summary sheet.   *Continued.*

B.   POSTURE
     Procedure: The child is observed in different positions such as
        sitting, standing, and executing locomotor acts. If the child
        does not spontaneously assume the different positions, the
        observer may specifically request them.

     0 Sits, stands, and walks erectly
     1 Carries head slightly forward or to the side
     2 Carries head and shoulders forward or to the side
     3 Displays a generally slumping posture

C.   IMPOSED MUSCLE TENSION
     1. Rigid body
        Procedure: The child stands with feet together, arms and fingers
           tightened, eyes closed, mouth open wide, and tongue stuck out
           as far as possible for a period of 10 seconds. The observer
           watches the child's ability to tighten his entire body and
           any nonessential movements that may arise from the imposed
           muscle tension.

        Performance

        0 Can tighten entire body and hold tension for 10 seconds
        1 Can tighten entire body and hold tension for 5 seconds
        2 Uneven tightness in body limbs
        3 Hypotonic and unable to tense body

        Nonessential movements

        Right   Left
        0   0   No associated or involuntary movements
        1   1   One or two twitches, one or two writhing movements,
                          or slight finger tremor
        2   2   Three to five twitches, three to five writhing
                          movements, or marked finger tremor
        3   3   Constant nonessential movement in fingers and arms

     2. Loose wrist
        Procedure: The child drapes his hands loosely over the observer's
           arm or the back of a chair, then closes eyes hard, opens
           mouth wide, and sticks the tongue out as far as possible.
           The observer watches the child's hands and fingers for
           nonessential movements.

        Right   Left
        0   0   No finger movement
        1   1   Slight finger spreading
        2   2   Moderate spreading of fingers with some finger
                          and wrist extension
        3   3   Maximal spreading and extension of all fingers
                          and wrist

Fig. 7-5, cont'd. For legend see p. 65.

```
D.  LOCOMOTION
    1. Walking on heels
       Procedure: The child walks on his heels for 15 paces.

       Performance

       Right   Left
       0       0       Walks on heels for 15 paces
       1       1       Touches ball of foot to floor one or two times
       2       2       Touches ball of foot to floor three or four times
       3       3       Unable to walk on heels

       Nonessential movements

       Right   Left
       0       0       No obvious nonessential movements
       1       1       Some visible nonessential movements
       2       2       Marked elbow flexion and wrist hyperextension
       3       3       Marked elbow flexion and wrist hyperextension
                       plus upper arm abduction or facial movement

    2. Hopping on one foot
       Procedure: The child hops on one foot a maximum of 15 times.

       Right   Left
       0       0       Hops 15 consecutive times
       1       1       Hops 11 to 14 times
       2       2       Hops 6 to 10 times
       3       3       Hops 5 times or less

E.  BALANCE
    1. Backward line walk
       Procedure: The child walks backwards heel-to-toe along a
          straight line for 15 paces, keeping the body erect.

       0   Walks smoothly without deviating from the line more than
           two times
       1   Walks smoothly without hesitating or deviating from the
           line more than three times
       2   Hesitates or deviates from the line four times
       3   Hesitates or deviates from the line five times
```

Fig. 7-5, cont'd. For legend see p. 65.   *Continued.*

2. One-leg stand
   Procedure: The child stands on one leg for 15 seconds with his eyes closed.

Right	Left	
0	0	Stands for 15 seconds
1	1	Stands for 11 to 14 seconds
2	2	Stands for 6 to 10 seconds
3	3	Stands for 5 seconds or less

F. FINE MOVEMENTS
   1. Finger aiming
      Procedure: Keeping the elbow bent, the child aims his index finger and touches the index finger of the observer. Three tries are given for each hand with the finger traveling at least 10 inches.

Right	Left	
0	0	Touches fingertip accurately without tremor
1	1	Misses one time or has a slight tremor
2	2	Misses two times or has a moderate tremor when fingertip is approached
3	3	Misses three times or more or has tremor throughout entire movement

   2. Finger opposition
      Procedure: If child is under 5 years of age, eyes are opened; otherwise they are closed. The child touches each finger to the thumb (2, 3, 4, 5) and then reverses the sequence (5, 4, 3, 2, 3, 4, 5), completing five sequences for each hand.

   Performance

Right	Left	
0	0	Accurate and smooth finger transition
1	1	Touches thumb to same finger twice or hesitates or goes out of sequence one or two times
2	2	Touches thumb to same finger three or more times or hesitates or goes out of sequence three or more times
3	3	Cannot complete a sequence

   Nonessential movements (mirroring)

Right	Left	
0	0	No mirroring movements of opposite fingers
1	1	Slightly visible mirroring movements
2	2	Marked mirroring movements
3	3	Marked mirroring movements and wrist extension

Fig. 7-5, cont'd. For legend see p. 65.

3. Forearm rotation

   Procedure: The child stands facing the observer with one arm
   bent 90 degrees at the elbow and the other arm kept loosely
   at the side. On the word "go" the child rotates the forearm
   of the bent arm inward and outward as fast as possible.

   Performance

Right	Left	
0	0	Smooth rotation with less than 3 inches of outward movement of the elbow
1	1	Movement of elbow outward from 3 to 8 inches
2	2	Movement of elbow outward more than 8 inches
3	3	Unable to pronate and supinate forearm

   Nonessential movements (mirroring)

Right	Left	
0	0	No mirroring or nonessential movements of the opposite arm
1	1	Slight mirroring or flexion of opposite elbow
2	2	Marked pronation and supination of opposite elbow
3	3	Marked pronation, supination, and flexion of opposite elbow

4. Ball bounce

   Procedure: The child bounces and catches a tennis ball 10 times
   in a row while seated in a chair.

0	Bounces and catches tennis ball with one hand 10 times
2	Catches ball 8 to 9 times
4	Catches ball 6 to 7 times
6	Catches ball 5 times or less

Fig. 7-5, cont'd. For legend see p. 65.   *Continued.*

5. Pencil tracking
   Procedure: With the figure-of-eight track placed on its side,
     the child starts in the center and, using the preferred hand,
     attempts to draw a continuous line without leaving the paper.

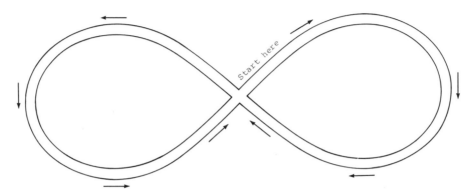

Note: Actual width of track should be 3/16 inch.
       Overall dimensions should be 8 inches by 3 inches.

0   Makes continuous line that does not touch or go outside of
    the track
2   Makes 1 or 2 errors
4   Makes 3 to 6 errors
6   Makes 7 to 10 errors

Fig. 7-5, cont'd. For legend see p. 65.

Fig. 7-5, cont'd. For legend see p. 65. *Continued.*

2

	GENERAL BEHAVIOR	LARGE-MUSCLE CONTROL	SMALL-MUSCLE CONTROL	NON-ESSENTIAL MOVEMENTS

E. BALANCE

Backward line walk

One-leg stand   R L

TOTAL SCORE [   ]

F. FINE MOVEMENTS

Finger aiming   R L

Finger opposition

   Performance   R L

   Nonessential movements   R L

Forearm rotation

   Performance   R L

   Nonessential movements   R L

Ball bounce

Pencil tracking

TOTAL SCORE [   ]

TOTALS

General Behavior

Large-muscle Control

Small-muscle Control

Nonessential Movements

ADDITIONAL COMMENTS:

Fig. 7-5, cont'd. For legend see p. 65.

view is to (1) talk generally with the family and determine their expectations from such a program, (2) evaluate the parent-child relationship, (3) carefully go over the forms for accuracy and completion, and (4) clarify any misunderstandings as to the offerings and limitations of the program.

It is extremely important for the therapist and parents to discuss the detailed contents of the child's medical and developmental history (see Appendix) since ideally it reveals selective information in six categories: general information, birth and health history, developmental events, school progress, family relationships, and the child's personality. Studying the information provided in each category, the interviewer can assess the child's past physical, maturational, and emotional health. From the history it can be decided whether or not the child needs medical, psychological, or educational services besides motor therapy. The interviewer also gains from the history a knowledge of special safety factors that should be considered and any activities that would be contraindicated. The final step taken to ensure that the child will profit from such a program is administering the individual motor behavior survey.

Individual Motor Behavior Survey

The Individual Motor Behavior Survey (IMBS) was developed in 1973 at California State University, Long Beach, (by Arnheim) as a nonstandardized tool to reveal obvious problems in movement (Fig. 7-5). A trained observer can normally give the IMBS in 15 minutes without hurrying the child. The IMBS does not give the observer definite answers as to why there are problems but does reveal a need for a special movement program. The IMBS is subjective and varies somewhat according to the background and knowledge of the observer. It is divided into six categories: general behavior, posture, imposed muscle tension, locomotion, balance, and fine movements. In each of these categories are tasks that are scored from 0 to 3 or 0 to

6 points, with 0 indicating the ideal response to the task and 3 or 6 points the worst possible response that could be made by the child. A low score indicates a high level of observed motor ability.

To further assist the observer in determining the motor behavior of the child, totals from the six categories are divided into three areas of motor behavior: large-muscle control, small-muscle control, and nonessential movements. With the understanding that this survey is subjective but at the same time discriminating in terms of general motor problems, the observer is able to make a reasonable decision about whether the child will benefit from a motor therapy program.

Category A, general behavior, is divided into two parts: cooperation and nongoal-directed responses. Throughout the entire survey session the child is observed as to how well he cooperates and follows directions (Fig. 7-6). The child is also observed to determine his ability to carry out purposeful movements and to determine the extent to which nonessential gross and fine movements are displayed. A high rating in nonessential movements may be indicative of hyperkinesia or a high level of anxiety.

Category B is used to determine the postural attitudes that the child habitually takes in sitting, in standing, and in gross movements. It should be noted that chil-

Fig. 7-6. Observing a child's general behavior in the testing situation.

dren who have motor difficulties often reflect them in posture malalignments.

Category C, imposed muscle tension, has two parts, the rigid body test and the loose wrist test. In the rigid body test the child stands with feet together, arms and fingers stiffened, eyes closed hard, mouth open wide, and tongue stuck out as far as possible for approximately 10 seconds. While in

this rigid state the child is observed for inability to totally stiffen (Fig. 7-7) or extraneous movements that may occur, particularly in the fingers and wrists in the form of tremors, writhing, or twitching. In the loose wrist test the child drapes his hand over the back of a chair or the observer's bent arm, his eyes are closed hard, and his mouth is opened wide with the tongue stuck out as far as possible (Fig. 7-8). Under these conditions the child's hands are observed for extraneous movements, extension of the wrists, and any spreading movement of the fingers (Towen and Prechtl, 1970).

Category D is concerned with locomotion. The first of the two parts is walking on heels for 15 paces, a test designed to indicate dynamic balance, large-muscle control, and presence of any nonessential movements such as elbow flexion, wrist hyperextension, or facial grimaces as the task is initiated (Fig. 7-9). The second part is hopping on one foot. Leaving the ground in a hop movement requires the child to have leg strength and balance. Successfully hopping a maximum of 15 times inde-

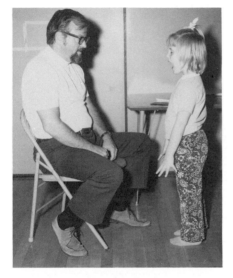

Fig. 7-7. Rigid body test.

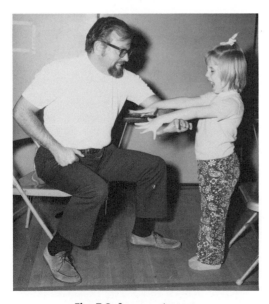

Fig. 7-8. Loose wrist test.

Fig. 7-9. Heel walking test.

pendently on each foot requires the ability to sequence movement effectively and at the same time coordinate leg muscles.

Category E is concerned with the ability to balance both dynamically and statically, walking backwards heel-toe on a line for 15 paces and standing on one foot for 15 seconds with the eyes closed. A child who hesitates or deviates five or more times while walking the line or is unable to stand on one foot for more than 5 seconds would be considered as having problems in the balance area.

Category F is concerned with fine movement responses and has five parts. The child demonstrates accuracy of performance with absence of nonessential movements. The first part of category F is finger pointing and requires the ability to accurately see, aim, and touch the examiner's fingertip straight out from the body without missing it, hesitating, or trembling (Fig. 7-10). The second part is finger opposition; the child touches each finger to the thumb with eyes open or closed depending on age. Also noted are mirroring movements of the other side of the body while the opposition test is being conducted (Fig. 7-11) Motor immaturity is indicated when the child dis-

plays obvious mirroring movements of the opposite wrist and hand. The third part is forearm rotation and requires the child to face the observer with one arm bent at 90 degrees and the other arm held loosely at his side. The child is then instructed to rotate the forearm as quickly as possible in an inward and outward manner. Three factors can be noted from the forearm rotation test: how accurately the child can quickly rotate the forearm, the extent to which the elbow must be moved out from the body in order to accomplish the task, and the extent to which the child does or does not demonstrate nonessential movement in the opposite arm. As in the finger opposition test, the child who demonstrates obvious mirroring may be reflecting a developmental delay or motor retardation, depending on his age. The fourth part in fine movements is the task of bouncing and catching a ball. The child is instructed to catch the ball with both hands without trapping it against his body. In a seated position the child attempts to bounce and catch the ball 10 times. Accomplishment of the ball bounce and catch test requires that the child coordinate his eyes and hands as well as adjust to the subtle perceptions

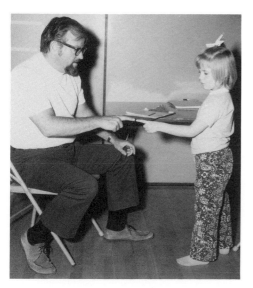

Fig. 7-10. Finger pointing test.

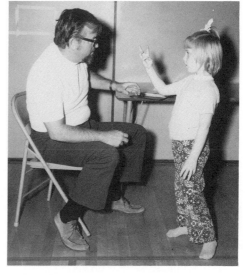

Fig. 7-11. Finger opposition test.

of ball speed and deflection from the floor. The reader should note, however, that ideally a test should be culture free, meaning the examinee need not have had prior experience in that activity. Ball bouncing is probably the least culture-free item in the survey. The fifth part requires that the child coordinate his hands and eyes by drawing a pencil line with the preferred hand within a very limited figure-of-eight track placed directly in front of the body. An error is counted each time the child stops and starts the line and each time that a mark touches the side or goes outside of the track.

After completing the motor survey the observer transfers the various responses to a summary sheet Computing the score in

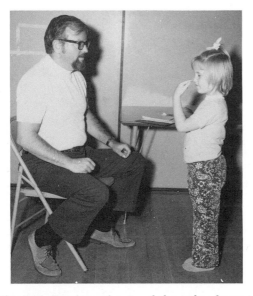

Fig. 7-12. Touching the tip of the index finger to the tip of the nose.

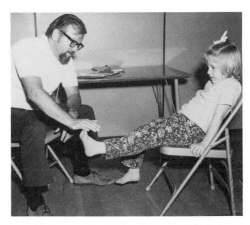

Fig. 7-13. Testing ability to kick the observer's hand when it is placed in different positions.

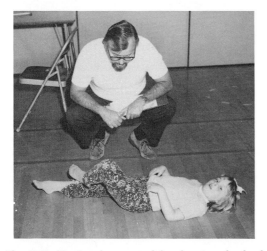

Fig. 7-14. Testing leg control by drawing the heel up the full length of the opposite leg.

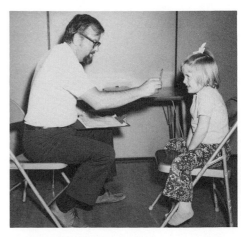

Fig. 7-15. Testing ocular convergence.

each area reveals the general areas of inco-ordination as well as problems in a specific category. Experience has shown that for a typical 3-year-old child 10 points on gross movements, 10 points on fine movements, and 12 points on nonessential movements would most likely be within the normal range. On the other hand, normal scores may be 6 points, 6 points, and 7 points, respectively, for a 4-year-old child and 3 points, 3 points, and 4 points, respectively, for a 5-year-old. Typical children 6 years of age and over should accomplish each of the tasks with no points in the gross and fine motor areas and only 2 or 3 in the nonessential movement area. It should be noted that some nonessential movement responses may normally linger through adulthood.

Additional observations of selected movement tasks should be made if further information is necessary or there is doubt as to the accuracy of responses indicated by the IMBS. Added to the survey may be observation of accuracy in touching the tip of the index finger to the tip of the nose with the eyes closed (Fig. 7-12), testing ability to kick the observer's hand when it is placed in different positions in relation to the seated child (Fig. 7-13), and testing ability to trace the heel up the length of the opposite extended leg (Fig.

7-14). Other observations may include factors of eye control such as the point of ocular convergence, which is normally about 9 inches from the nose (Fig. 7-15), ability to visually pursue a moving object (Fig. 7-16), and localizing sounds while blindfolded (Fig. 7-17).

The reader should be cautioned that children displaying obvious problems in performing motor tasks may require more definitive examination by a medical specialist such as a pediatric neurologist.

Child placement

Following the completion of the motor behavior survey, the observer confers with the parent in assessing all the information that has been provided about the child including the motor survey. At the conference a decision is made as to whether the child would profit from a motor therapy program and, if so, whether the best placement would be in an individual or group setting. Children with obvious moderate to severe motor problems coupled with severe emotional problems will at the outset of therapy find the greatest success in an individual-

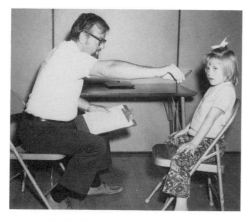

Fig. 7-16. Testing visual tracking.

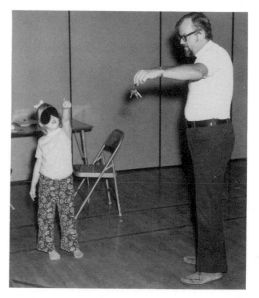

Fig. 7-17. Testing ability to localize sounds while blindfolded.

ized program. A child having mild motor deficits but severe emotional problems should also be considered a prime candidate for an individualized program. However, severely emotionally handicapped participants could profit from a highly structured social setting for the purpose of developing ego strength and a positive self-concept.

Group placement means putting together two or three children with common emotional and movement needs. Groups that are larger than three do not provide the individual control that is needed. However, when there is a need to play games requiring a larger number, several small groups are joined to provide the correct number of participants.

DISMISSAL FROM THE PROGRAM

Knowing when a child has gained the maximum benefit from therapy is difficult. To assist this judgment, constant reassessment of the child's progress must be made. This does not necessarily mean that formal testing must be administered continually; subjective indicators can be used. One of the best subjective factors to show that a child is benefiting is whether he looks forward to each session. Where there is a high level of motivation one can expect that positive changes will take place. Conversely, if there is a low motivation, it is doubtful that positive motor changes can take place. If the child appears to have made as much progress as possible in a particular movement area and a learning plateau occurs over a 1- or 2-week period, a complete change of activities can be made or the child maybe permitted a vacation from the program for a month or two. The decision to dismiss should not be made until all available information has been gathered and weighed as to its total effect on the child. Ideally, when the child is dismissed from the program, recommendations should be made as to how he might continue to improve his motor skills. Referral to other advanced programs is important and once the child has gained all the improvements that motor therapy can bring about, the logical continuance of this growth would be in programs offered by a parks and recreation department, YMCA, YWCA, or other public or private agency.

8

DIAGNOSTIC MOTOR ABILITY TEST

As discussed in Chapter 7, the clumsy child is admitted to the motor therapy program through a series of administrative procedures, one of which is a survey of motor responses. Once the instructor is convinced that a child will profit from a remediation program, an attempt should be made to determine specific problems through diagnostic measures. However, it has been clearly pointed out in Chapter 4 that diagnosis through any specific motor ability test is often inadequate. At this time highly discriminating tests are not readily available nor easily applied by the practitioner. We suggest the Moyes and Stott test or the Ayres battery when there is an opportunity for individual examination; however, when more than one child is involved in the evaluation, we suggest the Basic Motor Ability Tests.

The Basic Motor Ability Tests (BMAT) compiled by Arnheim and Sinclair (1974) and partially adapted from the Frostig Movement Skills Test Battery of 1972 are a battery of nine tests designed to evaluate the selected motor responses of small- and large-muscle control, static and dynamic balance, eye-hand coordination, and flexibility in children who range in age from 4 to 12 years. Each of the nine subtests is relatively easy to administer and requires little special training. An individual child can be tested in approximately 12 to 15 minutes and a group of up to five children in about 25 minutes by one tester. Norms were established by testing 1,065 children of various ethnic, cultural, social, and economic groups. Using various random samples, the retest reliability for the entire test battery was 0.89. Face validity was assumed since all the subtests were adapted from existing tests for which validity had previously been established.

SPECIFIC ADMINISTRATION AND SCORING PROCEDURES

The examiner must follow the administration and scoring procedures precisely. Before each subtest is administered, obvious permanent and temporary physical disabilities that would adversely affect the child's motor performance must be noted.

Fig. 8-1. Bead stringing.

Fig. 8-2. Target throwing.

It is also imperative that the child being tested thoroughly understand the directions to each subtest. Therefore the examiner must demonstrate as well as verbally explain each aspect of the test before it is executed. Establishing good rapport with the child and encouraging him to put forth his best effort cannot be overemphasized. The testing room also should be free from all distractions. It is desirable to follow the order in which the subtests are presented here to maximize performance and attention and keep muscular fatigue to a minimum.

SUBTEST 1: Bead stringing (Fig. 8-1)

PURPOSE: To test bilateral eye-hand coordination and dexterity.

MATERIALS: The ½-inch beads supplied with the Stanford-Binet test set, an 18-inch round shoe lace with a ¾-inch plastic tip and a knot tied at the end of the shoelace, a stopwatch.

PROCEDURE: Place the beads and lace before the child. Demonstrate by putting two beads on the lace while explaining that speed is essential. The beads merely have to be on the lace; he should not waste time stringing the beads all the way down to the knot.

TIME LIMIT: 30 seconds.

SCORING: Record the total number of beads strung in the 30-second period.

SUBTEST 2: Target throwing (Fig. 8-2)

PURPOSE: To test eye-hand coordination.

MATERIALS: A target consisting of three squares measuring 5, 11, and 18 inches on each side attached to a wall with the bottom 4 feet from the floor, fifteen 4 by 5 inch beanbags.

PROCEDURE: Children from 4 to 5 years of age stand behind a restraining line 7 feet from the target and those from 6 to 12 years of age stand behind a restraining line 10 feet from the target. The difference in throwing distances is to minimize the adverse effects of the lack of arm strength in younger children. The tester demonstrates by throwing two bags at the target while explaining that the small square has a value of 3 points, the middle square a value of 2 points, and the large square a value of 1 point. The child is then told to score as many points as possible in 15 throws.

SCORING: The total score is determined by adding the points earned in the 15 throws. If a beanbag lands on the line between two squares, the larger score is awarded.

Fig. 8-3. Tapping board.

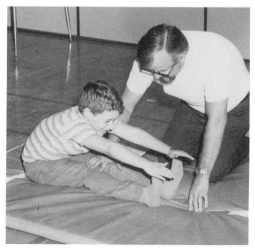

Fig. 8-4. Back and hamstring stretch.

SUBTEST 3: Tapping board (Fig. 8-3)

PURPOSE: To test the speed of hand movement crossing from one side of the body to the other.

MATERIALS: A table, a chair, and an electronic tapping board 18 inches long with an impulse counter are desirable but the test can be performed without the latter if the tester does the counting.

PROCEDURE: The child is seated at a table with the tapping board placed directly in front of him. The tester demonstrates the test twice while at the same time explaining that the tapping should be executed as quickly as possible with the preferred hand. The child reaches across his body, tapping once on each side of the board as rapidly as possible.

TIME LIMIT: 20 seconds.

SCORING: Record the total number of taps executed in the allotted time.

SUBTEST 4: Back and hamstring stretch (Fig. 8-4)

PURPOSE: To test the flexibility of back and hamstring muscles.

MATERIALS: A 3-meter rule or yardstick.

PROCEDURE: The child sits on the floor with legs fully extended and heels approximately 6 inches apart. The 3-meter rule or yardstick is placed between the child's legs with the 30 cm or 20-inch mark even with his heels. Keeping his knees straight, he bends forward, reaching down the rule as far as possible without bouncing. Three attempts are allowed.

SCORING: Record the farthest point reached by the child's fingertips in his three attempts. Measure to the nearest centimeter or ⅛ inch.

SUBTEST 5: Standing long jump (Fig. 8-5)

PURPOSE: To test the strength and power in the thigh and lower leg muscles.

MATERIALS: A 3-meter rule or yardstick, a nonslippery surface for taking off and landing.

PROCEDURE: First the tester demonstrates and explains the proper way to jump.

Then the test is executed by swinging the arms back, bending the knees, and swinging the arms forward and extending the legs at the moment of takeoff. A maximum of three trials is allowed.

SCORING: The longest jump of the three trials is recorded in centimeters or inches.

SUBTEST 6: Face down to standing (Fig. 8-6)

PURPOSE: To test speed and agility in changing from a prone to a standing position.

MATERIALS: A 4 by 6 foot mat or carpeted surface, a stopwatch.

PROCEDURE: The tester demonstrates twice while explaining that the child is to start on his stomach with his forehead touching the mat. On the command "Go," he rises to an erect standing position with his knees straight. He repeats this cycle as many times as possible.

TIME LIMIT: 25 seconds.

SCORING: Record the number of times the child is able to get to a standing position within the 25-second time limit.

SUBTEST 7: Static balance (Fig. 8-7)

PURPOSE: To test static balance first with eyes open and then with eyes closed.

MATERIALS: Blindfold, stopwatch, two balance boards—one with a width of 2 inches, the other with a width of 1 inch.

PROCEDURE: The tester demonstrates on each board, explaining that either foot may be used but the hands must be kept on the hips with the nonsupporting foot behind the other knee. First the child is given one trial on each board with his eyes open and then repeats with the

Fig. 8-5. Standing long jump.

Fig. 8-6. Face down to standing.

Fig. 8-7. Static balance.

eyes closed or blindfolded. If the child refuses the blindfold or is unable to keep his eyes closed, the test should be considered incomplete.

TIME LIMIT: 10 second per trial.

SCORING: Record the total number of seconds the child can maintain a balanced position. Criteria for discontinuing a trial are touching the foot to the floor, removing either hand from the hips, or opening the eyes.

SUBTEST 8: Chair push-ups (Fig. 8-8)

PURPOSE: To test arm and shoulder girdle strength.

MATERIALS: A stopwatch, a chair or bench measuring 14 to 18 inches above the floor, a wall against which the feet may be braced.

PROCEDURE: The examiner demonstrates twice while explaining to the child that a front-leaning rest position should be

assumed with legs together, feet against the wall, arms fully extended, and the body forming a straight line from head to feet.

TIME LIMIT: 20 seconds.

SCORING: The number of correct push-ups counted within 20 seconds.

SUBTEST 9: Agility run (Fig. 8-9)

PURPOSE: To test ability to rapidly move the body and alter direction.

MATERIALS: Four cones or chairs, a stopwatch.

PROCEDURE: The cones are placed 5 feet apart in a straight line. The examiner demonstrates the test and explains that on the command "Go" the child is to run as fast as possible in a zigzag pattern around the cones, starting on the right side of the first cone.

TIME LIMIT: 20 seconds.

SCORING: Scoring is based on the total number of cones that are passed in 20 seconds; for a complete run down and back the child would receive a total of 8 points.

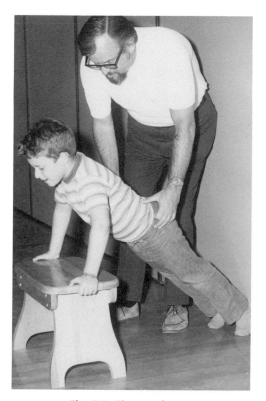

Fig. 8-8. Chair push-ups.

Fig. 8-9. Agility run.

Norms: Basic motor ability tests

Sex: Male   Age: 4 years

Per-centiles	Bead stringing	Target throwing	Tapping board	Back and hamstring stretch (cm)	(in)	Standing long jump (cm)	(in)	Face down to standing	Static balance	Chair push-ups	Agility run
90+	10	22	40	52	28¾	130	51¼	10	18	9	20
75	7	16	35	45	25⅞	100	39⅜	8	15	7	18
50	5	10	32	36	22⅜	89	35	6	10	5	16
25	3	3	20	27	18¾	60	23⅝	4	7	2	12
1	1	1	5	18	15¼	30	11¾	2	3	0	7

Sex: Male   Age: 5 years

Per-centiles	Bead stringing	Target throwing	Tapping board	Back and hamstring stretch (cm)	(in)	Standing long jump (cm)	(in)	Face down to standing	Static balance	Chair push-ups	Agility run
90+	12	24	54	52	28¾	139	54¾	11	22	15	22
75	9	19	46	44	25½	110	43¼	10	17	10	20
50	7	15	41	33	21¼	97	38¼	7	11	8	18
25	4	8	20	25	18	70	27⅝	5	8	7	11
1	1	5	15	15	14⅛	40	15¾	3	3	4	9

Sex: Male   Age: 6 years

Per-centiles	Bead stringing	Target throwing	Tapping board	Back and hamstring stretch (cm)	(in)	Standing long jump (cm)	(in)	Face down to standing	Static balance	Chair push-ups	Agility run
90+	14	23	59	50	27⅞	156	61⅜	15	27	18	28
75	11	17	52	42	24¾	133	52⅜	13	20	14	24
50	8	9	44	32	20¾	104	40⅞	10	16	9	22
25	5	1	37	22	16⅞	75	29½	7	8	4	17
1	1	0	28	13	13¼	49	19¼	5	3	1	11

Sex: Male   Age: 7 years

Per-centiles	Bead stringing	Target throwing	Tapping board	Back and hamstring stretch (cm)	(in)	Standing long jump (cm)	(in)	Face down to standing	Static balance	Chair push-ups	Agility run
90+	15	28	61	47	26¾	171	67¼	16	28	19	35
75	11	21	55	39	23½	146	57⅜	14	18	15	30
50	9	12	46	29	19⅝	115	45¼	11	16	10	28
25	6	3	39	19	15¾	83	32¾	8	9	5	21
1	3	1	30	10	12⅛	52	20½	4	4	1	17

Sex: Male   Age: 8 years

Per-centiles	Bead stringing	Target throwing	Tapping board	Back and hamstring stretch		Standing long jump		Face down to standing	Static balance	Chair push-ups	Agility run
				(cm)	(in)	(cm)	(in)				
90+	15	36	66	46	26¼	173	68⅛	15	30	14	37
75	12	28	59	38	23⅛	151	59⅜	13	20	15	33
50	10	18	51	28	19¼	123	48⅜	11	15	11	30
25	7	8	41	18	15¼	96	38¾	8	9	6	25
1	4	2	35	8	11¼	69	27¼	5	4	1	20

Sex: Male   Age: 9 years

Per-centiles	Bead stringing	Target throwing	Tapping board	Back and hamstring stretch		Standing long jump		Face down to standing	Static balance	Chair push-ups	Agility run
				(cm)	(in)	(cm)	(in)				
90+	15	34	69	47	26¾	185	72¾	18	30	19	37
75	13	28	62	39	23½	163	64¼	16	24	15	34
50	11	19	53	27	18¾	132	51	12	17	12	31
25	9	11	41	16	14½	102	40¼	8	10	7	27
1	6	2	37	5	10¼	72	28¼	5	4	3	19

Sex: Male   Age: 10 years

Per-centiles	Bead stringing	Target throwing	Tapping board	Back and hamstring stretch		Standing long jump		Face down to standing	Static balance	Chair push-ups	Agility run
				(cm)	(in)	(cm)	(in)				
90+	17	40	74	46	26¼	192	75⅝	19	30	21	42
75	15	32	60	45	25⅞	172	67¾	16	25	16	39
50	12	23	55	31	20⅜	148	58¼	12	18	11	34
25	8	14	47	17	14⅞	123	48⅜	8	11	6	32
1	5	5	42	4	9¾	99	39	5	5	1	24

Sex: Male   Age: 11 years

Per-centiles	Bead stringing	Target throwing	Tapping board	Back and hamstring stretch		Standing long jump		Face down to standing	Static balance	Chair push-ups	Agility run
				(cm)	(in)	(cm)	(in)				
90+	17	42	77	48	27⅛	207	81½	21	31	25	44
75	15	34	66	40	23⅞	181	71¼	17	26	19	39
50	12	24	61	29	19⅝	147	57⅞	13	19	12	35
25	10	14	57	19	15¾	121	47½	8	12	4	33
1	7	4	55	9	11¾	89	35	4	7	1	25

Sex: Male Age: 12 years

Percentiles	Bead stringing	Target throwing	Tapping board	Back and hamstring stretch		Standing long jump		Face down to standing	Static balance	Chair push-ups	Agility run
				(cm)	(in)	(cm)	(in)				
90+	16	42	86	52	28¾	208	81⅞	20	32	21	44
75	14	35	77	42	24¾	195	76¾	17	27	17	40
50	12	26	73	31	20⅜	166	65⅜	13	19	12	36
25	10	16	65	19	15¾	137	53⅞	10	10	7	34
1	8	7	63	7	10⅞	108	42½	5	7	3	27

Sex: Female Age: 4 years

Percentiles	Bead stringing	Target throwing	Tapping board	Back and hamstring stretch		Standing long jump		Face down to standing	Static balance	Chair push-ups	Agility run
				(cm)	(in)	(cm)	(in)				
90+	10	22	38	52	28¾	129	50¾	10	17	8	20
75	8	17	35	47	26¾	99	39	8	15	6	18
50	5	11	33	36	22⅜	89	35	6	11	5	16
25	3	3	19	28	19¼	60	23⅝	4	8	2	12
1	1	1	7	19	15¾	30	11¾	2	2	0	6

Sex: Female Age: 5 years

Percentiles	Bead stringing	Target throwing	Tapping board	Back and hamstring stretch		Standing long jump		Face down to standing	Static balance	Chair push-ups	Agility run
				(cm)	(in)	(cm)	(in)				
90+	11	22	53	50	27⅞	135	53⅛	10	21	15	21
75	9	18	45	43	22½	108	42½	9	19	10	20
50	7	14	41	32	20¾	95	37⅜	7	13	8	17
25	4	7	19	27	18¾	67	26⅜	5	9	7	11
1	1	4	13	15	14⅛	35	13¾	2	5	4	8

Sex: Female Age: 6 years

Percentiles	Bead stringing	Target throwing	Tapping board	Back and hamstring stretch		Standing long jump		Face down to standing	Static balance	Chair push-ups	Agility run
				(cm)	(in)	(cm)	(in)				
90+	13	16	56	54	29⅜	145	57⅛	16	28	16	28
75	11	11	51	46	26¼	125	49¼	13	22	14	24
50	8	6	42	35	22	100	39⅜	10	17	8	22
25	5	1	35	24	17⅝	74	29⅛	7	8	4	17
1	2	—	27	13	13	49	19¼	3	3	1	11

Sex: Female   Age: 7 years

Per-centiles	Bead stringing	Target throwing	Tapping board	Back and hamstring stretch		Standing long jump		Face down to standing	Static balance	Chair push-ups	Agility run
				(cm)	(in)	(cm)	(in)				
90+	14	15	58	48	27⅛	166	65⅜	16	31	16	33
75	12	11	50	41	24¼	141	55½	13	24	12	31
50	9	6	43	32	20¾	111	43¾	10	14	7	27
25	6	1	38	23	17¼	80	31½	7	8	3	20
1	3	—	27	14	13¾	49	19¼	4	3	—	16

Sex: Female   Age: 8 years

Per-centiles	Bead stringing	Target throwing	Tapping board	Back and hamstring stretch		Standing long jump		Face down to standing	Static balance	Chair push-ups	Agility run
				(cm)	(in)	(cm)	(in)				
90+	16	19	63	52	28¾	180	70⅞	15	25	16	35
75	13	11	54	43	25⅛	155	61	13	19	13	32
50	10	8	50	31	20⅜	121	47½	11	11	8	29
25	7	3	41	19	15¾	93	36½	8	6	4	24
1	1	—	33	8	11¼	63	24¾	5	3	—	18

Sex: Female   Age: 9 years

Per-centiles	Bead stringing	Target throwing	Tapping board	Back and hamstring stretch		Standing long jump		Face down to standing	Static balance	Chair push-ups	Agility run
				(cm)	(in)	(cm)	(in)				
90+	16	30	67	50	27⅞	178	70⅛	16	27	17	37
75	15	20	60	41	24¼	156	61⅜	14	20	14	35
50	11	17	50	30	20	130	51¼	11	13	9	32
25	8	14	39	20	16⅛	104	40⅞	8	7	5	30
1	5	11	35	9	11¾	78	30¾	4	4	1	20

Sex: Female   Age: 10 years

Per-centile	Bead stringing	Target throwing	Tapping board	Back and hamstring stretch		Standing long jump		Face down to standing	Static balance	Chair push-ups	Agility run
				(cm)	(in)	(cm)	(in)				
90+	17	32	72	54	29⅜	192	75½	16	30	19	38
75	14	25	57	45	25⅞	169	66½	14	27	14	36
50	12	18	52	33	21¼	140	55⅛	11	16	9	33
25	9	15	47	22	16⅞	112	44⅛	8	10	4	27
1	6	10	40	10	12⅛	84	33⅛	4	8	—	21

Sex: Female   Age: 11 years

Per-centile	Bead stringing	Target throwing	Tapping board	Back and hamstring stretch		Standing long jump		Face down to standing	Static balance	Chair push-ups	Agility run
				(cm)	(in)	(cm)	(in)				
90+	17	33	70	53	29⅛	206	81⅛	16	29	18	39
75	15	27	63	44	25½	183	72	14	24	14	37
50	12	19	58	32	20¾	154	60½	11	15	9	35
25	10	10	53	20	16⅛	124	48¾	9	12	3	30
1	6	2	45	9	11¾	95	37⅜	6	5	—	22

Sex: Female   Age: 12 years

Per-centile	Bead stringing	Target throwing	Tapping board	Back and hamstring stretch		Standing long jump		Face down to standing	Static balance	Chair push-ups	Agility run
				(cm)	(in)	(cm)	(in)				
90+	17	40	79	53	29⅛	207	81½	18	25	20	40
75	15	32	74	44	25½	189	74⅜	16	20	15	38
50	13	22	69	32	20¾	161	63⅜	12	14	8	35
25	10	12	60	20	16⅛	133	52⅜	9	7	2	31
1	8	2	50	9	11¾	104	40⅞	5	3	—	25

9

FROM THEORY TO PRACTICE

Before motor therapy can be effectively administered, all available information must be seriously scrutinized and a specific strategy decided on. Information provided by the physician, school, family, and other sources must be evaluated with the information provided during the parent-child-therapist interview. The therapist studies this information to find obvious trends or inconsistencies to determine target areas on which to concentrate in a therapy plan that includes both long-term and short-term objectives. The therapy plan represents the immediate and far-reaching strategies in assisting the child to overcome clumsiness.

LONG-TERM OBJECTIVES

The major long-term objectives in remediation of the clumsy child should be *effective total body management, object management, emotional control, ability to socialize effectively, a positive self-concept,* and *a sense of enjoyment in movement.* The long-term objective may require

months or even years to accomplish, depending on the seriousness of the problem. Before remediation is started, reasonable expectations must be established, including the types of activities to be learned, the time at which they should be introduced, and the length of time required to learn them.

SHORT-TERM OBJECTIVES

Six short-term objectives stand out as being extremely important to the therapy plan. *These are efficient execution of specific large-muscle tasks, efficient manipulation of specific objects, efficient reception and propulsion of specific objects, efficient body control when associated with apparatus and large objects, effective emotional control when experiencing specific stressful situations, and the ability to adapt and interact when a variety of social situations is presented.* As can be easily determined, it is desirable that the child develop efficiency in a great variety of movement situations while at the same time developing

89

confidence and self-control when confronted with a variety of external stressful situations. The most effective remediation program for the clumsy child should be keyed to adaptation and the providing of a rich environment of multisensory experiences.

BEHAVIORAL OBJECTIVES

In recent years there has been a trend in education to state both long- and short-term objectives in behavioral terms. To some degree this trend has been due to the computer age, Skinnerian psychology, and a desire to effectively manage human behavior. More specifically, however, the trend toward establishing behavioral objectives is an attempt to provide measurable changes in behavior and to be accountable for what has taken place through the process of education or therapy. The following questions should be considered when writing behavioral objectives (Yerkovich, 1972). (1) Is the objective stated clearly and concisely? (2) Is the objective related directly to the activity to be learned? (3) Is the objective presented as part of a large whole? (4) Is the objective measurable and verifiable? (5) Is the objective reasonable and within the ability level of the child? (6) Is the objective challenging? (7) Is the objective observable and accountable?

In discussing the writing of behavioral objectives, Davis (1973) indicates two essential parts, the observable behavior and the criteria for acceptable performance. An example of such an objective is as follows: "The child will be able to balance on one foot, with hands placed on hips, on a 2-inch balance board for 5 seconds by the end of the next therapy session." The ability to perform the act is the observable behavior and the time limit of 5 seconds indicates the acceptable performance. Additional elements that might be considered desirable or might increase the difficulty of the task, such as the maintenance of a specific form or posture, may be included. However, the more elements written into the performance criteria, the greater will be the expectations from the child and the therapist.

Specificity and concreteness

It is very important that behavioral objectives be stated in specific and concrete terms, using action words such as "distinguish," "interpret," "describe," "construct," "name," or "identify" but avoiding vague words such as "various," "fairly," or "almost."

Criteria for acceptability

Ideally, behavioral objectives should be stated for each individual. However, when providing therapy to small groups engaging in similar activities and tasks, the therapist may establish criteria for acceptable group behavior. If groups are well matched according to abilities, it is reasonable to expect success from 75% of the children attempting each task. However, criteria for acceptability vary with each individual, depending on the particular goals to be accomplished.

Evaluating progress

The outstanding benefit of establishing and carrying out behavioral objectives in a motor remediation program is that they provide for an ongoing evaluation process. They also provide an excellent means of testing the effectiveness of prescriptive activities. When a child is unable to accomplish a particular motor task, lower expectations or a change to an easier activity may be warranted. Also, the behavioral objectives approach works extremely well with the no-failure concept in developing a positive self-concept.

FAMILY INVOLVEMENT IN THE THERAPY PROCESS

To ensure the success of a motor therapy program there must be full cooperation by the child's family. Parents, siblings, and other immediate relatives work with the instructor to ensure success in remediation. To effectively bring this about there must be a program of family education and counseling. The extent to which this is carried out depends on three factors: availability of time, specific needs of the child, and receptivity of the family to help.

The rights of parents

Too often parents are kept in the dark by professionals who are working with their children. This is particularly true for physicians, psychologists, educational therapists, and teachers. A common reason suggested for not explaining to parents the specific problems of their child or the type of treatment being received is the lack of time needed to communicate properly. Another is that the parent will fail to understand and, as a result, probably overreact, to the detriment of the child. This point of view is unfortunate because in most cases parents are very interested in the welfare of their child and with proper explanation will react in an understanding and positive manner. We contend that parents should be informed and educated as to the needs of their child if the most effective therapy is to take place. Of course, as a member of the interdisciplinary therapy team, the motor therapist must never overstep his bounds by playing the role of another professional or placing doubt in the minds of parents as to the quality of care that is being provided by other professionals. The parent must have a clear understanding of the problems a child may have and the remediation that motor therapy is intended to provide.

Communicating with parents

There are four aspects of the motor therapy program that lend themselves to producing effective communication between parents and therapist. These include the *initial interview,* the *conference for interpreting the motor tests,* the *feedback conferences* immediately after therapy sessions, and *special programs* conducted for the express purpose of educating the entire family.

As discussed earlier, the initial parent-child interview with the therapist is essential to the understanding of child and parent expectations. During this initial interview, time is taken to fully discuss the program's purposes and objectives, how the child is to be approached, and what probable outcomes the parent should expect. The initial interview is designed to establish a climate of working together to assist the clumsy child in becoming a more efficient mover and having a greater sense of personal worth. We think that too often relieved parents who have sought and finally found help for their child totally relinquish their responsibility in this matter to the professional. Parents must come to realize that success is a matter of mutual concern and effort.

A second opportunity for communication between parents and therapist is immediately following motor ability testing. Parents are made familiar with the test, including its strengths, its weaknesses, and the interpretation of findings. During this conference a program of remediation is tentatively mapped out, with targets and strategies carefully explained to the parents.

A third opportunity for communication is the constant dialogue carried on as the therapy sessions progress. Time should be set aside periodically following a therapy session to discuss and exchange impressions on the child's progress in the program, both at home and at school. The relationship between therapist and parent should be developed as one of openness where questions for clarification can be made as they arise and problems can be dealt with immediately. However, discussion about the child should be conducted in the language that parents best understand, depending on their cultural background and education. In other words, the valuable time spent explaining a child's performance in the program should not be one of impressing the parents with the therapist's command of scientific language; it should be one of mutual education on behalf of the child.

The last but certainly not least important factor in the parent communication process is in periodic night meetings that both parents and interested family members can attend. The night meeting is an excellent time to show slides or other educational media and generally discuss the progress of the motor program as a whole as well as each child's progress within the program. A night meeting allows an opportunity to speak with parents who work during the day and to clarify questions and gain additional insights.

Parents as observers

When it is feasible, parents should be given opportunities to observe their child without being seen. Seeing the child interacting with the therapist and carrying out motor activities provides the parents with understanding that can be acquired in no other way. It is important that the parents see the child in relationship to other children who have motor difficulties. Observations by the parents should be planned, not indiscriminately allowed, to avoid misunderstandings and confusions when parents see specific techniques used in working with their child.

Parents as aides

For parents who have time and are genuinely interested in the program, acting as aides may increase their knowledge and understanding. As aides, parents must work with children other than their own who are completely unknown to them (Fig. 9-1). By working with other children parents gain sensitivity and insight into their own child's problems. However, before accepting aide positions they must be educated as to the proper procedures to follow and the limitations inherent in such a position. Parents acting as aides can add a great deal to the total therapy program by increasing assistance to the individual child as well as helping in the many routine activities that take the therapist's time away from working directly with the child.

Parents as home therapists

In our opinion, parents who are not carefully supervised generally are not effective home therapists. The analogy of a husband attempting to teach his wife to drive a car applies to a parent doing home motor therapy with a clumsy child in that the activity is too emotionally involving; it is extremely difficult to be objective. A parent who is normally reasonable and understanding may find it difficult to be nonjudgmental

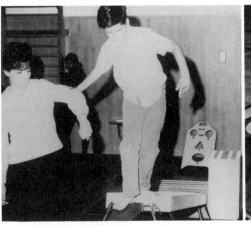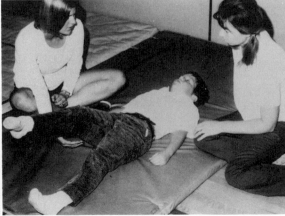

Fig. 9-1. Mother acting as an aide in the motor therapy program.

of his child's responses. It should be understood that the emotional climate in the home may be the very reason why the child is having motor difficulties. The impatience of parents when their child does not come up to an expected level makes them unsuitable as therapists. In general, home therapy programs designed for remediation of clumsiness only serve to increase the seriousness of the child's many problems.

The best approach, rather than having parents act as home therapists, is to give them hints on how to more effectively enhance their child's feeling of self-worth. Parents should praise the child for those things that he does well rather than dwelling on areas in which he has difficulty. The parents and child should engage in motor activity for the sheer fun of it rather than for improving any particular skill. In essence, motor therapy should be left to the teacher or therapist while the parents provide the most positive home atmosphere possible.

PART III

MOTOR THERAPY TASK CATEGORIES

Part III provides the reader with specific motor therapy task categories in which competence is necessary if a clumsy child is to become an efficient mover. Although the task categories are discussed as being autonomous, it should be understood that there is a great deal of overlapping of skills from one category to another. Innumerable cognitive, physical, and affective responses also are necessary to successfully complete each movement challenge. Presenting this information in separate categories is intended to give the reader a practical understanding of skill development but not to segment the child into discrete abilities.

10
TENSION RELEASE

A prerequisite to good body coordination and management is the ability to contract and relax muscles at will. This differential relaxation allows for coordinated and efficient movement without undue fatigue. Muscle tone is necessary for muscles to respond when needed. However, an abnormal amount of muscular tension may be related directly to emotion or indicative of some cerebral dysfunction. Whatever the etiology of excess muscular tension, conscious reduction will assist the child to develop better muscle synchronization and emotional control.

There are many means to muscle tension reduction; the most lasting are techniques that educate the child in consciously becoming aware of the state of abnormal muscle tone in the body and of when and how to reduce it. Such methods as imagery, rhythmical activity, play until physically fatigued, and muscle stretching exercises reduce tension to some degree; however, the most lasting approach is conscious tension reduction as suggested by Jacobson (1938). In his method of progressive relaxation, Jacobson first teaches the subject to be fully aware of excess tension and then to reduce it by focusing full attention on relaxing that tension.

The following is a program of tension-release activities designed for children who need to gain emotional and physical control through combining imagery, muscular tension recognition, and release.

TENSION REDUCTION THROUGH IMAGERY ALONE
Level I

Purpose. To help the child learn to reduce muscular tension through imagination.

Equipment and facilities. Necessary equipment includes a radio or record player to play relaxing background music or a metronome set between 48 and 68 beats per minute and a comfortable, quiet, dark place to recline. Lying on a soft mat is ideal; however, imagery can also effectively be carried out in a sitting position. The room should be darkened and the temperature no less than 74° F. If possible, extraneous noise should be held to a minimum so that just the voice of the instructor is heard. The child who has difficulty in keeping his eyes closed may wear a blindfold if he can do so without fear.

Position of therapist and child. While the child lies on his back the therapist sits nearby, close enough to be heard easily while speaking in a soft, low voice.

Preparation for imagery
1. Have the child stare at a spot on the ceiling without blinking until his eyes become tired; then instruct him to slowly allow them to close.
2. Have the child take five deep breaths, inhaling and exhaling slowly.

Imagery suggestions. The following is a list of images that can be suggested, depending on the age and interest of the participants.
1. Imagine that your body is very heavy and sinking into the floor.
2. Imagine you are a pat of butter in a warm frying pan, slowly melting.
3. Imagine yourself floating on a cloud.
4. Imagine yourself in a warm bath.
5. Imagine you are gliding along in a sailboat.
6. Imagine yourself in a warm, soft bed.
7. Imagine yourself lying on the front lawn, with the warm sun beating down, watching the clouds go by.
8. Imagine you are a soft marshmallow melting in a hot cup of cocoa.

Discussion. For imagery to be most effective, it is important that the child be able to conceptualize the difference between overt tension of the body and the physical release of that tension. To emphasize this point it may be advisable to contrast imagery by having the child become limp as a rag and then become heavy as a big rock or stiff as a board.

MUSCLE TENSION RECOGNITION AND RELEASE
Level II

Purpose. To assist the child in discovering his muscular tension level and to increase or decrease it at will in selected parts of the body.

Therapy hints
1. Prepare the child for relaxation by going through some imagery activities that last approximately 5 minutes.
2. In the first stages of learning the child should obviously stiffen and sag the body to develop the concept of tension and release. As control is gained, less obvious stiffening and sagging are required until finally all that is needed is to think about letting go of tension.
3. The concept of tension recognition must be introduced to the child gradually without a sense of urgency or forcefulness.
4. Depending on the ability of the child to concentrate, the relaxation period should not exceed 15 minutes. It should be noted, however, that in most cases a child who is hyperkinetic will not be able to maintain tension release as long as a normal child.
5. The best indication to the therapist that the child is learning to consciously release tension is the absence of resistance when a body part is lifted or moved. In the beginning sessions, resistance testing should automatically follow the relaxation of a given part. With this procedure the child has an immediate feedback as to the success of his efforts.

Muscle tensing sequences
1. Have the child stiffen his entire body for approximately 30 seconds to the point of fatigue (Fig. 10-1).
2. At the end of 30 seconds, have the child gradually decrease the stiffening and observe the degree of limpness in the body (Fig. 10-2).
3. Talk about how good it feels to be limp and relaxed in contrast to being stiff and tense.
4. When the child is limp, determine the lack of muscle tone in the body by lifting and dropping one arm. If the arm falls loosely to the floor without any visible restriction, then complete relaxation can be assumed to have taken place.

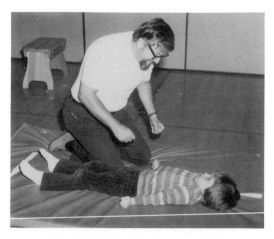

Fig. 10-1. Stiffening the entire body.

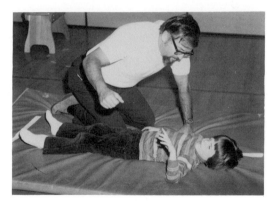

Fig. 10-2. Gradually decreasing stiffness.

However, if the arm resists falling, then it can be assumed that relaxation is not complete.

BILATERAL BODY CONTROL
Level III

Level III can be introduced to the child who is developmentally at least 7 years old (Arnheim and Pestolesi, 1973). It consists of bilateral body part tension recognition and release exercises.

1. When the child has successfully accomplished levels I and II, then level III is introduced; it mainly involves both upper and lower limbs.
2. As in level II, the child visibly brings tension into his limbs, gradually de-

creasing it until a relaxed state occurs.
3. The child clenches both hands as hard as possible, tensing the forearms and straightening the elbows until both arms are completely stiff. The child is then instructed to slowly let the upper arms "go loose," then let the forearms relax, and finally open the hands and allow the fingers to become limp.
4. As indicated earlier, stiffening of the limbs becomes less and less obvious as the concept of conscious tension reduction is learned. In other words, the child develops the ability to mentally control the muscle tone of the various upper and lower limb segments.
5. The legs are stiffened by first curling the toes down, then pointing the feet down, and finally locking the knees by fully extending the legs.
6. Like arm stiffening, leg stiffening is maintained for approximately 30 seconds and is followed by a gradual release of tension in the thigh, knee, lower leg, ankle, and then foot.
7. After he can perform the skill in both limbs the child is ready to learn unilateral body control.

UNILATERAL BODY CONTROL
Level IV

Level IV is concerned with development of unilateral body control through tension-release methods that normally can be attained by children with a motor development of 9 years of age.

1. Unilateral body control consists of controlling the muscular tension levels of only one side of the body, such as tensing the left arm and leg while completely relaxing the right side and then tensing the right arm and leg while relaxing the left side. In this way the child begins to more fully differentiate body parts as well as distinguish between the two sides of the body.
2. Level IV should be attempted only after successful execution of levels I, II, and III but, like the first three levels, should

be started with stiffening to the point of fatigue or for 30 seconds followed by gradual release of tension to the point of limpness.
3. When the child has learned to successfully control one side of the body, then he concentrates on the other.

RELAXATION OF SPECIFIC BODY PARTS
Level V

Level V is the relaxation of specific individual body parts. Success in level V indicates that the child can consciously reduce tension in most of the body's large muscles.
1. Full control of the tension levels of the large muscles normally requires a great deal of skill and is usually not achieved until the late teens or adulthood.
2. Level V is highly diagnostic, indicating the parts of the body with the most tension and those the individual has the most difficulty in controlling.

3. After the child's early attempts at gaining segmental control by consciously tensing and relaxing the therapist and child may determine the areas of the body that are most difficult to relax. Areas that are commonly difficult to control are the low back, the neck and shoulders, and the abdominal region.
4. When the child has mastered the ability to consciously relax the major portions of the body, he can concentrate on the more difficult areas rather than going over areas already mastered.

We consider tension recognition and conscious tension reduction as among the most valuable motor skills that can be acquired by the clumsy child. By progressing through the various levels, the child gains the ability to relax selected muscles, increase the sense of body awareness, and assist in the reduction of anxiety.

11

LOCOMOTION

As has been discussed in some detail in Chapter 1, the development of efficient upright posture (Fig. 11-1) and locomotion must be considered one of the greatest of human achievements. In the bipedal position a person is free to explore and manipulate objects with his hands. Purposeful mobility occurs when the infant is able to roll over from back to stomach, which occurs at about 3 months of age. From that time on the development of purposeful mobility is progressive, evolving to crawling, creeping in four-point position, and eventually the adult pattern of walking and running, which develops at about 4 years of age. To have success in each locomotor activity requires the ability to organize general motor behavior into specific motor skills. Fifty percent or more of children are able to sit without support at the age of 5½ months, to walk at about 1 year, to pedal a tricycle at 2 years, and to hop on one foot at 3½ years of age, all of which require skill in locomotion.

The clumsy child is often delayed in achieving locomotor skills, displaying ineptness in large- or small-muscle control. To offset these problems the clumsy child should be given the opportunity to experience and accomplish a large variety of locomotor skills such as rolling, crawling, creeping, walking, climbing, hopping, skipping, galloping, jumping up, jumping down, running, and leaping. Each skill should be given to the child in a progressive and logically sequenced manner with one task built on another until a level of locomotor efficiency commensurate with his physical maturity has been attained.

ROLLING, CRAWLING, CREEPING, AND CLIMBING
Level I

Level I is concerned with locomotor activities in which the child is almost completely grounded or securely close to the floor.

Purpose. To gain confidence, eliminate the fear of falling, and instill the courage to attempt new activities that provide less stability.

Equipment and facilities. Two tumbling mats measuring 5 by 10 feet should be put end-to-end for rolling activities. A 1-inch

Fig. 11-1. Determining postural alignment through the use of a grid.

tape line should be placed 1 foot from one edge and extended the full length of both mats. A second tape strip should be placed in the center and a third line 1 foot from the other edge.

Position of therapist and child. The therapist should position himself in such a way that he can give immediate directions to the child. It is important that manual guidance and immediate verbal feedback as to the accuracy of the activity be given continually for the child to develop an accurate sense of body positioning.

Therapy hints. It is essential that the child understand that the activity must be executed precisely. We suggest, therefore, that in the beginning each movement be done slowly, with a gradual increase in speed as control is gained. The therapist should keep in mind that locomotor skills are designed for both visual and large-muscle coordination and that the child should efficiently demonstrate each sequence before going on to the next more difficult task.

Activity progressions
Rolling

1. The child lies on his back with shoulders positioned on a side line, body fully extended, feet together, and arms held to the side. He rolls the full length of the two mats while trying to maintain his shoulders on the line. Each time the child makes a full revolution of the body he must become reoriented to the line. The head first turns in the direction of the roll, followed by the hips. The trunk is twisted, the shoulders lifted, and one thigh rotated inward and over the other thigh. In this manner, all segments of the body are aligned and maintained in good control. When the child is able to roll effectively in one direction, then rolling in the other direction should be attempted.

2. The child is now instructed to execute the same roll with the exception that each time he comes around he should sight along the line to end of the mat at an object such as a stick or brightly colored ball held in the therapist's hand. This task requires the child to orient his body and the object in a spatial relationship.

3. When the shoulder line roll has been accomplished in both directions, then the child is instructed to orient his hips to the center line (Fig. 11-2) and sight on the line at the end of the mat. When this is accomplished, the child orients his rolling by focusing on an object held in the therapist's hand.

4. Instead of placing his hips on the center line, the child is now instructed to place his knees there, following the same procedure as in No. 3.

Fig. 11-2. Attempting to roll precisely along a tape strip.

Fig. 11-3. Rolling like a ball.

5. The last rolling task is the placement of the ankles on a line and following the same procedure as in the other rolling tasks.

DISCUSSION. Successful completion of all rolling tasks indicates that the child has a good beginning for gross motor and posture control. The body's large muscles have an opportunity to operate in a synchronous manner and the eyes are used to orient the child to spatial relationships.

VARIATIONS OF ROLLING. When the basic rolling sequence has been successfully achieved, many variations can be included to offer additional challenges.
1. Rolling with hands clasped overhead
2. Rolling with one arm extended over the

head and the other arm held to the side of the body
3. Rolling under a string line that extends the full length of the mat and is placed above the child's shoulders, hips, knees, or ankles at a distance of 18 inches from the body (In this way the child is forced to orient to both the tape on the mat and the string, requiring an adaptation to two reference points.)
4. Rolling with the eyes closed and directing the body toward a sound made by the therapist
5. Rolling down the mat like a ball by grasping onto his knees and making himself as round as possible (Fig. 11-3)
Obviously rolling can eventually lead to execution of tumbling stunts, but these should be attempted only when it is apparent that the participant is ready for elementary gymnastics. Rolling activities as presented here should be the highest level attempted until some other higher level locomotor skills have first been mastered.

Crawling. Crawling is a natural extension of rolling. Like rolling, crawling provides the physically clumsy child with security because the body is fully in contact with a surface. The child moves along the floor in a prone (face-down) position by various movements of the arms and legs. Each crawling task must be executed in the proper form before the next higher level skill is attempted.
1. On his stomach, with arms at his sides and feet together, the child weaves back

and forth, attempting to propel himself forward. Instruction is given to maintain his arms at his sides, keeping his legs straight and moving his body as a single unit. Most likely, little forward progress will be made by the child. However, when the body can be moved as a unit equally well on both sides and can progress forward a foot or more, the child is ready for the next progression.

2. Crawling is next attempted in an amphibian fashion by moving the arm and leg on one side of the body in unison and then moving the limbs on the opposite side. The head should be either in a straight line with the eyes looking straight ahead or turned toward the side on which the limbs are flexed.

3. Movement is then introduced in which the opposite arm and leg are flexed and the other limbs extended. When the child can execute a cross-pattern movement with synchrony, variations are added.

VARIATIONS OF CRAWLING

1. Crawling sideways in each direction
2. Crawling backwards with feet first
3. Crawling under and over an obstacle
4. Crawling up and down an incline
5. Crawling forward on a narrow board

Creeping sequences. In creeping the child takes a quadrupedal (hands-and-knees) position. A well-skilled creeper maintains the trunk in line with the head and the shoulders. Keeping the body in good segmental alignment, the creeper should be able to move easily forward, backward, or even sideways. In general, like crawling, creeping is developed from less specific bilateral movements to unilateral and then cross-pattern movements. After the most sophisticated of creeping skills has been attained, then variations are introduced.

1. Maintaining good head and back alignment, the child moves forward by using the hands and the legs together in a homologous movement technique that is commonly described as a rabbit hop.

2. Following successful completion of homologous creeping, the child progresses to a unilateral pattern by moving first the arm and leg on one side and then both limbs on the other side.

3. Cross-pattern creeping is performed by extending one arm forward and placing the hand on the mat; the opposite knee follows. This movement alternates with movement of the other arm and knee (Fig. 11-4).

VARIATIONS OF CREEPING

1. The child executes the cross-pattern creeping technique moving backward instead of forward.

2. Rather than moving one limb at a time, the child moves the opposite arm and leg forward simultaneously.

3. Instead of moving forward the child

Fig. 11-4. Cross-pattern creeping.

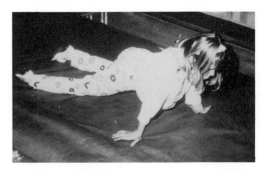

Fig. 11-5. Seal walk.

moves backward, moving the opposite leg and arm simultaneously.

4. The child moves sideways left and then right in the four-point position.

5. The child drags his legs like a seal (Fig. 11-5).

Ladder climbing. In some respects ladder climbing can be considered a direct extension of creeping because it involves the coordinated use of both legs and arms. In much the same way as crawling, creeping, and walking, climbing a ladder evolves from a unilateral skill to the most sophisticated cross-pattern skill.

1. Unilateral (homolateral) climbing is performed by placing the right foot on the rung, extending the right arm, placing the left foot on the rung, and extending the left arm.

2. Another type of unilateral climbing is performed by simultaneously moving first the right leg and arm and then the left leg and arm.

3. Cross-pattern climbing using one limb at a time begins with the right leg. Then the left arm is moved, followed by the left leg and then the right arm (Fig. 11-6).

4. In cross-pattern climbing incorporating simultaneous movements, the right leg and left arm move first, followed by the left leg and right arm.

NOTE: All of these sequences should include both climbing up and climbing down the ladder before the child goes on to level II.

WALKING AND STAIR CLIMBING
Level II

Level II introduces transport activities executed while in the upright posture and includes activities in which some part of the body is in contact with the supporting surface at all times, such as in walking on a level surface and stair climbing. Level II is a natural extension of level I, following the basic principles of developmental direction. At level I the child requires a great deal of physical support, while at level II he has progressed to the point that balance and locomotion are possible in the bipedal position.

Purpose. To execute a wide variety of bipedal movements, keeping one foot in contact with the ground at all times.

Fig. 11-6. Cross-pattern ladder climbing.

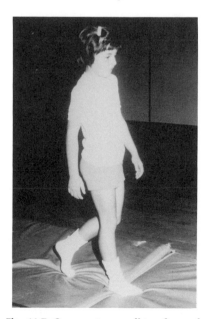

Fig. 11-7. Cross-pattern walking forward.

Equipment and facilities. A wide variety of outdoor terrain should be available, including differently textured surfaces, slopes, elevations, and stairs.

Position of therapist and child. The therapist should be positioned in such a way that he can give verbal direction easily and can spot when needed.

Activity progressions

Walking

1. Taking an upright position with good posture, the child propels himself forward with a cross-pattern technique, first swinging one arm and then the opposite leg. This is followed by an alternating of the other limbs (Fig. 11-7).
2. The child walks forward but moves opposite arms and legs simultaneously.

VARIATIONS OF WALKING

1. Walking unilaterally (moving the arm and leg on the same side in unison)
2. Cross-pattern walking backward (Fig. 11-8)
3. Walking backward in a unilateral pattern
4. Walking sideways to the left and then to the right
5. Walking forward, backward, and sideways on the toes (Fig. 11-9)
6. Walking forward, backward, and sideways on the heels
7. Walking with feet turned out
8. Walking with feet turned in
9. Walking on different textures, for example, grass, cement, sand, soft mat, wood floor, rug, gravel, dirt
10. Walking up and down inclines
11. Walking with the feet on different levels

Stair climbing. Ascending and descending stairs are natural extensions of creeping and walking. However, in remediation of the clumsy child, stair climbing should follow development of skill in walking. When the obstacle of a flight of stairs is presented to a toddler, he typically regresses to a unilateral style of locomotion in the quadrupedal position until maturation and confidence allow him to ascend and descend while standing upright.

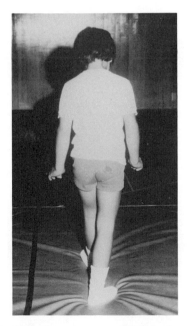

Fig. 11-8. Cross-pattern walking backward.

Fig. 11-9. Walking forward on toes.

1. Ascending stairs:
   a. Creeping upstairs in a unilateral fashion
   b. Creeping upstairs in a cross-pattern movement
   c. Walking upstairs in a unilateral fashion
   d. Walking upstairs in a cross-pattern movement (Fig. 11-10)
   e. Creeping upstairs in a supine position
   f. Walking upstairs backwards
2. Descending stairs:
   a. The child sits with hands flat on the same step and feet flat two or three steps lower. From this position the child moves down to the next step by first moving his seat, then both feet, continuing down the stairs like an inchworm.
   b. Following performance of bilateral scooting just described, the child moves down the stairs in a unilateral manner.

   c. The child descends using cross-pattern movements with feet first.
   d. Standing at the top of the stairs either holding on to a banister or free and maintaining good posture, the child steps down the stairs in a unilateral fashion always beginning with the right foot.
   e. As in d above, the child walks down the stairs, but always beginning with the left side (Fig. 11-11).
   f. Maintaining good posture alignment, the child descends the stairs in a cross-pattern fashion without holding on to a railing.

JUMPING, HOPPING, AND SKIPPING
Level III

The ability to propel the body upward from a supporting surface requires much strength, balance, and confidence, especially for the child who has not learned to jump. Jumping, hopping, and skipping are direct extensions of walking.

Fig. 11-10. Walking upstairs using cross-pattern movements.

Fig. 11-11. Cross-pattern descending of stairs.

Fig. 11-12. Jumping and landing on both feet.

Fig. 11-13. Low obstacle jumping.

Activity progressions
Jumping

1. Jumping with both feet together, leaving the ground, and landing with the body under control (Fig. 11-12)
2. Jumping with both feet together, swinging the arms, bending the knees, propelling the body over a line or very low obstacle such as the edge of a Hula-Hoop, and landing with both feet together under good control (Fig. 11-13)
3. Jumping over a 3-inch wide space with both feet
4. Jumping over a 6-inch wide space with both feet
5. Jumping over a 9-inch wide space with both feet
6. Jumping over a 12-inch wide space with both feet
7. Jumping with both feet over a space equal to the length of the child's lower leg

NOTE: Jumping farther than specified in No. 7 would be in the realm of motor fitness, which also includes such activities as running.

8. Jumping over a 3-inch obstacle with both feet

Fig. 11-14. Jumping with both feet over a 6-inch obstacle.

9. Jumping over a 6-inch obstacle with both feet (Fig. 11-14)
10. Jumping over a 9-inch obstacle with both feet
11. Jumping with both feet over an obstacle equal to the height of the child's knee

    NOTE: Jumping heights greater than the height of the knee should be considered high jumping, an area of motor fitness.

12. Jumping from a 2-inch step, landing with both feet together and the body under good control
13. Jumping from a 6-inch step, landing with both feet together and the body under good control
14. Jumping from two steps or a box approximately 18 inches in height, landing on both feet

15. Jumping from three steps or an equally high box, landing on both feet (Fig. 11-15)
16. Jumping with a two-foot takeoff over a space, landing in a balanced position on either the left or the right foot

    Hopping
1. Hopping once on the left foot
2. Hopping once on the right foot (Fig. 11-16)
3. Hopping twice on the left foot
4. Hopping twice on the right foot
5. Hopping three times on the left foot
6. Hopping three times on the right foot
7. Hopping forward on the left foot 10 times
8. Hopping forward on the right foot 10 times
9. Hopping backwards on the left foot three times
10. Hopping backwards on the right foot three times
11. Hopping backwards on the left foot 10 times
12. Hopping backwards on the right foot 10 times

Fig. 11-15. Jumping from a box with good body control.

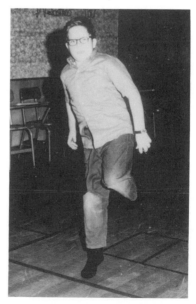

Fig. 11-16. Hopping on right foot.

13. Hopping sideways to the left on the left foot three times
14. Hopping sideways to the right on the left foot three times
15. Hopping sideways to the right on the right foot three times
16. Hopping sideways to the left on the right foot three times
17. Hopping once on the left foot and twice on the right
18. Hopping twice on the left foot and once on the right
19. Hopping blindfolded or with the eyes closed

Skipping. Skipping is a cross-extension movement of hopping, that is, a movement consisting of alternating hops on each foot to move forward.

1. Skipping forward
2. Skipping backwards
3. Skipping to the right
4. Skipping to the left
5. Skipping up a ramp
6. Skipping down a ramp
7. Skipping up stairs

RUNNING AND LEAPING
Level IV

The activities of level IV are the most difficult of the locomotor skills. They require the child to have a good foundation in the lower level skills.

Running. When the child gains confidence in the bipedal position, walking and running develop almost simultaneously; however, controlled running does not occur until after child has reached the toddler stage. Running is an extension of walking with the difference that there is no time when both feet are in contact with the ground. In essence, there are three phases in running: pushoff, flight, and landing. The faster a person runs, the more his body is inclined forward and the more he runs on the balls of his feet. As the person runs more slowly the pelvis is inclined backward and each foot is in contact with the ground for a longer time. In all running tasks the child should be encouraged to

Fig. 11-17. Attempting to run fast with the weight on the balls of the feet.

run in good alignment with arms and legs moving freely in a cross-pattern way. Deviation from this form produces inefficient running and expenditure of more energy than is necessary.

1. Running or jogging slowly with the feet flat
2. Running slowly with the weight slightly forward on the balls of the feet
3. Running forward at medium speed with the weight on the balls of the feet (Fig. 11-17)
4. Running forward fast with the weight on the balls of the feet
5. Running alternately slowly and then fast
6. Running backwards
7. Running slowly through a zigzag obstacle course
8. Running fast through a zigzag obstacle course
9. Running up a ramp
10. Running down a ramp
11. Running upstairs

Leaping. A leap is a synchronous movement that in most cases is an extension of running. In the leap one foot is used to push off and the other to land. The runner bends the knee of the leg that is in the back position and, with an exaggerated step of the front leg, lands on the front foot. The leaper attempts to literally sail through the air, making a landing that is as soft as possible.

1. Stepping and leaping, landing on the right foot
2. Stepping and leaping, landing on the left foot
3. Running slowly and leaping, landing on the right foot
4. Running slowly and leaping, landing on the left foot
5. Running fast and leaping, landing on the right foot
6. Running fast and leaping, landing on the left foot
7. Running, fast leaping over a knee-high hurdle, and landing on the left foot

NOTE: Leaping over a higher obstacle would be considered hurdling.

Gaining locomotor efficiency should be one of the most important goals for the clumsy child. Most gross and fine motor skills develop from an effective transport system.

12

BALANCE

Balance is the ability to maintain equilibrium while engaging in various locomotor or nonlocomotor activities. Equilibrium is maintained by the interaction of a number of neurophysiological structures, senses, and pathways, such as vision, labyrinthine or vestibular stimulation, neck reflexes, the tactile senses, and proprioception. The internal sense of proprioception and the vestibular system combine with vision to provide the individual with external information as to his position in space. The vestibular apparatus increases the individual's awareness of postural positions and changes in acceleration and coordinates with visual, tactile, and proprioceptive systems in providing movement guidance. If these systems do not function normally, the child experiences great difficulty in maintaining balance (Arnheim and Pestolesi, 1973).

There are three basic categories of balance. (1) Static balance is the ability to maintain a specific position for a given period of time. Standing at attention and maintaining a headstand are examples of activities involving static balance. (2) In contrast to static balance, dynamic balance is body control while moving. (3) Object balance is the ability to support some external object without letting it fall, such as balancing a stick on a finger or a beanbag on the head.

Since the force of gravity is continually acting on the human body, it must be taken into consideration in all balance activities. This force is always exerted in a vertical direction toward the center of the earth. It acts on all parts of the body and is particularly noticeable at the weight center of the body, which is known as the center of gravity. The center of gravity is located in the hip region; however, this should be considered only a reference point because any movement of the body can shift the center of gravity in the direction of the movement. It is conceivable that the center of gravity may be located outside the body if the skill being performed requires gross movement in a particular direction. Static balance can only be accomplished when the center of gravity is above the body's base of support. If the center of gravity is not above the base of support, maintaining a static position is difficult. To maintain dynamic balance the body must alternately lose and regain equilibrium.

PROGRESSIONS IN STATIC BALANCE
Level I: Static balance

Level I is concerned with activities for the remediation of static balance problems. They are based on the principle that activities designed for a specific movement problem progress from the simple to the more complex.

Equipment and facilities. One tumbling mat measuring 5 by 10 feet.

Position of therapist and child. The therapist should position himself in such a way that he can give immediate direction and manual assistance to the child.

Therapy hints. The therapist should keep in mind the following concept for minimizing difficulty in balance activities: *to provide more stability the base of support should be increased; when less stability is desired, it should be decreased.* Thus a static balance program should begin by providing the child with the largest possible base on which to balance. Gradually, motor tasks providing less stability are introduced. Ultimately the child develops a high level of static balance skill and the ability to perform a wide variety of activities.

Activity progressions. All balance postures in level I should be held for 10 seconds.

1. The child lies on his right side, with the arm underneath extended above his head and the arm on top placed against his side. Then he lies on his left side.
2. Sitting on the floor, the child lifts the legs while maintaining balance on the buttocks. Various combinations of arm and leg positions may be explored, such as sitting cross-legged with arms crossed.
3. The child assumes the following positions.
   a. Three-point position with the right knee off mat
   b. Three-point position with the left knee off mat
   c. Three-point position with the right hand off mat
   d. Three-point position with the left hand off mat
   e. Two-point position with the right hand and left knee off mat
   f. Two-point position with the left hand and right knee off mat
   g. Two-point position with the right hand and right knee off mat
   h. Two-point position with the left hand and left knee off mat
4. The child assumes the following positions.
   a. Three-point position with the right foot off mat
   b. Three-point position with the left foot off mat
   c. Three-point position with the right hand off mat
   d. Three-point position with the left hand off mat
   e. Two-point position with the right hand and left foot off mat
   f. Two-point position with the left hand and right foot off mat
   g. Two-point position with the right hand and right foot off mat
   h. Two-point position with the left hand and left foot off mat
5. The child is instructed to:
   a. Squat with arms crossed on chest and back held straight.
   b. Stand with feet together and hands placed on waist.
   c. Stand on tiptoes with feet together and hands placed on waist.
   d. Stand on heels with feet together and hands placed on waist.
   e. Stand heel-to-toe with right foot in front of left and hands placed on waist.
   f. Stand heel-to-toe with left foot in front of right and hands placed on waist.
   g. Stand on left foot with arms crossed.
   h. Stand on right foot with arms crossed.

i. Stand on left foot with arms crossed and eyes blindfolded.
j. Stand on right foot with arms crossed and eyes blindfolded.
6. While the feet remain stationary, the child explores the various movements that his upper body can make, for example, swinging, twisting, turning, bending, circling, and swaying.

Variations of level I

1. All activities are increased in time up to 15 seconds.
2. The child performs each task blindfolded after he can accomplish it with eyes open.
3. The child balances on a large rubber ball in a supine position and in a four-point stance (Fig. 12-1).

Level II: Static balance on a balance beam

Level II requires the child to perform many of the tasks in level I while balancing on a balance beam. Level II is a natural extension of level I that progressively increases the difficulty of the balancing tasks.

Equipment and facilities. One tumbling mat measuring 5 by 10 feet and one balance beam with the following dimensions: length, 10 feet; height, 4 inches; and width, 2 inches.

Position of therapist and child. The therapist should be positioned in such a way that he can easily give verbal directions and can spot the child when it is necessary.

Activity progressions. All balance postures in level II should be held for 10 seconds.

1. While balancing on the 4-inch side of the balance beam, the child is instructed to:
   a. Stand heel-to-toe, right foot in front of left, hands placed on the waist.
   b. Stand heel-to-toe, left foot in front of right, hands placed on the waist.
   c. Stand on the left foot with arms crossed.
   d. Stand on the right foot with arms crossed.
2. While standing heel-to-toe with feet remaining stationary, the child explores the various movements that his upper body can make, for example, swinging, twisting, turning, bending, circling, and swaying.

Variations of level II

1. All activities are increased in time up to 15 seconds.

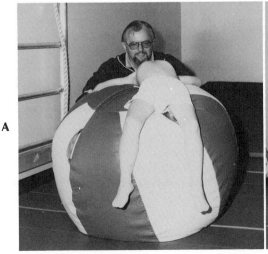

Fig. 12-1. Maintaining body equilibrium while balancing on a large rubber ball. **A,** In a supine position. **B,** In a four-point stance.

2. The child performs each task blind-folded after he can accomplish it with eyes open.
3. While lying in a supine position, the child performs a variety of synchronized movements such as alternating leg raises (Fig. 12-2).
4. The child performs all the tasks while balancing on the 2-inch side of the balance beam. (The beam should be stabilized with brackets.)

Fig. 12-2. Lying on a 4-inch balance beam.

5. The child balances on a variety of objects such as balance boards (Fig. 12-3), T-stools, and Bongo Boards (Fig. 12-4).

Level III: Static balance variations

Level III consists of tasks that require more strength than the other levels; some are gymnastic stunts.

Activity progressions

1. While balancing on a 2-inch balance beam, a 4-inch balance beam, or a T-stool, the child is instructed to:
   a. Play catch with a variety of objects (Fig. 12-5).
   b. Balance other objects such as sticks and beanbags on his head.
   c. Maintain balance using weights to change balance of a part of the body, for example, holding a weighted object in his right hand with his right arm fully extended parallel to the floor.
2. The child forms a tripod by placing his

Fig. 12-3. Maintaining balance in seated and standing positions on balance boards.

head and hands on the mat with knees resting on his elbows (Fig. 12-6).

3. To do a headstand using a wall for support, the child is instructed to:
   a. Face the wall and place his head on the floor 3 inches from the wall.
   b. Place his hands on the floor 12 inches from the wall.
   c. Raise one leg upward and gradually move up the other leg until both feet are resting side by side against the wall. In the final position the head, trunk, hips, and legs should be aligned (Fig. 12-7).
4. The child performs a headstand without support (Fig. 12-8).
5. To perform a frog stand supported only by the hands, the child begins in a squatting position. With hands on the mat, he bends his elbows slightly and places both knees on top of his elbows. The child rocks forward on his hands, raises his feet off the floor, and attempts to maintain a balance position for 10 seconds.
6. Standing with his feet shoulder-width apart and hands clasped together be-

Fig. 12-4. Balancing on a Bongo Board.

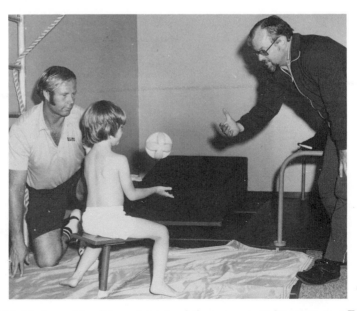

Fig. 12-5. Playing catch while maintaining balance in a seated position on a T-stool.

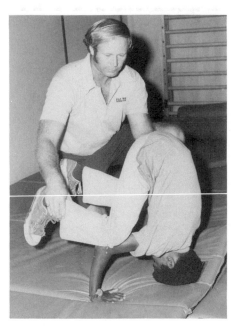

Fig. 12-6. Balancing in a tripod position using head and hands.

hind his back, the child kneels on both knees and then attempts to stand up without losing his balance or changing the position of his feet.

7. Standing on his right foot and grasping his left foot with his right hand, the child squats down and touches his left knee to the floor; then he stands up without touching any other part of his body to the mat or losing his balance.

8. The child stands on his left foot, bends forward, and places both hands on the floor. While keeping his right foot off the mat, he touches his head to the mat and returns to the original standing position without losing his balance.

9. Standing with both feet together, the child bends his knees, threads both arms between his legs, and grasps his ankles. He should maintain this position for 10 seconds without losing his balance (Fig. 12-9).

10. While standing, the child kicks his

Fig. 12-7. Headstand using wall for support.

Fig. 12-8. Unaided headstand.

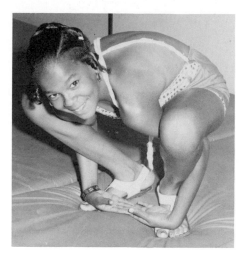

Fig. 12-9. Squat balancing.

right foot up to shoulder level without moving his left foot.

11. The child crosses both feet and sits down cross-legged with arms folded across his chest. He then returns to a standing position without unfolding his arms or moving his feet.

12. The child stands on his left foot with his right foot extended off the floor. He squats down on the heel of his left foot, and then returns to the original standing position without losing his balance or touching his right foot or either hand to the floor.

PROGRESSIONS IN DYNAMIC BALANCE
Level I: Dynamic balance

Level I is concerned with basic tasks that are conducted on the floor.

Position of therapist and child. The therapist should position himself in such a way that he can give directions to the child.

Activity progressions. The child is instructed to do the following tasks for 10 steps within a 4-inch track while maintaining good posture.

1. Walk forward heel-to-toe.
2. Walk backward toe-to-heel.
3. Walk sideways using a crossover step.
4. Walk on tiptoes.
5. Walk on heels.

6. Walk on toes with toes pointed out.
7. Walk with toes pointed out.
8. Skip.
9. Hop first on the right foot and then on the left.

Variations of level I

1. The child performs each task blindfolded after he can accomplish it with eyes open.
2. The child plays catch with a variety of objects while doing each task.
3. The child bounces a ball while doing each task.

Level II: Dynamic balance on balance beam or walking board

Level II involves activities that are conducted on a balance beam or a walking board.

Equipment and facilities. A balance beam 10 feet long, 2 inches thick, and 4 inches wide and a walking board 10 feet long, 2 inches thick, and 3 feet wide.

Position of therapist and child. The therapist should position himself in such a way that he can easily give verbal directions and can spot the child when necessary.

Activity progressions. The child is instructed to do the following tasks for 10 steps on a 4-inch balance beam while maintaining good posture.

1. Walk forward heel-to-toe (Fig. 12-10).
2. Walk backward toe-to-heel.
3. Walk sideways using a crossover step (Fig. 12-11).
4. Walk on tiptoes.
5. Walk on heels.

Variations of level II

1. The child performs each task blindfolded after he can accomplish it with eyes open.
2. The child plays catch with a variety of objects while doing each task.
3. The child bounces a ball while doing each task.
4. The child performs each task with the balance beam in various inclined positions.
5. The child maintains balance while ascending and descending a walking

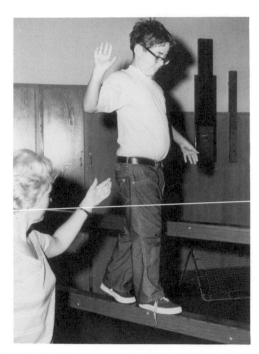

Fig. 12-10. Walking forward heel-to-toe on a balance beam.

Fig. 12-11. Walking sideways using a crossover step.

Fig. 12-12. Maintaining equilibrium while walking down an incline.

Fig. 12-13. Walking forward on a beam while balancing an object overhead.

Fig. 12-14. Balancing a beanbag on the head while negotiating an obstacle course.

board in various inclined positions (Fig. 12-12).
6. The child maintains balance on the balance beam while using weights to change the balance of a part of the body; for example, he holds a weighted object overhead with both hands or in either hand with his arm fully extended and parallel to the floor (Fig. 12-13).
7. The child walks forward and backward through an obstacle course, stepping over and between obstacles of different heights (Fig. 12-14).

Level III: Dynamic balance variations

Level III involves a variety of activities and equipment that is used for improving dynamic balance.

Position of therapist and child. The therapist should position himself in such a way that he can give verbal direction and spot when needed.

Activity progressions
1. Jumping rope
2. Riding on a scooter board
3. Riding a two-wheel bicycle
4. Walking on stilts
5. Skating on roller skates
6. Bouncing on a pogo stick
7. Playing hopscotch

PROGRESSIONS IN OBJECT BALANCE

Object balance deals with the ability of the child to balance an external object on a part of his body.

Equipment and facilities. One 5 by 10 foot tumbling mat, three beanbags, two broomsticks, five marbles, two ½-inch boards 4 inches square, and one ½-inch board 12 inches square.

Position of therapist and child. The therapist should position himself in such a way that he can give immediate direction and manual assistance to the child.

Activity progressions
Level I
1. Balancing a beanbag on the top of his head, the child is instructed to:
   a. Walk forward heel-to-toe.
   b. Walk backward toe-to-heel.
   c. Walk sideways using a crossover step.
   d. Walk on heels.
   e. Walk on tiptoes.
   f. Hop first on the right foot and then on the left.
   g. Skip.
2. The child is instructed to:
   a. Walk forward and backward with his head tilted back and a beanbag balanced on his forehead.
   b. Walk forward and backward with arms held out sideways and palms up while balancing a beanbag in each hand.
   c. Walk forward and backward with arms held out sideways and palms down while balancing a beanbag on the back of each hand.
   d. Walk forward and backward with arms held out sideways and palms down while balancing a beanbag on

Fig. 12-15. Balancing a beanbag on the back of the hand while moving from a seated to a standing position.

Fig. 12-16. Balancing a stick with the fingertips while walking forward.

the back of each hand and one on the top of his head.
  e. Crawl on all fours with a beanbag balanced on the back of his head.
  f. Crawl on all fours with a beanbag balanced on his back between his shoulder blades.
Level II
1. The child assumes a seated position on a tumbling mat and is instructed to:
  a. Stand up while balancing a beanbag on the back of one hand (Fig. 12-15).
  b. Stand up while balancing a bean bag on the top of his head.
  c. Stand up while balancing a beanbag on the back of one hand and another on the top of his head.
2. The child hops forward on one foot with a beanbag balanced on top of the other foot.
3. With a broomstick balanced in a vertical position in the palm of one hand, the child is instructed to:
  a. Walk forward (Fig. 12-16).
  b. Walk backward.
  c. Walk sideways using a crossover step.
  d. Hop forward first on the right foot and then on the left.
  e. Skip.

Fig. 12-17. Balancing a stick on the foot.

Fig. 12-18. Balancing Hula-Hoops on different parts of the body simultaneously.

Level III

1. The child walks forward and backward while performing the following tasks.
   a. Balancing a marble on a 4-inch square board in front and away from the abdomen

   b. Balancing a marble on a 4-inch square board held in a flat position by one hand with the arm fully extended sideways
   c. Balancing a marble on each of two 4-inch square boards held in a flat position by both hands with the arms fully extended sideways.
   d. Balancing five marbles at one time on a 12-inch square board held in a flat position by both hands in front and away from the abdomen.
2. The child balances a broomstick in a vertical position on the top of his foot (Fig. 12-17).
3. The child balances Hula-Hoops on different parts of the body simultaneously (Fig. 12-18).

One or more type of balance is involved in practically all motor skills. Consequently, if the clumsy child is to be able to participate on an equal basis with his peers, either in physical education classes or recreational play time, it is absolutely essential that the therapist include a sequence of balance activities at every session.

13

BODY AND SPACE PERCEPTION

How one perceives his body is an ever-growing and changing phenomenon. Many terms have been used to designate body perception, producing a great deal of confusion. Terms such as body awareness, body image, body schema, body concept, and body percept all refer in some way to how the body is perceived. In a brief overview of the literature on body concept, Morris and Whiting (1971) include the following factors that are associated with an individual's body perception: body sensations, imagination and mental imagery, ego development, affective development, cognitive development, acquisition of a sense of body boundary, and the development of kinesthetic sensitivity. Since all of these factors play an important part in body perception, it can be considered multi-dimensional rather than a result of one factor.

Body perception is directly affected by cognitive, affective, and psychomotor learning and has a direct relationship to the individual's understanding of space. To provide remediation, key factors of body perception must be lifted from the milieu and presented to the clumsy child in the form of specific tasks. The three areas of body perception that have been found to be most important are body knowledge, body image, and body-space relationships.

BODY KNOWLEDGE

As in the other aspects of body perception, knowledge of the body starts at birth and progresses throughout adulthood. As the child becomes organized through maturation and development, body knowledge is also acquired. Barsch terms the discovery of various body parts as learning "Who am I?" Accurate, specific knowledge about the body provides the child with a basis for both physical and mental development. The developing child first learns the large areas of the body and then the increasingly more discrete aspects of the external body. Body planes, body parts, body movements, laterality, and directionality are learned progressively until the child has acquired a keen knowledge of the body and its relationship to its surroundings.

BODY IMAGE

The image or feeling that the child has about his body results from the sum total of the child's experiences. Body image is the product of an individual's perception, attitudes, and values about the environment. It must be considered on a continuum that is always changing, being modified from birth till death. An image of the body stems from an interplay of all experiences. In essence, the child is what his thoughts and others' thoughts determine him to be. Before a child can successfully interact with the environment in ways that are meaningful and fulfilling, accurate body knowledge and a positive body image must be developed.

SPATIAL RELATIONSHIPS

The expanse that extends in all directions from the body outward to infinity is considered space. Material objects such as the human body are contained within, or occupy a portion of, that space. The human body becomes a reference point for identifying the position of objects in space. Near space is the space that immediately surrounds the person; middle space extends out from the individual for a distance of approximately 20 feet, and far space goes on into infinity. To function efficiently in this spatial world, the child must be able to accurately integrate all of his internal body sensations with his surroundings and make judgments as to distances, sizes, relative positions of objects, and the force that is applied to various projectiles.

Closely associated with body perception and spatial relationships is the awareness of the two sides of the body, called laterality. The projecting of laterality outward from the body into the spatial world is known as directionality. The acquisition of reading and writing skills is dependent on the awareness of left and right and the directional perception of up, down, back, and front; these provide spatial references for recognizing shapes, letters, and words. Children who are confused in the accurate perception of their bodies often have directional confusion that is reflected in an inability to effectively engage in classroom motor skills or to play games (Chapters 17 and 18).

CLUMSINESS AND BODY PERCEPTION

The individual whose problems include poor perception of his body often has difficulty in moving effectively in space. This problem can be observed when he inadvertently bumps into obstacles, drops objects, or knocks them over. It should be noted, however, that individuals can sense their bodies accurately but still be clumsy in their actions due to other difficulties such as problems in visual perception. For children who have obvious body perception problems a specific program should be instituted. The following activities are suggested for remediation of problems in body perception. Activity sequences are presented in the two categories of directive and reflective progressions. Directive activities are those activities initiated by verbal or tactile directions. Reflective activities, on the other hand, are initiated without verbalization or touching but are conducted by having the child mimic the therapist's body positions or copy the attitudes of some graphic display such as a picture.

Equipment and facilities. Body perception is best taught in an area that is uncluttered and has a nondistracting background such as a blank wall. A full-length mirror should be available so that both the child and the therapist can view themselves at the same time; a blindfold is also needed.

Position of therapist and child. In directive activities the therapist can either stand or lie on his back.

Therapy hints. The therapist should make his directions as concise and concrete as possible, omitting words that only tend to confuse the child. Each direction should be repeated twice and should be

Fig. 13-1. Touching the front of the body.

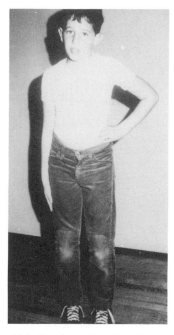

Fig. 13-2. Touching the side of the body.

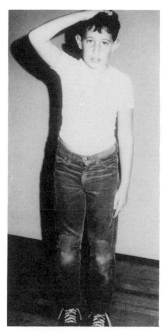

Fig. 13-3. Touching the top of the body.

Fig. 13-4. Touching the arm.

followed by an immediate positive response such as praise when the child successfully completes the task. However, if the child fails at a certain body perception task, a few more directives should be given to determine whether the missed task was an accurate indication of the child's functional level.

Directive progressions. The therapist gives the directions listed and the child carries them out.

Level I

1. Body planes (using one or both hands):
   a. Touch the front of your body (Fig. 13-1).
   b. Touch the back of your body.
   c. Touch the side of your body (Fig. 13-2).
   d. Touch the top of your body (Fig. 13-3).
   e. Touch the bottom of your body. (Child touches both hands to the bottom of the feet.)
2. Body parts:
   a. Touch your head.
   b. Touch your arm (Fig. 13-4).
   c. Touch your leg.
   d. Touch your foot.
   e. Touch your face.
   f. Touch your elbow (Fig. 13-5).
   g. Touch your knee (Fig. 13-6).
   h. Touch your nose (Fig. 13-7).
   i. Touch your ear (Fig. 13-8).

Fig. 13-6. Touching the knee.

Fig. 13-5. Touching the elbow.

Fig. 13-7. Touching the nose.

   j. Touch your mouth.
   k. Touch your eye.
   l. Touch your hand.
   m. Touch your stomach (Fig. 13-9).
3. Body movements:
   a. Bend your body forward (Fig. 13-10).
   b. Bend your body backward (Fig. 13-11).

Fig. 13-10. Bending the body forward.

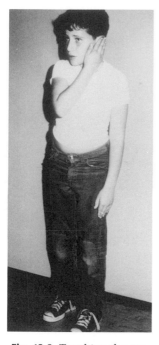

Fig. 13-8. Touching the ear.

Fig. 13-9. Touching the stomach.

Fig. 13-11. Bending the body backward.

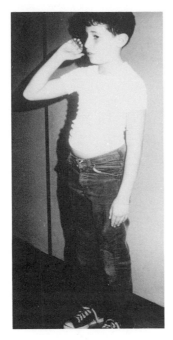

Fig. 13-12. Bending the elbow.

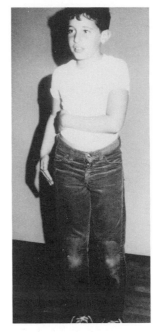

Fig. 13-14. Touching the right side.

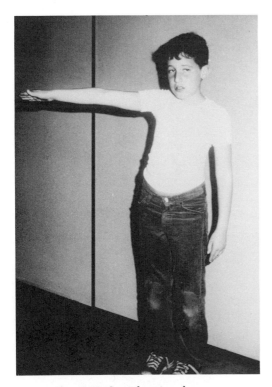

Fig. 13-13. Straightening the arm.

    c. Bend your body sideward.
    d. Twist or turn your body.
    e. Bend your knees.
    f. Stand on your tiptoes.
    g. Bend your head forward.
    h. Bend your head sideward.
    i. Bend your head backward.
    j. Bend your elbow (Fig. 13-12).
    k. Straighten your arm (Fig. 13-13).
Level II
1. Body parts:
    a. Touch your elbow.
    b. Touch your knee.
    c. Touch your shoulder.
    d. Touch your fingers.
    e. Touch your wrist.
    f. Touch your nose.
    g. Touch your mouth.
2. Body movements:
    a. Circle your head.
    b. Circle your arms.
    c. Circle your leg.
    d. Bend your fingers.
    e. Bend your toes.
3. Laterality:
    a. Touch your right arm.

Fig. 13-15. Holding up the right arm.

b. Touch your left knee.
c. Touch your right foot.
d. Touch your left eye.
e. Touch your right shoulder.
f. Touch your left elbow.
g. Touch your right side (Fig. 13-14).
h. Touch your right side against the wall.
i. Kneel on your left knee.
j. Hold something in your right hand.
k. Step up on the chair with your left foot.
l. Hold up your right arm (Fig. 13-15).

Level III

1. Body parts:
   a. Touch your thigh.
   b. Touch your wrist.
   c. Touch your upper arm.
   d. Touch your forearm.
   e. Touch your lower leg.
   f. Touch your kneecap.
   g. Touch your little finger.
   h. Touch your big toe.
   i. Touch your little toe.
   j. Touch your eyebrow.
2. Body movements:
   a. Straighten your leg.
   b. Straighten your arms.
   c. Circle your foot.
   d. Circle your hand.
   e. Spread your fingers.
   f. Spread your toes.
   g. Wiggle your nose.
   h. Stick out your tongue.
   i. Make a sad face.
   j. Make a happy face.
3. Laterality:
   a. Touch something to your right side.

b. Touch a ball to your left knee.
c. Touch something to your left elbow.
d. Touch something to your right ear.
e. With your right hand, touch your left foot.
f. With your left hand, touch your right ear.

g. With your right hand, touch your right ear.
h. With your left hand, touch your left shoulder.
i. With your right hand, touch your left elbow.
j. With your right hand, touch your left wrist.
k. With your left hand, touch your right eye.
l. With your right hand, touch your nose.
m. With your left hand, touch your knee.
n. With your left hand, hold on to your right ear.
o. With your left hand, grab your left ankle.

4. Directionality:
a. Touch another child's right hand.
b. Touch another child's left ear.
c. Touch another child's right shoulder.
d. Touch another child's right knee (Fig. 13-16).
e. Touch another child's right eyebrow.
f. Touch the left side of the chair. (Child stands facing a chair.)
g. Touch the right side of the chair.
h. With your left hand, touch the right side of the chair.
i. With your right hand, touch the left side of the chair.

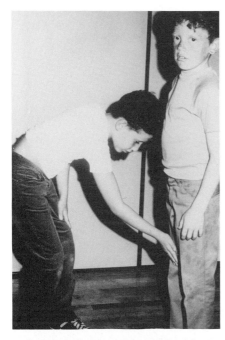

Fig. 13-16. Touching another child's right knee.

Fig. 13-17. Coloring and identifying the body parts represented in a self-silhouette.

j. With your right hand, touch the right side of the chair.

k. Tell me, what foot is another child standing on?

l. Tell me, what hand does another child have raised?

m. Stand with your right side against another child's left side.

n. Stand so that your left side is against another child's right side.

Variations of directive body perception

1. The child gives directions to the therapist.

2. The child gives directions to self aloud.

3. The child gives directions to another child.

4. After the child's silhouette is traced on a large sheet of paper, the child colors and identifies the body parts (Fig. 13-17).

5. On the directions of the therapist the child places his body part on the corresponding part of the silhouette tracing.

6. The child verbally identifies all body parts.

Reflective progressions. Reflective body perception tasks are designed to reveal how

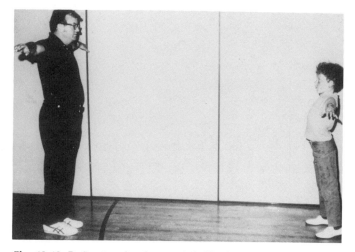

Fig. 13-18. Reflecting the therapist's half side spread of both arms.

Fig. 13-19. Staggering the right foot forward and the left foot back.

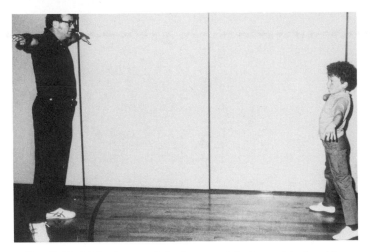

Fig. 13-20. Half side spread, both arms; right foot out to the side.

accurately a child copies the movements or poses of another person or an animal. The therapist can demonstrate in several ways, for example, by facing the child, with his back to the child, or by having both the child and the therapist face a mirror. When the therapist is facing him the child responds as if he were viewing himself in a mirror. If the therapist has his back to the child or they are both facing a mirror, the child attempts to mimic the therapist's moves exactly.

Level I. Child lies on a mat facing the therapist, who is standing at the child's feet.

1. Half side spread, both arms
2. Three-quarters side spread, both arms
3. One-quarter side spread, both arms
4. Half side spread, both legs
5. Three-quarters side spread, both legs
6. One-quarter side spread, both legs
7. Both arms spread overhead; half side spread, both legs
8. Half side spread, right leg
9. Half side spread, left leg
10. Half side spread, right arm
11. Half side spread, left arm
12. Half side spread, right hand; three-quarter side spread, left leg
13. Three-quarter side spread, right arm; one-quarter side spread, left leg

VARIATIONS OF LEVEL I

1. The child verbalizes how the arms and legs are to be moved and then the therapist and the child take that position.
2. The child watches therapist's movement and then mimics the movement with eyes closed.

Level II. Activities are conducted in a standing position with the child facing the therapist, who stands approximately 8 feet from the child. The child is instructed to follow the therapist's movements as if he were viewing himself in a mirror. All activity tasks are conducted in silence with no verbal instructions given except prompting by the therapist to clarify how the task is executed or to provide positive reinforcement.

1. Half side spread, both arms (Fig. 13-18)
2. Three-quarter side spread, both arms
3. One-quarter side spread, both arms
4. Three-quarter side spread, left arm; half side spread, right arm
5. Three-quarter side spread, right arm; one-quarter side spread, left arm
6. Half side spread, right arm; three-quarter side spread, left arm
7. Half side spread, left arm; three-quarter side spread, right arm

Fig. 13-21. Playing follow the leader in front of the mirror.

Fig. 13-22. Copying pictures with the body.

8. Right arm extended in front of face, left arm overhead
9. Left arm extended in front of face, right arm overhead
10. Both feet spread to side
11. Both feet together
12. Right foot out to side
13. Left foot out to side
14. Right foot forward, left foot back (Fig. 13-19)
15. Left foot forward, right foot back

VARIATIONS OF LEVEL II
1. The child plays follow the leader.
2. The child mimics different animals.

Level III. In contrast to level II, level III tasks include moving both arms and legs simultaneously.

1. Half side spread, both arms; right foot out to side (Fig. 13-20)

2. Half side spread, both arms; left foot out to side
3. One-quarter side spread, both arms; right foot forward; left foot back
4. One-quarter side spread, right arm; left arm extended overhead; left foot forward; right foot back
5. Both arms extended at shoulder level, both feet spread

VARIATIONS OF LEVEL III
1. The child follows the therapist as they both stand in front of the mirror (Fig. 13-21).
2. The therapist shows the child drawings of figures assuming various positions and the child assumes the same positions (Fig. 13-22).
3. The therapist instructs the child to take the position opposite the one demonstrated.

14

RHYTHM AND TEMPORAL AWARENESS

Rhythm may be considered the ordering of energy. Time and rhythm are interdependent. Rhythms are patterns of movement joined together in a synchronized way to produce efficiency in movement, whereas time is the experience of duration (Bateman, 1968). All coordinated movement requires an accurate sense of space, time, and force; without it there is dysrhythmia. In general, life has both time and rhythmic factors that are extrinsic and intrinsic to the human organism. In an attempt to organize his world, man has created events, milestones, and periods as well as clock and calendar time. These time periods provide man's life with a sense of predictability and a stable base from which to operate. The child who lacks coordination is asynchronous and expends unnecessary energies in order to perform a given task. The individual who has a good inner sense of rhythm and timing is usually graceful, while one who displays asynchronous motor behavior is unable to make the correct application of muscular effort.

Laban and Lawrence (1947) proposed that four components of effort are involved in carrying out a motor task. They are weight, time, space, and flow. Each of these components is further divided—weight is firm or light, time is sudden or sustained, space is direct or flexible, and flow is bound or free. A child who uses the components of effort inappropriately moves in an uncoordinated manner. A planned intervention program of rhythm can be successfully employed with children who are asynchronous and can also help them to gain emotional control and learn to socialize. The teacher or therapist should be able to easily move into and out of different rhythms, for example, immediately changing a fast run to a slow walk or bouncing a ball quickly and then slowly.

CADENCE TRAINING

In remediation of clumsiness, cadence training provides sequenced learning for synchronizing body movement (Figs. 14-1 and 14-2). Barsch (1968) suggests an en-

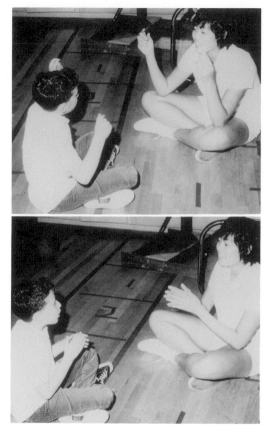

Fig. 14-1. Learning to coordinate hand movements to a rhythmical pattern.

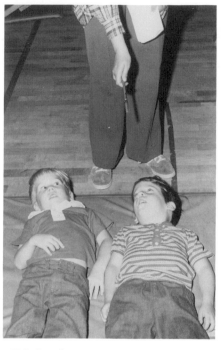

Fig. 14-2. Synchronizing eye tracking movements.

tire program of rhythm learning through metronomic pacing, starting at 48 beats per minute. He suggests taking the child progressively from unilateral to bilateral and then to cross-lateral body movements. Cadence training should progress from very simple movements to the more complex, depending on the specific abilities of the child. Almost any noisemaker can be used for cadence training, including such percussion instruments as drums, rhythm sticks (Fig. 14-3), metronomes, bells, or clapping hands. Cadence training can involve a full range of body movement possibilities to challenge even the most physically capable person. The following are cadence progressions based on levels of difficulty with the child in a back-lying position.

Level I

Unilateral cadence training of upper limbs
1. Grip and spread the fingers.
2. Rotate the forearm inward and outward.
3. Flex and extend the forearm.
4. Keeping the elbow straight, lift the arm to approximately 18 inches in front of the body.
5. Keeping the elbow straight, lift the arm so that it is positioned directly over the face.
6. Keeping the elbow straight, lift the arm over the head.
7. Bending the elbow halfway, rotate the arm at the shoulder from across the abdomen to the side of the mat.
8. Keeping the elbow straight, lift the arm halfway to the side of the body.

Fig. 14-3. Keeping time to the beat of a metronome with rhythm sticks.

9. Keeping the elbow straight, lift the arm to the side of the head.
10. Shrug one shoulder, keeping the arm straight at the side of the body.

Bilateral cadence training of upper limbs. Instead of performing the cadence activities on just one side of the body, the child moves both upper limbs simultaneously.

Unilateral cadence training of lower limbs
1. Point the toe down and return it to a straight position.
2. Rotate the foot inward.
3. Rotate the foot outward.
4. Rotate the leg out and inward.
5. Bend the knee upward 45 degrees and return the leg to a straight position.
6. With the leg straight, slide it to the side 45 degrees and return to the straight position.

Bilateral cadence training of lower limbs. The child moves both legs together instead of performing the cadence activities on just one side.

Unilateral cadence training of upper and lower limbs. The child moves the arm and leg on the same side of the body (Fig. 14-4).

Level II

Cross-lateral cadence training of upper limbs. Cross-lateral refers to moving one limb and then the other in an alternating fashion. The child performs the activities in the sequence given for level I unilateral cadence training.

Cross-lateral cadence training of lower limbs. Using the cross-lateral method, the child performs the sequences given for level I.

Trunk cadence training
1. Lift the pelvis up and down.
2. Bend the trunk to the left.
3. Bend the trunk to the right.
4. Arch the trunk.
5. Roll the trunk to the left.
6. Roll the trunk to the right.

Head and face cadence training
1. Lift the head up and down.
2. Bend the head to the left.
3. Bend the head to the right (Fig. 14-5).
4. Arch the head backward.
5. Blink the left eye.
6. Blink the right eye.
7. Wiggle the nose.
8. Make a smile.
9. Make a sad face.
10. Stick the tongue in and out.

Level III: Combining movements

1. Lift the right leg and arm halfway.
2. Lift the right leg and arm halfway and bend the head to the right side.
3. Lift the right leg and right arm half-

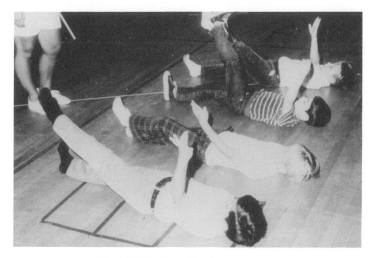

Fig. 14-4. Unilateral cadence training.

Fig. 14-5. Bending the head to the right.

way, bring the head to the right side, and blink the right eye.

4. Squeeze the right hand and then bend the right elbow.
5. Squeeze the right hand, bend the right elbow, and blink the right eye.
6. Bend the right elbow halfway and lift the left leg halfway.
7. Bend the left elbow halfway and lift the right leg halfway.
8. Rotate the left leg and the right arm outward.

9. Rotate the right leg and right arm outward.
10. Blink the left eye and bend the right knee; then alternate sides.

Variations of cadence activities

1. Decrease the pace of the cadence.
2. Increase the pace of the cadence.
3. Alternately increase and decrease the pace of the cadence.
4. Perform the activities with eyes closed.
5. Perform the activities standing up.

Fig. 14-6. Marching provides an excellent means of synchronizing movement.

6. Perform the activities lying on the stomach.
7. Perform the activities lying on the side.
8. Perform the activities in a swimming pool.
9. March to a cadence (Fig. 14-6).
10. Run to a cadence.
11. Skip to a cadence.
12. Hop to a cadence.
13. Gallop to a cadence.
14. Jump rope to a cadence.
15. Jump on a trampoline to a cadence.
16. Tumble to a cadence.
17. Track a ball to a cadence.

SPECIAL RHYTHM THERAPEUTICS

When creating a therapy program to remedy the problems of clumsiness, the therapist can use all types of rhythm and dance activities commonly found in textbooks of elementary physical education.* In

---

*For example, see Arnheim and Pestolesi (1973) and Anderson et al. (1966).

addition, two methods of rhythm therapy are not normally found in physical education and recreation books. They are dance therapy and the music education approach of Orff-Schulwerk; both are extremely well suited to assisting the clumsy child.

Dance therapy

Dance therapy is an expanding profession that helps to solve emotional and movement problems through dance. It assists participants in finding self-expression through the medium of nonverbal communication, increases self-awareness, and increases positive self-esteem. Dance therapy has been found to be particularly successful with mentally ill and emotionally disturbed individuals. Programs that emphasize rhythmical movement provide an important tool in psychotherapy because of the strong relationship between motor behavior and feelings (Bernstein, 1972). The point is particularly stressed in *The Language of the Body* (Lowen, 1958), which vividly depicts how the body's movement patterns vary according to individual personality differences and emotional reactions. Emotional disturbances adversely alter muscular tension levels and reciprocal contractions. Rhythmical movements skillfully employed by a therapist can provide a highly effective means for intervention. Habitual body behavior patterns can reduce abnormal muscle tension levels, restoring free-flowing and graceful movements through subtle techniques. A child who is both tense and emotionally withdrawn can be gradually encouraged to "open up" and learn to become more expressive physically. A highly nervous, apprehensive, and jittery child can learn to become confident and relaxed, and the outwardly antagonistic child can learn to be less aggressive through dance therapy.

Orff-Schulwerk therapy

Orff-Schulwerk therapy is a musical approach to educating the child. Orff originally intended that his approach would encompass all areas of education besides

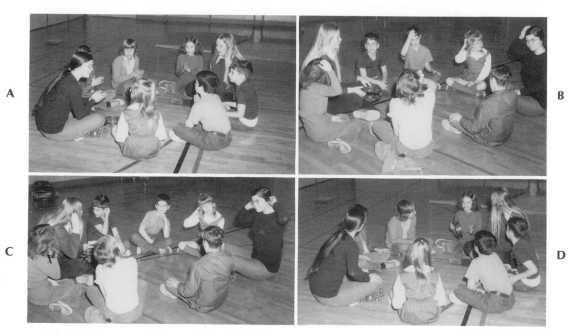

Fig. 14-7. Learning body control and the ability to socialize through the Orff-Schulwerk rhythm method. **A,** All clapping hands together at the same time. **B,** Identifying where the head is. **C,** Touching the ear. **D,** Striking the tamborine to the rhythm of a name.

orienting young children to the joys of playing music. Although Orgg-Schulwerk therapy is considered by many as a very good approach to learning reading and arithmetic, we have found it effective for use with the clumsy child, primarily in the area of socialization. The Orff techniques in confidence building and socialization for the retarded have been used successfully at the Fairview State Hospital in Costa Mesa, California. The participants often showed remarkable improvements in ability to relate to therapists and peers as a result of an increase in confidence and self-esteem; this led to better adjustments to all aspects of institutional life. Because the no-failure concept is strictly adhered to, every child finds success regardless of his level of proficiency.

Particular success occurs with rhythmical activities conducted in a circle in which each child participates by vocalizing and playing a percussion instrument (Fig. 14-7). In starting out the activity, each child in the circle says his own name rhythmically, as "Mar-y" or "Dan-ny,"

while at the same time beating out the tempo with hands or other rhythm makers. As the responsibility for saying his name passes to each child, different expressions are encouraged; then all the children in the circle copy the leader. As participants increase in confidence, activities of greater difficulty, such as the following poems, can be instituted.

I see the moon,
And the moon sees me.
The moon sees someone
I would like to see.

Beanbag, beanbag
In your hand.
Can you, can you
Toss it in the pan?

Mules go up
And names go down.
Show us how
Your name sounds.

A tree, a tree, a tree
What is more lovely than
A tree, a tree, a tree?
I think that I shall be a tree.

Jump one, jump two,
Rumble, rumble, roar,
Jump three, jump four,
Right out the door (or across the floor).

Pumpkin, pumpkin,
Diddle, diddle, bumpkin,
Pumpkin, pumpkin,
Diddle, diddle, say . . .

The worms wiggle in
And the worms wiggle out.
How do you
Wiggle them out?

Alike and different,
Alike and different,
We are both alike
And different.

Up in the air,
Down on the floor.
What will you bring
From the store?

Stamp one foot,
Keep the other foot still,
Stamp both feet,
Stamp and move at will.

A parrot sings
A sound you say.
Who will sing
The sound you play?

Trampoline, trampoline,
Who likes to trampoline?
Trampoline, trampoline,
Do your thing.

Ring, gong, ring,
Sing, gong, sing.
Take a message
To the king.

The witch has an itch,
The witch has an itch.
Where, oh where is the
Witch's itch?

Almost any nursery rhyme or poem can be adapted for use by Orff-Schulwerk participants. Children are encouraged to bring their own rhymes to share in their group and to innovate sounds by striking different materials.

Body ego technique

The body ego technique is a nonverbal teaching approach that has been developed from modern dance principles. It is currently being used primarily for treatment of psychiatric patients and individuals with severe disturbances in body perception and self-esteem. The body ego technique is similar to movement education in that it uses the movement elements of space, force, and rhythm. Unlike movement education, however, the body ego technique provides a highly structured environment in which the participants gradually gain a sense of ego boundary that ultimately leads to more effective communication (Salkin, 1973). Through this approach, basic movement patterns can be gained as well as the even more sophisticated movement skills characteristic of modern dance. Besides motor skill development, and perhaps even more important, the performer learns to express internal feelings and thoughts, producing an emotional catharsis that reduces abnormal fears and muscular tensions.

In the beginning of body ego therapy the therapist takes on the same motor and emotional characteristics as the subject. As the therapist enters the movement behavior world of the child, he gradually makes changes covertly rather than requiring the individual to overtly adjust to a new set of movement patterns. Also, postural attitudes and feelings can be redirected gradually by the therapist who poses special movement problems for the child to solve.

Depending on the developmental level and the particular problem of each individual, the body ego technique attempts to manipulate the individual in such a way that permanent changes are made in both verbal and nonverbal expressive behavior. It has been well documented that an individual cannot overtly express a particular attitude and at the same time think or feel opposite to that attitude; therefore changes in movement expression make changes in emotion and attitudinal behavior. Schoop (1974) expresses this point very well when she states that the "mind and body are in constant reciprocal interactions, so that whatever the inner self experiences comes full realization in the body, and whatever the body experiences influences the inner self." Besides dealing with serious emotional problems, the body ego technique is highly successful with individuals who generally feel inadequate in their ability to move effectively.

• • •

In essence, the rhythm and dance media can be used to make positive changes in social behavior, such as assisting a child in controlling his impulses, increasing body awareness (specifically as it concerns the self-concept), providing an emotional catharsis to release abnormal tensions, and providing the physical abilities necessary for efficient movement. (Williams, 1974).

15

REBOUND AND AIRBORNE ACTIVITIES

In German the word "trampoline" means springboard, and that is what a trampoline offers to the child—a springboard to worthwhile and enjoyable learning experiences. Through trampoline activities, children discover a new freedom that comes from being temporarily suspended in the air, overcoming the restraints of gravity. The upward force imparted by the trampoline momentarily assists the child in overcoming the gravitational pull, requiring a continuous adjustment of muscle tensions during the course of the activity.

Cratty (1969) points out that there are several ways in which trampoline activities can aid the development of body image in children. While springing up and down the child becomes aware of the body's position in space in terms of top and bottom, right and left, and back and front. The child also gains a better understanding of the differences in location and movement of specific body parts as the body adjusts to the forces imposed by the trampoline. More specifically, some of the values that can be ob-

tained from performing on the trampoline are (1) developing confidence and self-reliance, which in turn improve the child's self-concept, (2) developing motor fitness, and (3) developing a sense of enjoyment through personal accomplishment.

SAFETY

Although the trampoline is one of the most enjoyable of activities, it can be one of the most dangerous if it is improperly used. Therefore the therapist must remember that the soft, springy bed of the trampoline creates an illusion of safety for beginning participants. This attitude may lead to showing off or taking unnecessary chances and may consequently cause serious injury. To make trampolining safe, the following safety precautions should be followed.

1. Good equipment that is properly maintained is a prerequisite.
2. The trampoline must never be left unsupervised and should be folded up and stored away when not in use.

3. The trampoline should be inspected before and after it has been used for worn springs and tears in the bed.
4. Children should never be allowed to wear street shoes on the trampoline because they may tear the canvas bed.
5. There should be a minimum of one spotter for each exposed side on the standard 10 by 17 foot trampoline. If the trampoline is used indoors, it can be placed in a corner, necessitating the spotting of only two sides. There is still a risk of the child hitting a wall, but this is far safer than falling off the trampoline and hitting the floor.
6. Safety pads should be used to cover the exposed metal frame as well as the area around the base.
7. All objects should be removed from pockets and necklaces or chains should be put inside the shirt; ideally the child should wear gym clothes.

Tennis shoes should be worn on a trampoline with a nylon bed; bare or stocking feet are appropriate on one with a canvas bed.
8. The first skill taught to the beginning student should be the importance of staying in the middle of the trampoline and learning to stop a bounce by flexing the knees immediately on landing.
9. The learning progression of simple to difficult should be strictly adhered to.
10. A sequence of skills should take less than one minute to perform, minimizing the possibility of the child losing control due to fatigue.
11. A safety belt should be used in learning the more difficult stunts such as front and back flips.
12. Before dismounting from the trampoline the child should come to a complete stop, sit down, and place his hands on the frame for additional stability.
13. Above all, horseplay should never be tolerated.

LEAD-UP TO TRAMPOLINE
Level I: Airborne activities

Level I is concerned with rebounding and airborne activities that can be used as a lead-up to the trampoline.

Purpose. To gain postural control while in the air.

Equipment and facilities. Flex boards, tires, or springboards.

Position of therapist and child. The therapist should position himself in such a way that he can give immediate directions and manual assistance to the child if necessary.

Activity progressions. The child performs the following activities.

1. Jump up and down with both feet (Fig. 15-1).
2. Jump up and down with the right foot.
3. Jump up and down with the left foot.
4. Jump up and down, alternating feet.
5. Jump forward to mat.
6. Jump backward to mat.

Fig. 15-1. Jumping with both feet on a tractor tire.

Fig. 15-2. Playing catch while bouncing on the Spring-o-line.

7. Jump and twist one-fourth turn first to the right and then to the left.
8. Jump and twist one-half turn first to the right and then to the left.
9. Jump and twist three-fourths turn first to the right and then to the left.
10. Jump and twist completely around first to the right and then to the left.
11. Jump and catch an object in the air (Fig. 15-2).
12. Jump and throw an object at a target.
13. Jump over objects of different sizes (Fig. 15-3).

TRAMPOLINE PROGRESSIONS
Level II: Trampoline activities

Therapy hints
1. Two middle springs on one long side of the trampoline can be removed, enabling the therapist to stand between the frame and bed; this provides a greater advantage for spotting specific stunts.
2. If the bed of the trampoline is too rigid

Fig. 15-3. Jumping over a box.

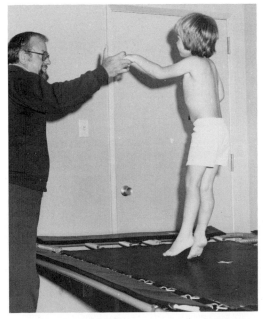

Fig. 15-4. Ideally, the small trampoline should be used as a lead-up to the regulation size.

for the smaller children, removing additional springs will make the bed more resilient.

3. Bouncing on the bed of the trampoline is very similar to bouncing on a springboard or the child's bed at home. In starting the jump the feet must be kept about shoulder-width apart; the legs are drawn together while in the air. The knees should be bent slightly when the feet first contact the bed and straightened as the body is projected upward. The arm movement is one of lifting on the upward bounce of the body and dropping down as the body returns to the bed in preparation for the next bounce. The arm movement is essentially like scooping water up to the face. Effective use of the arms facilitates better control of the body and at the same time adds more power to the upward thrust of the jump.

4. A small trampoline can be used as a lead-up to the regulation size trampoline (Fig. 15-4).

   Activity progressions

1. The following lead-up activities should precede any jumping activities on the trampoline.

a. The child performs side rolls on the trampoline bed.

b. The child crawls around the perimeter of the trampoline bed first to one side and then to the other to become acquainted with its size (Fig. 15-5).

c. The child walks around the perimeter and diagonally across the middle of the trampoline.

NOTE: These activities help the child develop an awareness of the size of the trampoline and discover that the center is softer and more resilient than the sides.

2. The child and therapist perform the following sequence.

a. The therapist bounces the child while he lies in a prone and supine position.

b. The child tries to initiate his own bounce while in a prone and supine position.

Fig. 15-5. Crawling around the edge of the trampoline bed.

Fig. 15-6. Bending the knees and pushing hard against the trampoline bed with the feet to propel the body upward.

c. Activities a and b are repeated with the child in a seated position.

d. Activities a and b are repeated with the child in an four-point position.

e. Activities a and b are repeated with the child in a kneeling position.

f. The child tries to bounce and turn clockwise and then counterclockwise in a four-point position. To provide motivation the child is encouraged to imitate the sounds of different animals while bouncing.

g. The child stands in the middle of the bed and tries to propel himself upward by merely bending his knees and thrusting against the bed with his feet (Fig. 15-6). If the child has difficulty or shows signs of fright, the therapist should reassure him verbally and provide stability with his arm.

h. When a child can demonstrate three or four bounces in a row he is instructed to stop bouncing by a quick bend of the knees. The child should practice this skill until it becomes second nature.

i. The child executes quarter turns both to the left and right. In producing a twist he should pull one hand across the chest and raise the other arm above the head.

j. The child executes both half and full turns to the left and right.

k. The child executes a tuck bounce by springing straight up, drawing the knees to the chest while grasping the shins with the hands, releasing the tuck, and returning to the starting position.

Level III: Beginning stunts

Knee drop (Fig. 15-7). As the child bounces into the air, he bends his lower legs under him and lands on his knees, shins, and insteps with his legs kept slightly apart for balance. The arm motion is the same in the knee drop as in regular bouncing, and it is important that the back be

Fig. 15-7. Executing a knee drop. This stunt is dangerous if the child is unable to keep his back straight.

kept straight to avoid injury. If the child has difficulty in maintaining the back in a straight line, the knee drop should be omitted and replaced by the seat drop.

Seat drop (Fig. 15-8). The child bounces into the air, extending his legs straight out in front of him to form an **L** shape with his body and legs. He lands on the bed in a sitting position, and the full length of the legs strike the trampoline bed simultaneously. The fingers are pointed forward and the hands are kept flat on the bed 6 to 8 inches behind and to the side of the hips. As the child rebounds from the bed, his arms reach upward and his feet return to their original position.

Front drop (Fig. 15-9). The child first bounces into the air, kicking his legs out to the rear and lowering the trunk until the entire body is in a prone position parallel to the bed of the trampoline. On landing the arms are extended forward with the elbows slightly bent and palms down. The child should land simultaneously on the palms, forearms, abdomen, lower chest, and thighs. As the child contacts the bed, he pushes with his hands and forearms, raising his head; as he springs upward, he places his feet back under the hips. The two most common mistakes made are landing on the knees first and diving forward and landing on the hands first.

Combined activities. The child performs

Fig. 15-8. Executing a seat drop.

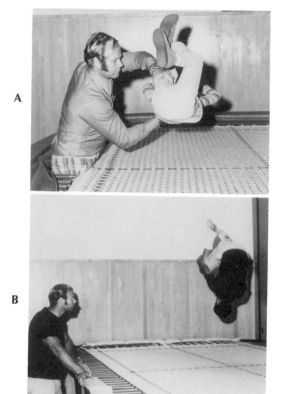

Fig. 15-10. Learning, **A,** and executing, **B,** a front somersault.

Fig. 15-9. Executing a front drop.

these combinations of previously described skills: (1) 3 feet bounces, 1 knee drop, 1 foot bounce, 1 front drop, back to feet and (2) 3 feet bounces, 1 knee drop, 1 seat drop, 1 front drop, back to feet.

Level IV: Intermediate stunts

Back drop. The child bounces upward, leans back, raises his legs, and lands on the bed in a supine position with the legs in a straight vertical position. The hands are placed on either side of the thighs with the head forward and the chin touching the chest.

Half-swivel hips. From a knee drop landing the child lifts his arms overhead and extends his legs downward. He twists his hips a half turn and swings his legs under his body in a pendulum fashion. After the half twist is completed he fixes the hips into a seat drop position and lands on his seat. The same precaution is taken on the knee drop portion of the half-swivel hips as on the basic knee drop.

Full-swivel hips. This skill is identical to the half-swivel hips except that it is performed from a seat drop instead of a knee drop.

Level V: Advanced stunts

Front somersault (Fig. 15-10). The child bounces upward and leans forward with his chin touching his chest. The child grasps his shins with his hands and pulls his knees into his chest in a tight tuck. The tuck should be held until the somersault is almost completed. Then the legs are extended downward toward the bed, leaving the arms up and forward of the chest.

Back somersault. The child bounces upward, raising the chest into the air and pressing away from the bed with the legs. At the same time he lifts his arms up past the chest and tilts his head backward. After leaving the bed he brings his knees up to his chest with his hands grasping shins and pulling the body into a tight tuck. He continues to tilt the head backward till the somersault is near completion; then he releases the tuck and extends the legs downward for the landing. NOTE: A spotter should always be used when the child is learning the technique.

Dual activities

The following activities may be introduced when the basic skills on the trampoline have been mastered.

Jumping activities

Rope jumping. Two students turn the rope, or one end may be attached to the wall.

1. The children swing the rope in pendulum fashion, making quarter turns.
2. The rope is turned in complete circles in each direction.
3. The child holds and turns his own rope in each direction.
4. The child holds and turns his own rope in each direction, completing two revolutions between landings.

Hula-Hoop jumping

1. The child jumps through a Hula-Hoop feet first while turning it in a clockwise direction a half revolution for each bounce.
2. The child jumps through a Hula-Hoop feet first while turning it in a complete revolution for each bounce.
3. The child performs Hula-Hoop activities head first turning the hoop counterclockwise.

Catching and throwing

1. The child catches objects of different

Fig. 15-11. Catching a ball while bouncing on the trampoline.

sizes and shapes while he is in the air between bounces (Fig. 15-11). After the child has caught the object he may perform a variety of skills such as knee drops and seat drops.

2. The child throws objects of different sizes and shapes while in the air between bounces. After the child has thrown the object, he may perform a variety of skills such as knee drops and seat drops.

The trampoline can be used in a variety of ways when working with the clumsy child. In addition to the trampoline's versatility and the children's inherent desire to bounce, the trampoline generates a great deal of enjoyment for the participants. Since enjoyment motivates intensive participation, we think that the trampoline, if utilized by a properly trained therapist, can be one of the best single pieces of equipment used in remediation of clumsiness in children.

16

PROJECTILE MANAGEMENT*

Team and individual games that involve projectile handling skills play a dominant role in normal physical education classes as well as in free play and recreational activities. The child who is successful at skills that consist of propelling and retrieving various objects receives a great deal of self-gratification and praise from his peers. Unfortunately the clumsy child may lack the eye-hand and eye-foot coordination necessary for effectively managing objects in play. As a result, he is chosen last for teams or, even more often, made fun of for his lack of skill. The child who has delayed motor development can overcome many of these deficiencies with the help of a therapist who persistently applies proper lead-up sequences, instructs the child in precise skill techniques, and delivers appropriate praise.

*All of the skills in this chapter will be described for the child who is right-handed.

THROWING AND CATCHING
Throwing

Throwing is probably second only to running as the most common element in games and sports; therefore it is exceedingly important that it be taught properly. Throwing is a skill that involves the release of an object with one or both hands in one of three basic patterns: (1) underarm pattern, (2) sidearm pattern, or (3) overarm pattern.

Equipment and facilities. Basketballs, soccer balls, plastic or rubber playground balls measuring 9 inches in diameter, balloons, beanbags, Fleece balls, rubber and plastic balls measuring 4 to 8 inches in diameter, and deck tennis rings as well as rug and paper balls constructed by the child.

Therapy hints
1. It is imperative that each child be afforded ample opportunity to handle a variety of projectiles. In a group situa-

149

Fig. 16-1. Underhand throw using the simultaneous coordination of both hands.

Fig. 16-2. Two-hand chest pass using a 16-inch diameter ball.

tion each child should have his own object to play with.

2. The child should start with large rubber balls (9 inches in diameter) because of their ease of handling.

3. When object rolling is being taught, the body should be lowered by bending the knees with the back straight and head up.

4. Throwing is a motor act that demonstrates the physics principle of a summation of forces—the total force of all the muscles and levers in the body moving in a sequential pattern. Since the object is controlled by the speed and direction of the hand doing the throwing, to improve a child's throwing ability the teacher or therapist must consider methods for developing speed and controlling the direction of the hand movement.

5. The longer the backswing, the more time there is to develop momentum.

Fig. 16-3. Two-hand overhead pass using a 16-inch diameter ball.

The backswing can be increased by turning the side opposite the throwing arm toward the direction of the throw, rotating the body away from the direction of the throw, and placing the foot opposite to the throwing arm forward.

6. Movement of the body in the direction of the throw adds force to the throw if the contributing body parts move in the proper sequence.

Activity progressions

Level I: Large ball activities

1. Rolling a ball underhand using two hands

    PURPOSE: To develop coordination between movements of both arms as a lead-up skill for the two-hand underhand throw.

    ACTION: The hands are placed on opposite sides of the ball with palms facing each other and fingers apart and pointing down. The ball is held in front of the body. As it swings forward, the child should flex his knees and release it on the ground by extending his elbows and wrists.

    VARIATIONS: The therapist sits on the floor opposite the child and they roll a large ball back and forth. As the child becomes proficient, the distance can be increased.

2. Throwing a ball underhand using two hands (Fig. 16-1)

    PURPOSE: To develop the coordination of moving both arms simultaneously.

    ACTION: The hands are placed on opposite sides of the ball with palms facing each other and fingers apart pointing down. The feet are shoulder-width apart with the ball held directly in front of the body. As the ball is projected forward, the child steps forward with the left foot, quickly extending the elbows and wrists.

3. Two-hand chest pass (Fig. 16-2): The two-hand chest pass consists of pushing

Fig. 16-4. Rolling a large ball through an obstacle course to improve eye-hand coordination.

Fig. 16-5. Throwing through a series of Hula-Hoops to improve accuracy.

the ball forward from the upper chest with a thrusting or pushing away movement by the arms, wrists, and fingers. The child holds the ball about chest high with his hands approximately 1 inch behind the center of the ball and his fingers spread on the ball's surface. The child starts the arm action by applying a forward push and by extending the arms, wrists, and fingers. The child stands with his feet parallel; as the ball moves forward, he steps forward with his left foot, transferring the weight of the body to it.

4. Two-hand overhead pass (Fig. 16-3): The ball is held in both hands directly overhead. It is held with hands on opposite sides of the ball and fingers apart and pointing up and back. The throw entails a quick extension of the elbows and wrists.

VARIATIONS

a. While seated the child throws a playground ball with both hands from an overhead position to the therapist, who is 3 feet away.

b. While kneeling the child throws the playground ball with both hands from an overhead position to the therapist, who is 3 feet away.

Level II: Large ball activities with Hula-Hoops

1. Rolling a ball underhand through a series of Hula-Hoops using two hands (Fig. 16-4)
2. Throwing a ball with a two-hand chest pass through a series of Hula-Hoops (Fig. 16-5)

   PURPOSE: To improve eye-hand coordination in throwing.

Level III: Small ball activities

1. One-hand underhand object throw: The ball is held on the child's right side approximately at waist level. It is clamped firmly between the fingers and thumb. As the ball swings forward, it is kept close to the side, the child's weight shifts forward on the left foot, and the wrist snaps quickly as the ball is released.
2. Throwing a ball overhand with one hand: The right arm is brought back and over the shoulder with the hand behind the ball and the fingers apart and pointing up. The left side of the body is turned toward the target. As the child steps forward with his left foot, he pivots his body toward the target and permits his right arm to draw back in readiness for its forward movement. As the body moves forward and the upper arm approaches a position straight out from the shoulder, the forearm is extended quickly and the wrist snapped as the ball is released.

   VARIATIONS

   a. The child attempts to toss a ball into a box or wastebasket.
   b. The child attempts to throw the ball as far as he can using one hand.
   c. Using two hands, the child attempts to throw the ball as far as he can with the overhead throw and the chest pass.
   d. The child attempts to throw the ball as high as he can using one hand.
   e. The child attempts to throw the ball as high as he can using two hands.

Fig. 16-6. Using both hands to catch a large rubber ball. Note the forward-backward stride position of feet and the hand alignment.

Catching

Therapy hints

1. The therapist should stress the fact that the eyes must remain open and watching the ball at all times.
2. The thought of catching a ball induces fear in many children. To minimize the anxiety as much as possible a light plastic or rubber ball approximately 9 inches in diameter should be used at first.
3. When catching a ball, the child should position his feet in a forward-backward stride position to enlarge the base of support in the direction of the oncoming ball and thus improve stability (Fig. 16-6). The force from the ball can be reduced by pulling the hands toward the body as they contact the ball. The position of the hands is most important to avoid possible injury to the fingers. When the ball approaches at the child's waist level, his palms should be facing each other with his fingers pointing straight ahead. The fingers should be pointing upward if the hands are above waist level, thus exposing the palms to the force of the ball.

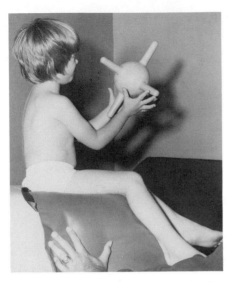

Fig. 16-7. Catching odd-shaped objects to develop eye-hand coordination.

Fig. 16-8. Developing catching skills with the aid of a Tooti Launcher.

Activity progressions

Level I. The child is instructed to do the following.

1. While seated, trap a rolling 9-inch rubber playground ball between his legs.
2. While in a kneeling position, stop a rolling 9-inch rubber playground ball with both hands.
3. While standing, drop a 9-inch rubber playground ball, allowing the ball to bounce once before catching it.
4. While standing, toss a 9-inch rubber playground ball upward, allowing the ball to bounce once before catching it.
5. While standing 10 feet in front of a wall, toss a 6-inch rubber ball against the wall and allow it to bounce once before catching it.
6. While standing 6 feet in front of a wall, toss a 6-inch rubber ball against the wall and catch it before it bounces.
7. While seated and while standing, catch odd-shaped objects such as a satellite ball (Fig. 16-7).

Supplemental throwing and catching activities

Level II: Activities using a bean bag. A beanbag is a versatile piece of equipment that can be used in many ways to augment the development of ball handling skills by children. A beanbag is relatively easy to throw and catch because it conforms to the contours of the child's hand. Use of beanbags reduces much of the child's fear of catching because it does not hurt if he is struck by it. The child is instructed to do the following.

1. Toss a beanbag underhanded and catch it first with both hands and then with one hand.
2. Toss a beanbag overhand and catch it first with both hands and then with one hand.
3. Toss a beanbag, turn a complete circle, and catch the beanbag first with both hands and then with one hand.
4. Toss a beanbag, move to a sitting or kneeling position, and catch the beanbag.

Fig. 16-9. Using the pitchback device to improve throwing and catching skills.

5. Toss a beanbag, turn halfway around, and catch it behind his back.
6. Toss a beanbag, bend over, and catch it behind his back.

Activities using a Tooti Launcher. The Tooti Launcher is composed of two pieces of wood. The larger piece acts as a lever and the smaller piece as the fulcrum of the lever. An object such as a beanbag or a Tooti is placed on one end of the board and the child stomps on the other end of the board, which acts as a third-class lever in

propelling the object into the air. This piece of equipment can be used to develop the eye-hand coordination necessary in ball handling skills (Fig. 16-8). The child is instructed to do the following.

1. Catch a Tooti with both hands.
2. Catch a Tooti with one hand.
3. Turn completely around and catch a Tooti.
4. Move to a sitting or kneeling position and catch a Tooti.
5. Spring the Tooti high enough to move under it and catch it behind his back.
6. Turn halfway around and catch the Tooti behind his back first with both hands and then with one hand.

Activities using a pitchback device. A pitchback device is just what the name implies. The child tosses an object into it and the object is rebounded back to the child. It can be used to develop eye-hand coordination and proper techniques used in throwing and catching (Fig. 16-9).

KICKING

Kicking involves propelling an object with either foot. Contact with the object is made on the inside, the outside, or the instep of the foot. With the exception of the position of the foot, the basic mechanical principles are the same in all types of kicking.

Therapy hints
1. The therapist should stress the importance of keeping the eyes open and watching the ball until it is contacted with the foot.
2. The child should begin with a rubber playground ball approximately 9 to 12 inches in diameter. As skill is developed, smaller and more rigid objects can be used.

Activity progressions
Level I
1. Kicking a stationary ball (Fig. 16-10): The child stands behind and slightly to the left of the ball. His left foot should be to the side and approximately 6 to 10 inches behind the ball. The right leg is drawn backward with the knee bent;

Fig. 16-10. Kicking a rubber ball from a stationary position.

it is then brought forward with a brisk extension of the knee. The foot is held at right angles to the shin and the ankle is held rigid at the moment of contact.

VARIATIONS

a. The child stands and kicks a stationary ball demonstrating proper technique.

b. The child takes one step and kicks a stationary ball using proper technique.

c. The child takes several slow steps and kicks a stationary ball using proper technique, gradually increasing his speed and the number of steps taken.

d. The child stands and kicks a stationary ball through a series of Hula-Hoops (Fig. 16-11).

2. Kicking a rolling ball: The techniques

Fig. 16-11. Kicking a rubber ball through Hula-Hoops to develop eye-foot control.

Fig. 16-12. Dribbling a ball with the feet through an obstacle course.

involved in kicking a rolling ball are precisely the same as those used in kicking a stationary ball. A rolling ball just adds another dimension to the task, that of judging the speed and direction of the oncoming ball. The child must time the kick to maintain his established stride while making contact with the ball. Each step in the following sequence should be practiced and mastered before progressing to the next level. The child is instructed to do the following.

a. Stand and kick a ball that is rolled to him, with the therapist progressively increasing the speed of the ball.

b. Take one step and kick the rolling ball.

c. Take several steps and kick the ball as the therapist progressively increases the speed of the ball and encourages the child to move as fast as possible while maintaining proper kicking techniques.

Level II

1. Punting: To begin the child should use a lightweight rubber playground ball approximately 12 inches in diameter. The ball is held approximately waist high at arms length and the fingers are spread on opposite sides of the ball. To generate more power the child should take one or two steps forward before punting. The ball is dropped vertically as short a distance as possible to reduce any error made in dropping the ball. Contact is made on the instep of the foot with the leg fully extended. The foot should also be extended so that it is parallel to the leg. The swing of the leg is toward the median line of the body so that after the follow-through the foot finishes in front of the opposite shoulder.

2. Dribbling the ball with the feet (Fig. 16-12): Dribbling is a skill that is used primarily in soccer. It is the technique of moving a ball down a field by a series of light taps or kicks with the sides of the feet. The child should be instructed not to kick the ball too far to avoid losing control. The child begins by walking, kicking the ball every few steps on the inside of the foot, alternating feet. As the child becomes more proficient in dribbling, he gradually increases his speed until he is running.

STRIKING

Therapy hints

1. The child starts with his feet shoulder-width apart. The child's left side faces the direction of the oncoming ball. The bat should be held securely with the right hand on top of the left hand. The bat is held off the shoulder with the tip pointing up and back. As the ball is about to be thrown, the child transfers his weight to the right foot. He pushes off from the right foot; the left foot should step slightly away from the oncoming ball. As the left foot is placed, the body begins to rotate at the shoulder

Fig. 16-13. Using a light plastic bat to develop a kinesthetic awareness of proper batting techniques.

and hips. Just prior to contact with the ball the forearms are extended, and as the ball is met, the wrists are extended quickly.

2. Activities should start with a light plastic ball and bat (Fig. 16-13); the ball should be approximately 8 inches in diameter.
3. The head should be kept as still as possible; tracking should be done primarily with eye movements.
4. The child rotates the bat back as far as possible before striking the ball in order to permit the development of maximum momentum.
5. The child should not stride too far forward, which locks the hip and causes the body to fall away from the ball; the result is a loss of force. For striking to be most effective the body must be moving forward when contact is made between the ball and the bat.
6. Since the distance the ball goes is directly proportional to the amount of force generated, and since mass is a component of force, the child should choose the heaviest bat he can swing

Fig. 16-14. Hitting an 8-inch rubber ball off a cone used as a batting tee.

without retarding the speed of the swing.

7. The weight of the bat and the strength in the child's grip, wrists, and arms dictate the position of the hands on the bat. The child who has a weak grip should

Fig. 16-15. Striking a Whiffle ball off the top of a cone.

Fig. 16-16. Batting a beanbag and a tennis ball thrown underhand from a distance of 10 feet.

choke up on the bat and spread his hands. This shortens the hitting area of the bat and enables the child to control his swing more effectively.

Activity progressions

Level I. The child is instructed to do the following.

1. Toss a balloon upward and attempt to keep it in the air by striking it.
2. Hit a balloon back and forth from one hand to the other.
3. Hit a balloon back and forth with a partner.
4. Hit a balloon with a table tennis paddle.
5. Hit a balloon with a light plastic bat.
6. Hit a stationary ball resting on a batting tee (Figs. 16-14 and 16-15).

Level II. The child is instructed to do the following.

1. Hit a variety of airborne balls (Fleece ball, tennis ball, 6-inch playground ball, etc.) with the plastic bat (Fig. 16-16).
2. Hit a ball moving at a very slow rate of speed; then gradually increase the speed.

BOUNCING

Bouncing the ball with one hand, or dribbling, is basically an arm-wrist-finger action (Fig. 16-17). When learning to dribble, the child should start by leaning slightly forward with his knees bent and his forearm parallel with the floor. The ball should not be slapped or hit downward. The child

Fig. 16-17. Bouncing a rubber ball with the dominate hand.

Fig. 16-18. Bouncing a ball inside a large tire to develop control.

pushes the ball down with his fingers and lets his fingers and hand ride back up with the ball. For better control the child's fingers should be in contact with the ball for as long as possible during the upward and downward movements.

Level I. The child is instructed to do the following.

1. Bounce a ball first with both hands and then with each hand individually.
2. Alternate hands while bouncing a ball.
3. Bounce a ball while moving in various directions.

Level II. The child is instructed to do the following.

1. Practice bouncing a ball while looking straight ahead.

2. Dribble between cones arranged in a zigzag path, keeping the body between the ball and the cones by alternating hands while dribbling.
3. Dribble around and through a series of obstacles such as tires (Fig. 16-18).

Throwing, catching, kicking, and striking objects are primarily sports activities. A great deal of the child's initial success in physical education and playtime activities depends on his proficiency in these particular motor skills. To help the clumsy child overcome his deficiencies in these particular areas, the therapist should follow a success-oriented program, exposing the child to a variety of objects differing in size, shape, and weight.

17

MANAGEMENT OF DAILY MOTOR ACTIVITIES

The activities described in this chapter are designed to help the clumsy child improve motor skills that are involved in daily living. It deals with simple and common activities such as walking without bumping into a desk, lacing one's shoes, or cutting paper with scissors, all of which require synchronization of small and large skeletal muscles as well as visual adaptation.

MANIPULATION
Level I: Manipulative activities

Level I deals with activities that are designed to augment the development of visual perception and finger dexterity.

Equipment and facilities
1. Beads of various sizes, shapes, and colors
2. Forty pennies
3. Twenty 1-inch cube blocks
4. Forty marbles
5. Forty "kitchen size" matches with heads removed

6. Open wooden or plastic box (3 by 3 inches)
7. Pencils and paper
8. Scissors
9. Twelve-hole pegboard

Position of therapist and child. The therapist should be positioned in such a way that he can give immediate direction and manual assistance to the child.

Activity progressions

Sorting activities. At first the objects being sorted should be easily discernible by color, shape, and size (Fig. 17-1). Sorting should become progressively more difficult as the child develops in perceptual ability. The child is instructed to sort:
1. One-inch blocks according to color (Fig. 17-2)
2. Beads according to shape
3. Various objects according to color, size, and shape
4. Beads on an abacus according to numbers (Fig. 17-3).

Fig. 17-1. Placing blocks in the appropriate spaces according to size and shape.

Fig. 17-2. Grouping blocks according to color.

Picking up objects

1. Picking up sticks: Matchsticks are placed in various configurations such as circles and squares on all four sides of the box. The child is instructed on the word "go" to pick up the sticks from

Fig. 17-3. Using an abacus to develop concepts of sorting.

Fig. 17-4. Pegboard activities.

each side of the box with the thumb and index finger and drop them into the box, alternating from the left and right to the far and near sides of the box.

2. Picking up coins: Coins are placed in various configurations such as circles and squares on all four sides of a box 3 inches square with a slit in the top just big enough to allow the coins to drop through. On the command "go" the child picks up the coins from each side of the box and drops them into the box, alternating from the left and right to the far and near sides of the box.

Circle tracing. The child is given a blank piece of paper cut into a circle measuring 6 inches in diameter. The child tries to draw as many circles as possible on the paper without any of the circles crossing.

Bead stringing. The child is instructed to string beads:

1. At random
2. At random as fast as possible
3. According to a shape the therapist has designated
4. According to a color the therapist has designated

Scissors activities. The child cuts:

1. Along a line previously drawn on the paper
2. Simple shapes
3. Patterns that have been drawn on the chalkboard

Pegboard activities (Fig. 17-4). The child places the pegs:

1. In a straight line from the top to the bottom of the board
2. In a straight line from left to right across the board
3. In a diagonal line from the upper left-hand corner to the lower right-hand corner. (The child can then start another line in the lower left-hand corner, finishing in the upper right hand corner, thus completing the letter X on the board.)

As a variation the child may insert the post of one magnetically charged cone into the hole of a second cone with the same magnetic charge (Fig. 17-5).

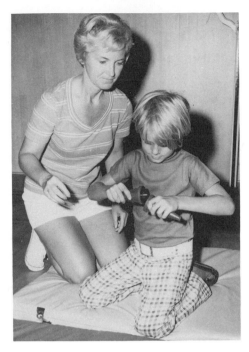

Fig. 17-5. Developing eye-hand coordination. The metal area surrounding the hole in the left cone is magnetically charged so that it will repel the post in the right cone if it is not inserted precisely into the hole.

Piercing. The child, using a pencil, pierces holes approximately ¼ inch apart in paper:

1. Along a line of dots previously drawn on the paper
2. Forming patterns that have been drawn on the chalkboard, such as geometric patterns or pictures of animals

Lacing. The child threads a lace back and forth through holes in a lacing board.

EYE AND HAND CONTROL
Level II: Eye tracking and chalkboard routines

Level II activities concern the development of left-to-right eye movements, laterality, directionality, eye-hand coordination, and tracking objects across the midline of the body.

Equipment and facilities. Chalk, a chalkboard, a flashlight, and a ball suspended on a string.

Position of therapist and child. The therapist should position himself in such a way that he can direct the activities and give assistance whenever necessary.

Activity progressions

Tracking activities

1. Following the ball: A ball is suspended on a piece of string and held directly in front of the child's nose. The therapist swings the ball and the child follows its path by moving only his eyes and not his head.
2. Flashlight chase: One student shines his flashlight on the chalkboard and a second child tries to catch the light with his flashlight.

Chalkboard routines

1. The child draws circles, both clockwise and counterclockwise, using the dominant hand first and then the nondominant hand.
2. The child marks an X on the chalkboard directly opposite his nose. Keeping his eyes focused on the X the child draws a lazy eight using the X as the midpoint of the eight. The eight can be drawn first with the dominant hand and then with the nondominant hand.
3. The child draws an X on the board directly opposite his nose. Keeping his eyes focused on the X he draws circles with both hands, using full arm movement. Variations include the following.
   a. Circles are drawn with both hands first moving in a counterclockwise direction and then in a clockwise direction (Fig. 17-6).
   b. Circles are drawn with both hands first moving toward a mark on the board designated as the midpoint and then moving out from the midpoint.
   c. Circles are drawn with one hand moving in a clockwise direction and the other hand moving in a counterclockwise direction.
   d. Circles are drawn with one hand moving toward the midpoint and the

Fig. 17-6. Clockwise and counterclockwise circle drawing while balancing on a beam.

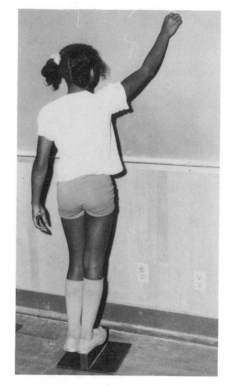

Fig. 17-7. Connecting numbers in ascending order by a straight line while balancing on a beam.

other hand moving out from the midpoint.

   e. Similar drawing and movement are done with other geometric shapes.

4. One child marks two dots on the chalkboard and a second child connects the two dots with a straight line. The first child then continues to make a series of dots while the second child continues to connect them with straight lines.

5. One child marks a series of dots in a horizontal pattern on the chalkboard. Another child connects all the dots moving in order from left to right.

6. A child marks a series of dots on the chalkboard in any configuration he wants. Another child tries to reproduce the shape by connecting the dots in any order he wishes.

7. The therapist draws a circle on the chalkboard with letters and numbers surrounding the perimeter of the circle. A child draws an X in the middle of the circle directly opposite his nose. Keeping his nose lined up on the X, the child places his right hand on a designated number and his left hand on a designated letter. As a variation, the child may draw a line from one designated number or letter to another (Fig. 17-7).

SIMULTANEOUS MOTOR CONTROL
Level III: Locomotor activities in the classroom

Level III is concerned with facilitating simultaneous motor activities such as walking and talking or walking and carrying an object.

Position of therapist and child. The therapist sits at his desk and directs the following activities, giving advice and assistance whenever necessary.

Activity progressions. The child is instructed to do the following activities without touching anything in the room.

1. Walk anywhere in the room and count up to 10.

Fig. 17-8. Carrying and walking.

2. Keep one hand overhead while walking around the room.
3. Carry a glass full of water without spilling it while walking around the room.
4. Walk and carry a heavy object (Fig. 17-8).
5. Push an object and walk (Fig. 17-9).
6. Walk on his toes.
7. Walk on his heels.
8. Walk while carrying books in his hands.
9. Walk while balancing a book on his head.
10. Walk at different speeds, take large steps, and take small steps.
11. Walk while bending some part of his body.
12. Walk as if he were stepping over big boxes.
13. Walk with a partner, trying to keep in step.
14. Walk backward.

NOTE: Variations include having the child run, skip, or hop through the previously listed activities.

15. Walk through an obstacle course arranged by using chairs, desks, books,

Fig. 17-9. Pushing and walking.

brooms, etc. The child is required to go under, over, around, and through a variety of obstacles of different shapes and sizes, and the following variations are possible.

a. The child goes through the course forward and then backward.

b. The children move freely through the obstacle course and around the room without touching any of their classmates or objects in the room. The activity begins with just one or two children moving and the rest standing still. More children are selected to move until the entire group is moving at the same time.

18

SELECTED PLAY SKILLS

Movement skills that are competitive within age groups are extremely important to any child. The clumsy child, who is unable to participate on a par with children down the street or at the playground, may feel left out of the mainstream of society. Therefore an effective remediation program must not discount selected play skills. When a child has the maturity that allows for the learning of specific activities, opportunities to do so must be provided. The teacher or therapist should find out which skills the child wants to learn and which ones will make him successful in his community. Often these selected motor skills can be taught on a task-sequenced basis, providing a successful experience that could not be gained in any other way. The following skills are examples of popular activities that can be broken down into a logical sequence of movement.

ROLLER SKATING

Roller skating, like ice skating, is a natural extension of walking and running in locomotion and dynamic balance (Fig. 18-1). Before the child attempts to learn

roller skating, these lead-up patterns should be mastered: (1) walk a 10-foot balance beam heel-to-toe with hands on hips; (2) walk forward, backward, and sideways on tin can stilts; (3) with socks on the feet, slide forward on a slippery floor in a cross-pattern fashion; (4) with a plastic skate on one foot only, slide forward on grass; (5) with plastic roller skates on each foot, walk forward on grass; (6) with plastic roller skates, skate on grass with a walking action, allowing the forward skate to slide; (7) with a metal roller skate on one foot, propel the body forward and coast on cement; (8) with metal roller skates on both feet, coast on cement after his body is propelled forward; and (9) walk on level cement with metal skates on both feet. From this point the child should be able to progress to the full roller skating pattern.

RIDING A BICYCLE

Riding a bicycle requires the child to have basic abilities in a wide variety of locomotor activities, particularly those requiring cross-pattern leg movements. The child should also be able to maintain both

Fig. 18-1. Roller skating is an important movement challenge.

dynamic and static balance in a variety of activities such as walking a balance beam, standing on one foot for 10 seconds, or maintaining balance while jumping from a chair or box. Normally the riding of a bicycle progresses from the use of two training wheels to one, and then to none. It requires the proper use of pedals and steering with the handlebars.

The first consideration in riding a bicycle is the reciprocal movement of the legs on the pedals that gives impetus to the forward movement of the bicycle. If the child has not had the opportunity to ride a tricycle or other vehicle propelled by foot action, he may have to be shown this particular pattern of movement. Also, if he has difficulty in keeping his feet on the pedals, they may have to be strapped in place to provide the constant pressure required for control.

The task sequence in teaching a child to ride a bicycle is as follows:

1. With the feet in place on the pedals, the therapist manually puts the child's foot through the full range of pedal movement and verbally indicates when he should push and which foot should apply the pressure.
2. The child is then instructed as to the proper use of the handlebars and steering. It may be appropriate to have the child disregard the foot movement and concentrate on steering until confidence is gained in this particular skill.
3. Once the child has acquired skill in both pedal action and steering, the two skills may be combined.
4. When control of the bicycle is assured, one of the training wheels may be removed.
5. At this time the therapist encourages the child to concentrate on attempting to balance the bicycle on its own two wheels.
6. When it appears that the child has the ability both to steer directly and to propel accurately and is able under many circumstances to balance without the

aid of the single training wheel, the remaining training wheel is removed.

7. Children should never be forced to go beyond their capabilities; however, they should be encouraged to try. When the last remaining training wheel suddenly is removed from the bicycle, the child may become frightened at the possibility of falling; the therapist should concentrate on balancing the two wheels, momentarily forgetting about the pedal and steering action. A good technique in helping a child to balance a bicycle is to find a slight incline bordered by a grassy or soft dirt area. The child is then encouraged to coast down the incline without particular concern about steering or pedal action (Fig. 18-2). If the child feels that he is going too fast and is getting out of control, he is instructed to put his feet down on the ground and use them as brakes or to steer onto the soft grass.

8. Once coasting balance has been learned, the child can concern himself with steering in a straight line (Fig. 18-3) and then with correct pedal action (Fig. 18-4).

ROPE JUMPING PROGRESSIONS

Jumping rope has long been a popular activity for both girls and boys. The ability to jump rope requires an ability to jump with both feet together or to hop on either foot while staying in one position (Fig. 18-5). Skill should be gained in jumping both the long rope, which is about 10 to 12 feet in length, and the individual short rope of 5 to 6 feet in length.

Fig. 18-2. Coasting down an incline.

Fig. 18-3. Steering comes before using the pedals.

Fig. 18-4. The final step in riding a bicycle is to be able to balance, use the pedals, and steer straight.

Long-rope jumping

Long-rope jumping requires two people to hold the ends of the rope or one end of the rope can be tied to a support and the other end held by one person. The progressions are as follows:

1. A 1-foot square is drawn on the ground so that the long rope passes through its middle. The child then proceeds to jump sideways over the rope and back again, staying within the square.
2. As in No. 1, the child jumps sideways over the rope while standing in the box. He turns to face in the opposite direction each time he jumps.
3. The long rope is wiggled back and forth while the child attempts to step over the "snake."
4. As in No. 3, the rope is wiggled back and forth, but this time the child tries not to have the rope touch him.
5. The rope is pulled to an elevation of about 2 inches above the ground and kept stationary. The child is then instructed to jump with both feet together back and forth, staying inside the square.
6. The child stands in the square and the rope is moved gently back and forth (known as "bluebells"). Each time the child jumps over the rope without leaving the square.
7. As in No. 6, the rope is moved back and forth. This time the child faces the rope, jumping over it with both feet forward and backward and staying within the square. At this point a verse may be added to the activity, such as "bluebells, cockleshells, Ivy, Ivy over."
8. On the word "over" the rope is turned over the jumper's head; he attempts to stay within the square without stepping on the rope.
9. A child first learns to coordinate a rope that goes over his head with jumping and staying within the box. Then he adds the skill of standing back from the jumping square, running to the rope, and beginning to jump while it is being turned. A lead-up to this activity is to run and jump from different positions to a rope that is swung back and forth.
10. When the child can sustain a jump while the rope is being turned over his head, the following variations may be added.
    a. Jumping to a rhythm, music, or a metronome
    b. "Front doors," in which the child

Fig. 18-5. Just being able to jump over a rope once may be a challenge.

Fig. 18-6. Coordinating rope jumping with another child is an advanced motor skill.

runs in as the rope is turned toward him and then runs out again

c. "Back door," in which the child runs in as the rope is turned away from him, jumps into the turning rope with a partner, jumps, and runs out (Fig. 18-6)

d. Bouncing a ball while jumping

e. Playing catch while jumping

f. Jumping and turning

g. Jumping and touching the ground

More difficult jumping activities can be added with the use of another long rope.

Individual rope jumping

Individual rope jumping is done with a short rope; the child holds one end with each hand, swings the rope over his head, and jumps through the loop. The object is to continue swinging the rope and jumping without missing. Individual rope jumping is an extension of the locomotion in long-rope jumping and requires the performer to be able to jump, step, and hop over a low obstacle repeatedly. Lead-up activities for individual rope jumping are as follows:

1. The child jumps in place to the rhythmical clap of the teacher.

2. The child imitates the teacher jumping rope.

3. The child holds both ends of the rope in one hand and swings the rope in such a way that the middle hits near the outside of one foot. Each time the rope hits the ground, the child jumps up. When he can execute this effectively with one hand, he then changes hands and practices with the other hand.

4. Holding an end of the rope with each hand, the child places the loop of the rope over his head, strikes the ground in front of the toes, and then steps over the rope. When the arm movement has been properly executed, the child is encouraged to swing the rope over the head and then jump with both feet over the loop of the rope when it strikes the ground.

5. The child is encouraged to sustain the jump by starting to jump as soon as he can hear the sound of the rope striking the floor. When the child can jump repeatedly with both feet for 10 jumps, he then executes the single jump over the rope. He then performs the double jump; the sequence is as follows: swing, jump, jump, swing, jump, jump.

6. Following double jumping with both feet, the child is taught to jump with one foot and then jump with the other foot as follows: swing, jump on left foot, swing, jump on right foot.

7. After the single jump with one foot is

Fig. 18-7. Playing jacks requires a high level of dexterity and eye-hand coordination.

accomplished the child can go to the double jump on one foot as follows: swing, jump on left foot, jump on left foot, swing, jump on right foot, jump on right foot.

Variations of rope jumping

As discussed earlier, rope jumping is one of the best activities for coordination and stamina. The following are some variations that can be included to make rope jumping more interesting to the child.
1. Skipping rope by running and jumping with the rope propelling the body across the floor
2. Skipping rope forward, backward, and sideways
3. Jumping with feet together, feet apart, forward, backward, and sideways
4. Hopping, tapping the toe in front and back, and then alternating feet
5. Hopping, swinging the foot forward and backward
6. Double jumping, in which two children face each other and jump in unison with one swing of the rope

PLAYING JACKS

Jacks has been a popular activity for many years; it requires dexterity and hand-eye coordination (Fig. 18-7). The specific abilities necessary in playing jacks are the bouncing and catching of a small rubber ball and the movement of picking up jacks and placing them into the palm of the opposite hand. The following progressions can be used to teach jacks playing.
1. The child sits kneeling or cross-legged on the ground and bounces and catches a tennis ball with one hand.
2. The child bounces and catches a small rubber ball normally used for jacks.
3. Without the ball the child picks up 1-inch blocks with the same hand that he normally used to bounce the ball and places them one at a time into the opposite hand.
4. Tossing the jack ball up, the child picks up a block with the same hand and then, keeping the block in that hand, catches the ball.
5. The child throws the ball up, picks up a block with the opposite hand, keeps the

block in that hand, and catches the ball with the same hand used to throw it.

6. The child throws the ball up, picks up a block with the same hand, transfers the block to the opposite hand, and catches the ball before it bounces twice.

7. No. 6 is repeated with the ball allowed to bounce only once.

When the child seems proficient in the use of the ball and blocks, regular jacks should be introduced.

Variations of playing jacks

1. Picking up two jacks and transferring them to opposite hand
2. Picking up three jacks and transferring them to opposite hand
3. Picking up four jacks and transferring them to opposite hand
4. Picking up five jacks and transferring them to opposite hand
5. Throwing the ball up, slapping the ground once with that hand, picking up a jack and transferring it to the opposite hand, and then catching the ball before it bounces twice
6. Same as No. 5 except that the child slaps the floor twice

Any motor skill can be taught by breaking it down into its component parts. The important factor to remember is that the parts should be skills in themselves that, when put together, form the larger whole of the skill to be learned.

19

MOTOR FITNESS

Fitness is one of the most controversial expressions in the field of physical education. Fitness has been generally referred to as an individual's capacity to survive and live effectively in his environment (Barrow and McGee, 1971). It is obvious, however, that these "necessary qualities" or the state of preparedness vary from one individual to another. Many variables must be considered in determining the level of fitness necessary for any given individual. These are factors such as body type, age, sex, and requirements for adjusting to an ever-changing environment. The American Association for Health, Physical Education and Recreation (AAHPER) has defined fitness as the state that characterizes the degree to which a person is able to function most effectively. The ability to function optimally depends on the state of physical, mental, emotional, social, and spiritual components, all of which are related and interdependent (AAHPER, 1956).

Through the years interest in physical fitness has been somewhat cyclic in nature, being affected by draft records, the emphasis on fitness during wartime, and more recently by President John F. Kennedy when he stated that intelligence and skill can only function at the peak of their capacity when the body is healthy and physically fit (Clarke, 1967). This launched a wave of concern for the physical fitness of American youth that has been perpetuated through subsequent presidencies.

COMPONENTS OF MOTOR FITNESS

Physical fitness is one phase of a child's total fitness; the term often is used interchangeably with "motor fitness." Other phases of total fitness include social, emotional, and intellectual components, which are discussed in other chapters of this book. The term "motor fitness," while commonly used synonymously with physical fitness, was coined to include all the various neuromuscular coordination skills that make up general motor ability as well as basic physical fitness. Thus motor fitness is most concerned with the efficiency of movement, involving the primary factors of muscle power, agility, speed, and balance. Motor fitness is the major component of total fitness that most so-called physical fitness tests actually measure. This is primarily because motor fitness is gauged by performance that can best be measured in terms of quantitative scores; the scores can be developed into normative data through statistical treatment. Motor fitness is most commonly divided into the categories of (1) muscular strength, (2) muscular endurance, (3) power, (4) speed, (5) agility, (6) balance, (7) flexibility, and (8) cardiorespiratory endurance.

Muscular strength

Strength is defined as "the capacity of a muscle to exert force" (Physical Education Framework, 1973). Increases in strength generally parallel increases in body mass, and the strength of a muscle is in proportion to its effective cross section. As children approach sexual maturity, muscular strength increases markedly, boys exhibiting much greater increases than girls. The early work of Dimock (1935) and later research of Jones (1949) clearly shows that postpubescent boys are as much as 30% stronger than prepubescent boys of the same chronological age. Jones attributes this difference to the fact that boys who mature early are for the most part mesomorphs who are by nature well muscled and inclined to participate regularly in athletic activities. The difference in the pattern of growth in strength of adolescent girls is less dramatic than in boys, although early maturers are on the average stronger than late maturers up to the age of 17.

The significant relationship between strength and motor performance can hardly be questioned, since motor acts are the product of muscular contraction. This relationship becomes apparent in activities requiring large-muscle responses. In pullups, for example, muscular strength becomes a dependent factor; therefore success is determined by the number and intensity of contractions made by the muscle groups involved in the work. Muscular force is also needed to develop the acceleration required for all types of running and jumping activities.

Overload principle. In order for strength to develop, there must be an increase in the resistance, duration of contraction, or rate of muscle action. Overloading can also be initiated by increasing the weight or friction that is necessary to overcome a particular resistance. Duration can be increased by lengthening the time a muscle contracts while maintaining a constant resistance. Rate, on the other hand, is raising the number of repetitions performed in a given period of time while keeping the resistance constant. Caution must be taken when requiring young children to execute repeated maximal muscular contractions because the muscles of the growing child are often stronger than their bony attachments and may produce avulsion fractures.

Muscular endurance

Muscular endurance is the ability of a muscle to repeat identical movements or to maintain a degree of tension over a period of time. Muscular endurance can be either static or dynamic in nature. Many studies have been made as to the value of the major types of resistance exercising to develop strength and muscular endurance. Isometric contractions are those in which a maximum static muscular contraction is held against an immovable object. The child exerts great muscular effort against a resistance, but there is neither perceptible muscle movement nor movement of the object involved.

Isotonic strength development exercise in which the child is able to move the resistance (ideally through a full range of joint movement) is a second type of exercise. Studies have shown that both forms of exercise improve muscular strength; however, the isotonic type favors the improvement of muscular endurance and the retention of both muscular strength and endurance for a longer period of time (Conrad, 1971). Isotonic exercise strengthens the points were resistance is applied.

Researchers have found a high positive correlation between muscular strength and muscular endurance, substantiating that the two variables are interrelated (deVries, 1972). Muscular endurance can be tested by having the child execute identical repetitions of movement through a designated distance or maintain one continuous muscle contraction for an unlimited amount of time. Activities such as push-ups, pull-ups, sit-ups, and flexed arm hangs can be used.

Power

Power is "the capacity of the muscles to move the entire body or any of its parts with explosive force" (Physical Education Framework, 1973). Power entails an explosive type of action and is equal to the product of force times velocity, where force has to do with muscle strength and velocity with the speed with which strength is used in motor performance. Power is an essential element where great distance or heights must be obtained in such activities as jumping, throwing, kicking, and hitting. Power is measured in terms of the distance through which the body or an object is propelled through space.

Speed

Speed is "the rate at which an individual can propel his body, or parts of his body, through space" (Johnson, 1970). "Speed has very little generality; consequently, a child with a fast arm movement can conceivably have a slow leg movement, in fact, this specificity extends to the type of task and the direction of movement" (deVries, 1972).

Agility

Agility is the ability of an individual to rapidly change body position in space. The importance of agility can be seen in many activities such as a fast game of hopping, jumping, or bouncing on a trampoline. Agility is usually measured by some test that involves rapid changes in movement,

such as the side step, zigzag run, obstacle run, and shuttle run.

Balance

Balance is the ability to assume and maintain any body position against the force of gravity or any other external force that the body is subjected to. Maintenance of balance results from the use of the senses and the interaction of the muscles working to keep the body's center of gravity aligned over its base of support (Chapter 12). Good balance plays a significant part in many sport activities as well as in daily living. Both static and dynamic balance are measured primarily by one's ability to maintain equilibrium either in a stable position or in moving from one point in space to another.

Flexibility

Flexibility is the capacity to move a particular joint through a range of motion. This range of movement is dependent on the flexibility and extensibility of the ligaments and muscles surrounding the joint. Good flexibility permits greater freedom of movement in activity and increases the child's capacity to avoid soft tissue injuries such as muscle and ligament tears. Flexibility is measured by determining the amplitude of a part as it moves in relation to an adjacent part.

Cardiorespiratory endurance

Cardiorespiratory endurance is determined by the ability of the heart and lungs to deliver oxygen to the body. Exercise designed to increase cardiorespiratory endurance places a measured amount of stress on the heart and respiratory systems. There are many activities that meet this stress requirement. According to Cooper (1970), the term "aerobics" refers to exercises that stimulate heart and lung activity for a time that is long enough to produce beneficial changes in the body. If an exercise or sport is not demanding enough to be classified as aerobic, modifications should be introduced if endurance is desired. For example, see forty-niner softball, p. 189.) There have been many misconceptions about the physiological capacity of children in elementary school to indulge in vigorous activities; consequently, most elementary school programs do not stress enough aerobic exercises. Research has shown that the cardiorespiratory system of the child in elementary school is as competent to deliver oxygen to exercising muscles as that of the adult (Bookwalter, 1964).

The main objective of an exercise program that emphasizes cardiorespiratory endurance is to increase the maximum amount of oxygen that the body can process within a given period of time. This is what determines the individual's aerobic capacity. Consequently, aerobic capacity depends on efficient lungs, a powerful heart, and a good vascular system. Since the aerobic capacity reflects the conditions of these vital organs, it is the best index of overall physical fitness.

There have been a number of tests devised to measure cardiovascular function. Cooper (1968) developed a 12-minute run-walk scoring scale for people to evaluate their own condition. Doolittle and Bigbee (1968) reported that the 12-minute run-walk had a correlation of 0.90 with maximum oxygen intake and was thus a highly valid indicator of cardiorespiratory fitness.

MOTOR FITNESS AND THE CLUMSY CHILD

The clumsy child's awkwardness makes him reluctant to participate in motor activities; consequently, in most instances he is below average in motor fitness. There is a vicious circle of mutual dependence between motor ability and fitness; when one is neglected, they both suffer. The following exercise program has been devised to aid the teacher or therapist in improving the level of fitness in the child so that his low level of fitness will not be a handicap to him in game skills with other children.

Strength and muscular endurance

The following section is concerned with exercises designed to develop strength and muscular endurance in the child. The exercises are listed in a sequential order, progressing from a low to a higher level in terms of difficulty.

Equipment and facilities. Horizontal ladder, tumbling mats, weight-lifting equipment (either commercial or homemade bar and weights), and climbing ropes.

Position of therapist and child. The therapist should position himself in such a way that he can give immediate direction and manual assistance to the child.

Activity progressions
Level I
1. Head circles
   PURPOSE: Strength, endurance, and flexibility of neck muscles.
   EQUIPMENT: None.
   STARTING POSITION: The child stands erect and rotates his head in complete circles both clockwise and counterclockwise.
2. Modified push-ups
   PURPOSE: Arm and shoulder strength and muscle endurance. (This is a lead-up exercise to regular floor push-ups.)
   EQUIPMENT: Tumbling mat.
   STARTING POSITION: The child assumes a front-leaning position with body and arms straight and hands and knees acting as the base of support. To perform the push-up the child bends his elbows and lowers his body close to the mat; then he pushes himself up.
3. Horizontal ladder straight arm hang (Fig. 19-1)
   PURPOSE: Arm and shoulder girdle strength and muscle endurance.
   EQUIPMENT: Horizontal ladder.
   STARTING POSITION: The child holds on to the ladder with palms out and hangs as long as possible. The child should be spotted throughout the stunt.

Fig. 19-1. Arm hang.

4. Arm circles

PURPOSE: Arm and shoulder girdle strength and muscle endurance.

EQUIPMENT: None.

STARTING POSITION: The child stands erect with arms laterally extended, parallel to the floor.

MOVEMENT: The child moves his arms in circles ranging in size from 6 inches in diameter to as large a circle as he can make. The movement should come from the shoulder joint.

5. Abdominal curl with arms at sides

PURPOSE: Upper abdominal muscle strength and endurance.

EQUIPMENT: Exercise mat.

STARTING POSITION: The child assumes a supine position with knees bent, feet flat on the mat, and arms at his sides.

MOVEMENT: The child lifts his head until his chin touches his chest, rolls both shoulders forward, and returns to the starting position.

6. Leg thrusts

PURPOSE: Lower abdominal muscle strength and endurance.

EQUIPMENT: Exercise mat.

STARTING POSITION: The child assumes a supine position with arms behind his head and legs fully extended.

MOVEMENT: The child draws his knees up to his chest, then thrusts his legs straight out, not allowing them them to touch the mat.

7. Back raise

PURPOSE: Extensor strength and flexibility in the lower back.

EQUIPMENT: Flat surface.

STARTING POSITION: The child stands in an erect position with feet shoulder-width apart and hands interlaced behind his head.

MOVEMENT: Keeping his legs straight and elbows even with his ears, the child bends down from the waist as far as possible and returns to starting position.

8. Side bends

PURPOSE: Strength and flexibility of trunk muscles.

EQUIPMENT: Flat surface.

STARTING POSITION: The child stands in an erect position with feet shoulder-width apart with hands interlaced behind his head.

MOVEMENT: The child bends down as far to one side as possible, returns to starting position, and bends to the other side.

9. Trunk rotation

PURPOSE: Strength and flexibility of trunk muscles.

EQUIPMENT: Flat surface.

STARTING POSITION: The child stands in an erect position with feet shoulder-width apart and hands interlaced behind his head.

MOVEMENT: The child moves his trunk

in a circular motion, leaning to the front, side, back, and other side.

10. Hopping

PURPOSE: Leg strength, coordination, and muscle endurance.

EQUIPMENT: Flat surface.

STARTING POSITION: The child stands in an erect position, balancing on one foot with the other leg bent at the knee at a 90-degree angle to the floor.

MOVEMENT: The child hops through a designated course on his right foot and returns on his left foot.

Level II

1. Head lifts

PURPOSE: Strength, endurance, and flexibility of neck muscles.

EQUIPMENT: Tumbling mat.

STARTING POSITION: The child is in a supine position with his arms and legs down. On the first command the child lifts his head into a vertical position with eyes focused on his toes. On the second command the head is lowered back to the mat.

2. Push-ups (Fig. 19-2)

PURPOSE: Arm and shoulder strength and muscle endurance.

EQUIPMENT: Tumbling mat.

STARTING POSITION: The child assumes a front-leaning position with body and arms straight and hands and feet acting as the base of sup-

Fig. 19-2. Push-ups.

Fig. 19-3. Bench press.

Fig. 19-4. Horizontal ladder travel.

port. The child then lowers his body close to the floor and raises himself to the starting position.

3. Bench press (Fig. 19-3)

    PURPOSE: Arm, shoulder girdle, and chest strength and muscle endurance.

    EQUIPMENT: Bench, bar, and weights.

    STARTING POSITION: The child lies in a supine position with hands grasping the bar and shoulder-width apart. The child pushes up the bar to full arm extension 10 times, exhaling on the way up. The child then lowers the bar onto his chest, inhaling on the way down.

4. Horizontal ladder corkscrew hang

    PURPOSE: Arm and shoulder girdle strength and muscle endurance.

    EQUIPMENT: Horizontal ladder.

    STARTING POSITION: The child hangs with one hand on a rung, twisting the body as far in one direction as it will go and then back again in the other direction.

5. Horizontal ladder travel (Fig. 19-4)

    PURPOSE: Arm and shoulder girdle strength and muscle endurance.

    EQUIPMENT: Horizontal ladder.

    STARTING POSITION: The child is positioned at one end of the ladder.

MOVEMENT: The child tries to reach the other end of the ladder employing a variety of methods such as moving forward or backward using every other rung, skipping one or two rungs, or traveling on the side rails.

6. Seal walk

    PURPOSE: Arm and shoulder girdle strength, muscle endurance, and coordination.

    EQUIPMENT: Exercise mats.

    STARTING POSITION: The child assumes a front-leaning position with fingers pointing laterally away from him. The legs are extended and relaxed.

    MOVEMENT: The child imitates a seal walking, dragging his legs behind him.

7. Crab walk (Fig. 19-5)

    PURPOSE: Arm and shoulder girdle strength, muscle endurance, and coordination.

    EQUIPMENT: Exercise mats.

    STARTING POSITION: The child assumes a face-up position supporting his weight on his hands and feet.

Fig. 19-5. Crab walk. Note that the hips should be even with the knees.

Fig. 19-6. Wheelbarrow walk. Caution should be taken to avoid back arching.

MOVEMENT: Keeping his seat off the mat, the child walks feet first to the end of the mat and head first back to his starting position.

8. Wheelbarrow walk (Fig. 19-6)

    PURPOSE: Arm and shoulder girdle strength, muscle endurance, coordination, and working together with a partner.

    EQUIPMENT: Tumbling mats.

    STARTING POSITION: Working with a partner, the child assumes a front-leaning position with hands on the mat and the arms fully extended. The partner grasps the child's ankles and lifts his legs up.

9. Abdominal curl with arms folded across chest

    PURPOSE: Upper abdominal muscle strength and endurance.

    EQUIPMENT: Exercise mat.

    STARTING POSITION: The child assumes a supine position with knees bent, feet flat on the mat, and arms folded across his chest.

    MOVEMENT: The child lifts his head up until his chin touches his chest and then rolls both shoulders forward and lifts his back from the mat to a full sitting position.

10. Leg lifts

    PURPOSE: Lower abdominal muscle strength and endurance.

    EQUIPMENT: Exercise mat.

    STARTING POSITION: The child assumes a supine position on the mat with hands behind his neck and legs extended.

    MOVEMENT: The child lifts his legs as high as he can without bending his knees. Then he lowers his legs under control to the starting position.

11. Upper back lift

    PURPOSE: Upper back muscle strength.

    EQUIPMENT: Exercise mat.

    MOVEMENT: Keeping his back straight and his toes touching the mat, the child lifts head, chest, and shoulders off the mat and holds this position for at least 10 seconds.

12. Lower back lift

    PURPOSE: Lower back strength.

    EQUIPMENT: Exercise mat.

    STARTING POSITION: The child assumes a prone position with hands clasped behind his head.

    MOVEMENT: Keeping his chest and shoulders on the mat with knees straight, the child lifts his legs at least 10 inches off the mat and holds the position for a minimum of 10 seconds.

13. Traveling jumps

    PURPOSE: Leg strength and muscle endurance.

    EQUIPMENT: Flat surface.

    STARTING POSITION: The child stands in an erect position with both knees bent.

    MOVEMENT: The child makes consecutive maximum jumps along a designated course.

Fig. 19-7. Leapfrog for developing leg strength and body coordination.

VARIATIONS: The child may perform traveling jumps with his feet together, apart, or alternately together and apart, or the child may play leapfrog with other children (Fig. 19-7).

Level III

1. Flexed arm hand

   PURPOSE: Arm and shoulder girdle strength and muscle endurance.

   EQUIPMENT: Horizontal ladder or bar.

   STARTING POSITION: Hands are shoulder-width apart with palms outward. Chin is over the bar.

   MOVEMENT: The child hangs as long as possible in the starting position.

2. Rope or pole climb

   PURPOSE: Arm, shoulder girdle, and upper body strength and muscle endurance.

   EQUIPMENT: Climbing rope or pole approximately 20 feet long with protective mat underneath.

   MOVEMENT: At first the child climbs the rope with the aid of his feet and legs; ultimately he climbs the rope with just his hands and arms. For the beginning child the leg-around technique is advised. This entails keeping the rope between the thighs and wrapping the right leg completely around the rope. The bottom of the rope crosses over the instep of the right foot from the outside. The left foot stands on the rope as it crosses over the instep, providing pressure to prevent slippage.

3. Swinging and vaulting

   PURPOSE: Arm and shoulder girdle strength, muscle endurance, coordination, and agility.

   EQUIPMENT: Rope and mats.

   STARTING POSITION: The child grasps the rope with his hands, standing in an elevated position.

   MOVEMENT: The child swings off a platform and vaults for distance, landing on both feet and finishing with a forward roll.

4. Pull-ups

   PURPOSE: Arm, shoulder girdle, and upper body strength and muscle endurance.

   EQUIPMENT: Horizontal ladder or bar that can be grasped and is high enough that the child can hang without his feet touching the floor.

   MOVEMENT: The child grasps the bar with an overhand grip with arms fully extended. He pulls his body upward, placing his chin over the bar, and then returns to his original position.

Fig. 19-8. Parachute play for developing upper body strength and muscle endurance.

5. Parachute play

PURPOSE: Arm and shoulder girdle strength, muscle endurance, and coordination.

EQUIPMENT: Parachute measuring 12 to 20 feet in diameter.

STARTING POSITION: Fifteen to thirty children are evenly spaced around the perimeter of the parachute. Each child stands erect and grasps the edge of the parachute with an overhand grip.

MOVEMENT: The children stretch the parachute tight at waist level; on the command "down" they lower the parachute edge to the ground. On the command "up" the children pull upward until their arms are fully extended above their heads (Fig. 19-8).

6. Abdominal curl with hands clasped behind neck (Fig. 19-9)

PURPOSE: Upper abdominal muscle strength and endurance.

STARTING POSITION: The child assumes a supine position with knees bent, feet flat on the floor, and hands interlaced behind his head.

MOVEMENT: The child lifts his head until his chin touches his chest, rolls his shoulders forward, lifting his upper back off the mat and touching his elbows to his knees, and then returns to the starting position.

VARIATIONS: The following variations increase the difficulty and/or effectiveness of the exercise.

a. The child performs a curl-up by lifting his head up, rolling his shoulders forward, simultaneously drawing his knees toward his elbows, and making contact between the elbows and the knees.

b. The child performs an alternating curl-up, touching his right elbow to his left knee and his left elbow to his right knee.

c. The child performs a curl-up on a board inclined at various angles.

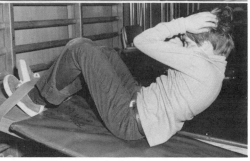

Fig. 19-9. Abdominal curl.

d. The child performs a curl-up on an incline board with additional weights added behind the neck.

7. Hanging hip curl

PURPOSE: Lower abdominal muscle strength and endurance.

EQUIPMENT: Horizontal bar.

STARTING POSITION: The child grasps a horizontal bar or ladder and keeps his feet together.

MOVEMENT: Keeping his arms straight, the child raises both knees and curls his lower trunk upward as far as possible, uncurling very slowly to his starting position.

8. Leg throw downs

PURPOSE: Lateral and lower abdominal muscle strength and endurance.

EQUIPMENT: Exercise mat.

STARTING POSITION: The child pairs off with a partner. The first child assumes a supine position with his

Fig. 19-10. Leg press.

Fig. 19-11. Hamstring and lower back stretch.

head between the second child's feet, grasping his ankles.

MOVEMENT: The first child lifts up his feet and legs to a vertical position. The second child pushes the first child's feet down toward the mat first to the left, then straight down, and then to the right. The first child attempts to stop his feet from touching the mat.

9. Lateral abdominal curl

PURPOSE: Lateral abdominal muscle strength and endurance.

EQUIPMENT: Exercise mat.

STARTING POSITION: The child assumes a side-lying position with his legs straight and together and with his arms folded across his chest.

MOVEMENT: The child raises his top leg upward and curls his trunk sideward toward his raised leg.

10. Leg press (Fig. 19-10)

PURPOSE: Leg strength and muscle endurance.

EQUIPMENT: Leg press machine.

STARTING POSITION: The child sits in the machine with his feet against the foot pedals and legs bent at a 90-degree angle.

MOVEMENT: The child presses the maximum amount of weight he can for 15 repetitions.

11. Half squat and toe raises

PURPOSE: Leg strength and muscle endurance.

EQUIPMENT: Flat surface.

STARTING POSITION: The child stands erect with feet shoulder-width apart and hands on the hips.

MOVEMENT: Keeping his back straight, the child squats, returns to a standing position, and raises up on his toes and back down to the starting position.

Flexibility

This section is concerned with exercises designed to facilitate the child's ability to move the joints in his body through their full range of motion.

Equipment and facilities. Tumbling mats.

Position of therapist and child. The therapist should position himself in such a way that he can give immediate direction and manual assistance to the child if necessary.

Activity progressions

Level I

1. Hamstring and lower back stretch (Fig. 19-11)

PURPOSE: Flexibility in the legs, shoulders, and back.

EQUIPMENT: Exercise mat.

STARTING POSITION: The child sits on

the mat with legs extended and toes pointed.

MOVEMENT: The child grasps the outer borders of feet and pulls head downward. He holds this position for a minimum of 30 seconds.

Fig. 19-12. Toe pointer.

Fig. 19-13. Shoulder stretch.

2. Toe pointer (Fig. 19-12)
   PURPOSE: Leg flexibility.
   EQUIPMENT: Exercise mat.
   STARTING POSITION: The child sits on the mat with his feet, toes, and ankles stretched backward.
   MOVEMENT: The child leans backward as far as possible with hands behind him to balance weight and holds the position for a minimum of 30 seconds.
3. Shoulder stretch (Fig. 19-13)
   PURPOSE: Flexibility in the shoulder joint.
   EQUIPMENT: Flat surface.
   STARTING POSITION: The child assumes an erect position with feet shoulder-width apart.
   MOVEMENT: The child reaches over his right shoulder with his right hand. He brings his left hand up from the left side and clasps the fingers of both hands together. The procedure is repeated on the opposite side and is held for a minimum of 30 seconds on each side.

Level II
1. Upper trunk stretch (Fig. 19-14)
   PURPOSE: Flexibility in the back.
   EQUIPMENT: Exercise mat.
   STARTING POSITION: The child assumes a prone position, keeping his pelvis on the mat.
   MOVEMENT: The child pushes up, extending his arms for a minimum of 30 seconds.
2. Lower trunk stretch (Fig. 19-15)
   PURPOSE: Flexibility in the back, legs, and shoulders.
   EQUIPMENT: Exercise mat.
   STARTING POSITION: The child assumes a prone position on the mat.
   MOVEMENT: The child reaches back and grasps his ankles, keeping his head up. He holds this position for a minimum of 30 seconds.
3. Upper and lower back stretch (Fig. 19-16)
   PURPOSE: Flexibility in the back and legs.

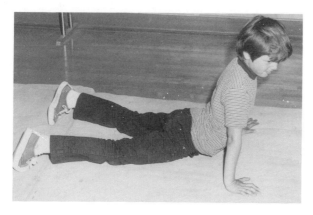

Fig. 19-14. Upper trunk stretch. Caution should be taken not to overarch to the point of pain.

EQUIPMENT: Exercise mat.

STARTING POSITION: The child assumes a supine position on the mat.

MOVEMENT: The child raises legs up and overhead, touching toes to the floor and leaving hands and arms on the floor. The position is held for a mimimum of 30 seconds.

General strength, agility, and large-muscle coordination

Activity progressions
Level I
1. Zigzag run

PURPOSE: Agility and leg strength.

EQUIPMENT: Any objects such as desks, chairs, or wastepaper baskets that can be positioned to provide an obstacle course.

MOVEMENT: The child stands in an erect position and on the word "go" runs as fast as possible between the obstacles in a zigzag fashion.

Level II
1. Side-straddle hop

PURPOSE: Agility, coordination, arm and leg conditioning, leg strength, and muscle endurance.

EQUIPMENT: None.

STARTING POSITION: The child stands erect with arms at sides and feet together.

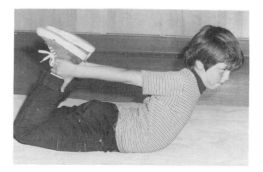

Fig. 19-15. Lower trunk stretch. Caution must be taken to maintain the hips and lower abdomen flat on the mat.

Fig. 19-16. Upper and lower back stretch. The child should avoid supporting weight just on the neck region.

MOVEMENT: On the count of 1 the child jumps to a straddle position with arms overhead. On the count of 2 he returns to the starting position.

2. Squat thrust

PURPOSE: Agility, coordination, and trunk and leg strength.

STARTING POSITION: The child stands erect with arms at sides and feet together.

MOVEMENT: The child bends knees and places hands on the mat in a squat position. He thrusts his feet and legs backward to a front-leaning rest position with the body straight from shoulders to feet, returns to a squat position, and stands erect.

Level III

1. Three-man roll

PURPOSE: Agility and coordination.

EQUIPMENT: Exercise mat.

STARTING POSITION: Three children get on their hands and knees on a mat 3 feet apart and facing in the same direction.

MOVEMENT: The child in the center rolls to his left; the child on the left projects himself over the oncoming child and rolls toward the child on the right. The child on the right projects himself over the oncoming child. Thus each child assumes the center position and rolls toward and under the outside child. The children must be instructed that as soon as they roll to the outside, they must immediately get ready to go over the oncoming child from the center.

2. Obstacle course

PURPOSE: The course should be designed to include all phases of fitness, including such activities as running, jumping, vaulting, climbing, and crawling.

EQUIPMENT: The course can be a permanently established or temporary portable installation made up of readily available physical education equipment such as mats, parallel bars,

Fig. 19-17. Jog and walk.

horizontal ladder, benches, balance beams, and high jump standards.

Cardiorespiratory endurance

Level I

1. Jog and walk (Fig. 19-17)

PURPOSE: Cardiorespiratory endurance, leg strength, and muscle endurance.

EQUIPMENT: Area for jogging.

STARTING POSITION: The child stands erect with arms at sides.

MOVEMENT: The child walks, jogs, or runs a prescribed distance or length of time.

Level II

1. Running in place

PURPOSE: Cardiorespiratory endurance, leg strength, and muscle endurance.

STARTING POSITION: The child stands erect with arms in a loose thrust position.

MOVEMENT: The child alternately lifts his left and right knees to a 90-degree angle, swinging his arms forcibly in opposition. Endurance can be developed by increasing the tempo and duration of the exercise.

Fig. 19-18. Forty-niner softball. A batting tee is used to develop skill level.

Level III

1. Running up and down stairs

   PURPOSE: Cardiorespiratory endurance, leg strength, and muscle endurance.

   EQUIPMENT: Stadium bleachers or flights of stairs.

   STARTING POSITION: The child stands erect with arms flexed at his sides.

   MOVEMENT: The child runs up and down a flight of stairs or stadium bleachers.

   PROGRESSION: The time allowed to complete a cycle is decreased, and the number of cycles the child has to accomplish is increased.

2. Forty-niner softball (Fig. 19-18)

   PURPOSE: This is a modified softball game designed to develop cardiorespiratory endurance along with softball skills.

   EQUIPMENT: Softball diamond, 9 bats, 9 balls, and 4 bases.

   RULES: All positions, rules, and strategies are the same as in regular softball with the exception of the following rules.

   a. Regardless of what happens to the ball, 5 seconds are allowed between pitches.

   b. Each batter receives only one pitch. A strike or foul ball constitutes an out.

   c. Ten outs retire the side.

   d. The batters must carry their bats with them as they round the bases.

   e. A runner dropping his bat retires the side.

   f. Runs are scored by touching third base with the baseball bat held overhead.

   g. Batters with bats line up along the third-base line behind a restraining line 5 feet behind the batter's box. When one batter is done, the next batter proceeds to the plate. He has 5 seconds to get ready for the pitch.

   h. A player designated as the retriever is positioned next to the pitcher to retrieve all the balls coming in from the field. The pitcher must have an ample supply of balls within reach to continue to deliver a pitch every 5 seconds.

   PROGRESSIONS: For small children and beginners the 5-second limit between pitches may be increased to 10 seconds. As the children's knowledge of the game and their skill level increase, the time limit can slowly be decreased.

PRINCIPLES OF EXERCISE

It takes time for a child to develop optimum fitness; consequently, the principles on which a personal exercise program should be planned are (1) warming up, (2) exercise tolerance, (3) progression through overloading, and (4) warming down.

Warming up

The child should begin at a slow pace with light, rhythmical exercises to raise the body and deep muscle temperatures, followed by stretching and deep breathing. This type of warm-up will stretch the ligaments and connecting tissues, thereby preparing the body for vigorous activity, and will help lessen the chance of injury and discomfort during strenuous exercise.

Exercise tolerance

Exercise tolerance refers to the greatest work load that a child can sustain without undue discomfort or fatigue. Exercise programs should be adapted to each individual's tolerance level. To ascertain a child's tolerance level a physical fitness test should be administered to each of the children in the class before a precise program is developed.

Progression through overloading

For performance to improve the intensity or the duration of the exercise must be increased. A good exercise program must provide progression, which may be accomplished by increasing either the intensity or the duration of the exercise. In most situations increasing the tempo or the amount of work done is more important than increasing the duration of the exercise. Progression should begin with easy exercises that gradually increase in difficulty, always keeping within the child's tolerance level.

Warming down

Just as the child needs to warm up properly he needs to warm down properly after exercise. The exercise program should finish with the child easing off gradually, thus assisting in bringing the blood back from the extremities to the heart and reducing the body temperature back to normal.

20

AGGRESSION MANAGEMENT

Aggression as it relates to children can present problems of overaggression and overpassivity. In many instances the clumsy child, because of a poor self-image, timidity, and lack of confidence, may refuse to stand up for himself or may run away when play becomes too rough. On the other hand, pent-up frustrations, feelings of hostility, and failure at establishing satisfying relationships with other children may result in the clumsy child finding expression in inappropriate behavior such as temper tantrums, destructiveness, preferring to play by himself, or other aberrations caused by an inability to cope with aggressive feelings. In this chapter we will describe activities that may be used as an outlet for emotional stress or as vehicles to aid the clumsy child in coping with his aggressive feelings. The environmental situations for aggression management must be highly structured and rigidly controlled. Safety must be paramount in the therapist's mind. Time limits must be imposed on certain activities to prevent accidents from occurring as the child becomes overly tired, tempestuous, or unmanageable. The entire activity area should be matted and uncluttered to avoid unnecessary collisions that may result in injury. The therapist must carefully explain to the participants that combative activity is only appropriate under specific situations that are strictly controlled by rules. It must be made clear to the child that testing his strength or other abilities against another child in a direct confrontation can be fun and should not lead to hurting or being hurt. It must also be made clear that activities of this type are only appropriate in the controlled setting of the designated activity area.

Level I: Object striking activities

Level I is concerned with activities that involve kicking or hitting with hands or inanimate objects.

Equipment. Balloons, 8 by 12 inch sheets of paper, cloth bags, and jousting clubs.

Position of therapist and child. The therapist should be positioned in such a way that he can easily give verbal directions.

Activity progressions

Striking balloons. The child assumes a two-point stance with feet shoulder-width apart. The therapist tosses up a balloon and the child tries to hit it as many times as he can with this left fist before it falls to the mat.

VARIATIONS OF STRIKING AND KICKING

1. The child strikes the balloon with the right hand.
2. The child strikes the balloon with both hands, starting with the left and alternating.
3. The child strikes the balloon with a jousting club held in both hands.
4. The child kicks the balloon first with one foot, then alternating left and right feet.
5. Ordinary 8 by 12 inch writing paper can be substituted for the balloons whenever necessary. The therapist drops the flat sheet of paper from an overhead position, and as the paper floats down, the child tries to strike it.

Striking a cloth bag. The child assumes a basic hitting stance with feet shoulder-width apart, the left foot in the lead, and the right toe lined up on the left heel. The child then strikes the bag with his fists in the following sequence.

1. With left hand only
2. With right hand only
3. With both hands, alternating between them

VARIATIONS OF STRIKING CLOTH BAG. The therapist can regulate the activity by setting either a number of strikes per hand or a definite time limit. For instance, the child could be given the task of striking the bag with his left hand only as many times as he can within 1 minute.

Level II: "One against one" activities

Purpose. These activities can be used in developing self-confidence or as an outlet for emotional stress.

Equipment and facilities. Jousting clubs, ropes, and tumbling mats or a covered area that protects against falls.

Position of therapist and child. The therapist should be positioned in such a way that he can give verbal directions easily and can intervene physically between the children if necessary.

Activity progressions

Indian wrestling. The children place the sides of their right feet against each other and at the same time grasp each other's right hand. The left foot is firmly

Fig. 20-1. Team tug-of-war.

positioned to the rear and used to support and balance. On the word "go" each child pushes and pulls the other in an effort to force the opponent's back foot to move.

Individual tug-of-war. Each child faces the other across a line with the rope secured by wrapping it around their hands. On the word "go" each child attempts to pull the other over the line. Many variations could be initiated, such as using only one hand and pulling while back to back with the rope over either shoulder or through the legs.

Team tug-of-war (Fig. 20-1). Two teams approximately of the same weight and height face each other across a line on opposite ends of a rope at least 20 feet in length. A cloth should be tied in the middle of the rope to indicate when one team has passed a certain point. Two parallel pieces of tape are placed on the mats, with the rope being equally divided between the two teams. Each team tries to pull the cloth over the piece of tape on their side.

Cock fight. Each child stands on one foot with the other leg held in a bent position by the hand on that side. Each child tries to bump another off balance so that he will let go of the supported leg. Children must be instructed not to continue bumping after an opponent has let go of his leg.

VARIATIONS OF COCK FIGHT

1. The bent leg is supported with opposite hand.
2. The children try to force each other out of a designated area.
3. The children select teams and compete on a team basis, with the team or individual maintaining balance the longest winning.

Jousting activities

1. King of the mat (Fig. 20-2): With the jousting clubs held in both hands, the children face each other on opposite sides of a circle measuring at least 10 feet in diameter. Each child tries to use his club to bump his opponent out of the circle.

Fig. 20-2. King of the mat.

Fig. 20-3. King of the beam.

Fig. 20-4. Referee's position used for push and pull and "one against one" activities.

Fig. 20-5. Child attempting to roll onto his stomach while being prevented by an opponent.

VARIATIONS
   a. The child balances on one foot and tries to force his opponent to drop his foot to the mat.
   b. The children select teams and compete on a team basis, trying to force the members of the other team out of a circle or to drop their legs. The team or individual lasting the longest is the winner.
2. Beam jousting: With the jousting clubs or bataccas held in both hands, the children face each other on opposite sides of a balance beam. On the word "go" each child tries to bump the other off the beam.
   VARIATION: Each child may try to push or pull the other off the beam (Fig. 20-3).

Wrestling activities. As a safety precaution all wrestling activities are executed in a three- or four-point position on the mats. Use of these positions prevents being thrown to the mats from a standing height and resulting in an injury. The most desirable position used is called the referee's position; one child assumes a bottom position and the other a top position. The child on the bottom is well balanced on his hands and knees as in a creeping posture. The

child on top places one arm around the other child's waist and the other hand just above his elbow (Fig. 20-4).

The wrestling holds described in this section are common to organized wrestling; however, they have been modified to suit the specific needs of the clumsy child. Even with simplication the described holds may be difficult without proper lead-up activities. The instructor should not be concerned with how well the maneuvers are performed but with what benefits are derived from the actions of pushing and pulling.
1. Far ankle and near waist
   PURPOSE: Used by child on top to take opponent to the mat.
   STARTING POSITION: Both children assume the referee's position. The following sequence is described in terms of the top child being on the right side.
   ACTION: The top child reaches across with his left hand and grasps his opponent's left ankle, while placing his right arm around his opponent's waist. He then pulls his left ankle forward, either taking him down on the mat or keeping him under control.

2. Sit out

   PURPOSE: This maneuver is designed for the child on the bottom to escape the grasp of his opponent.

   STARTING POSITION: Both children assume the referee's position, with the child on top on the left side of his opponent.

   ACTION: The child on the bottom brings his right foot forward and shifts his weight to his right foot and left hand. He then throws his left foot forward as far as he can, dropping on his left elbow and turning in to face his opponent.

   VARIATIONS

   a. One child lies on his back with the other child on top of him. The bottom child tries to roll over on his stomach while his opponent tries to keep him on his back (Fig. 20-5).

   b. One child lies on his stomach with the other child on top of him. The bottom child tries to get to his hands and knees while his opponent tries to keep him in a prone position.

3. Crotch and half nelson

   PURPOSE: Used by the child on top to get his opponent on his back and pin him.

   STARTING POSITION: Both children are in the referee's position, with the child on top on the right side.

   ACTION: The top child hooks his left leg around his opponent's ankle, reaches under him, grasps his left arm just above the elbow, and pulls it toward him, at the same time reaching around his right leg. The child on top then tries to push his opponent over on his back for a pin.

The activities covered in this chapter are just a few of the many types of combative activities that children can participate in. If properly supervised, they can be relatively safe and at the same time assist in helping the child effectively deal with aggression.

21

WATER ENVIRONMENT: AN IMPORTANT DIMENSION

Teaching motor skills to the clumsy child in a water environment is comparable to teaching on dry land. However, a pool does introduce a new concept to the child; that is, buoyancy accentuates the resistance and variations of pressure imposed on the body as movement takes place. If the new environment of water is properly used, it can augment the teaching of space, body perception, physical fitness, and many other selected movement factors.

ORIENTATION

When the child is brought to the pool site, safety instructions and orientation must be explained thoroughly before he actually goes into the water. Nothing must be left to chance, and routine pool procedures must be spelled out in clear, concise, and understandable language. Participants need to know where the toilet facilities are located, their proper use, the operation of

showers, and the proper use of locker room facilities, particular emphasis being placed on general health and safety procedures. The child should be oriented to the pool itself by a carefully directed tour. The therapist should point out the shallow-water section for beginners, the rope dividing the shallow water from the deep water, the deep water for advanced swimmers, the diving board, the diving area, specific rules for diving, and procedures for exiting from the pool. All safety rules must be gone over several times on different days to ensure understanding by all participants.

Level I: Entering and water adjustment

Position of therapist and child. While in the water the therapist should position himself in such a way that he can support the child and at the same time give verbal reinforcement.

Therapy hints. No other point in the pro-

Fig. 21-1. Entering the pool.

Fig. 21-2. Water adjustment.

gram is more critical to success than the initial stage of water adjustment. It is imperative that the child have fun and overcome any preconceived fear about the water as soon as possible. Each child's timetable for progress must be respected by each therapist; this is especially true in the initial stages of development.

Activity progressions

Entering the water (Fig. 21-1). At first the hesitant child is encouraged to sit on the side of the pool and dangle his feet in the water. To make him feel at ease in the water the child is encouraged to splash water on various parts of his body. When he has begun to feel relaxed and confident in the pool environment, he should go through basic movement patterns that include walking, running, jumping, hopping, skipping, galloping, and leaping (Fig. 21-2). Going through basic locomotor patterns helps the child become accustomed to the water.

Children who have a serious fear of water must be given special individual assistance. The instructor should hold the hand of the fearful child, walk with him in the shallow water, bounce up and down together, and at all times have fun. To gain rapport and confidence the instructor should talk to the child about his interests. The instructor should never break his word to the student; for example, if a student is told that he will not have to put his face under the water, the instructor must take extreme caution that at all times the child's head stays above water.

BREATH CONTROL
Level II: Breath control activities

Purpose. Breath control is necessary before additional skills can be learned by the child.

Activity progressions. The child is instructed to do the following.
1. Breathe only through his mouth.
2. Hold both hands together in a cupped fashion, catch water in his hands, and blow bubbles in it.
3. Put his mouth in the water and blow bubbles.
4. Put his face in the water.
5. Put his head underwater.
6. Duck underwater and blow bubbles.
7. Stay underwater and count to 5.
8. Stay underwater and count to 10.
9. Duck underwater, touching the bottom of the pool with both hands.

SPACE AND BODY AWARENESS
Level III

Activity progressions
1. Stretch a rope across an area in the shallow water and have the child:
   a. Step over the rope.
   b. Jump over the rope with both feet and then backward with both feet.
   c. Hop forward and backward over the rope with the right foot.
   d. Hop forward and backward over the rope with the left foot.
   e. Go over the rope headfirst in a semiprone position.
   f. Go over the rope feetfirst in a semiprone position.
   g. Go under the rope hands first, headfirst, and feetfirst.
   h. Go under the rope sideways and backward.
   i. Hold on to a kickboard and go over the rope in both prone and supine positions with the board held out in front.
   j. Think up different ways of going over and under the rope.
2. Using a Hula-Hoop, the child is instructed to do the following.
   a. Hold the hoop in a horizontal position under the water and try to step into it first with the right foot, then with the left foot, and then with both feet.
   b. Go in, over, and through, a floating Hula-Hoop headfirst.
   c. Using five hoops of one color and five of another color, go over and through hoops of the first color and under and through hoops of the second color (Fig. 21-3).
3. A pool obstacle course can be constructed by tying together a variety of floating devices such as Hula-Hoops, sticks, and balls. Some of the devices should be floating horizontally on the top of the water and others should be submerged and maintained in vertical positions by weights. The child goes through the obstacle course:
   a. Headfirst and with hands first
   b. Headfirst with hands and arms at his sides
   c. Feetfirst
   The child thinks of other ways he could go through the course, such as:
   a. Without use of legs
   b. With one hand at his side and the other over his head

Level IV: Body perception

Purpose. To reinforce the child's concepts of laterality and directionality by

Fig. 21-3. Moving over and through Hula-Hoops.

using the additional dimensions of buoyancy and water resistance.

Activity progressions. The child is instructed to do the following.

1. Stand on his right foot.
2. Stand on his left foot.
3. Balance on his right foot and left hand.
4. Balance on his left foot and right hand.
5. Balance on his right foot and right hand.
6. Balance on his left foot and left hand.
7. Place his left hand on the bottom of the pool and put his right hand above his head.
8. Place his right hand on the bottom of the pool and put his left hand above his head.
9. Place his left hand on the bottom of the pool and put his right hand and leg above his head.
10. Place his right hand on the bottom of the pool and put his left hand and right foot above his head.
11. Place his left hand on the bottom of the pool and put his right hand and right foot above his head.
12. Place his right hand on the bottom of the pool and put his left hand and left foot above his head.
13. Sit on the bottom of the pool and touch the bottom with both feet and hands.
14. Sit on the bottom with his left hand and right foot on the bottom and his left foot held in his right hand.
15. Sit on the bottom with his right hand and left foot on the bottom and his right foot held in his left hand.
16. Sit on the bottom with his right hand and foot on the bottom and his left foot held by his left hand.
17. Sit on the bottom with his left hand and foot on the bottom and his right foot held by his right hand.
18. Sit on the bottom with his right hand holding his right foot and his left hand holding his left foot. Arms and legs can be crossed in a variety of positions while sitting on the bottom.
19. Place both feet, knees, and hands on the bottom.
20. Place both feet and knees on the bottom.
21. Place his left foot, left knee, and right hand on the bottom.
22. Place his right foot, right knee, and left hand on the bottom.
23. Place his left knee and right foot on the bottom.
24. Place his right knee and left foot on the bottom.
25. Place his right knee and right foot on the bottom.
26. Place his left knee and left foot on the bottom. His buttocks should go higher than his head.
27. Stoop down and put his right elbow, then his left elbow, and finally both elbows on the bottom of the pool.
28. Place a certain number of parts on the bottom of the pool. (The number is chosen by the therapist.)
29. Hold on to the edge of the pool and stretch out in a prone float, draw the knees up to the abdomen, and stand up.

FLOATING
Level V: Basic floating progressions

Purpose. To develop the feel and concept of buoyancy, an acquatic survival skill that is fundamental to moving in water and recovering from various horizontal positions.

Position of therapist and child. The therapist should position himself in such a way that he can support the child in various floating positions, gradually releasing him but always reassuring him that supporting hands are close by if needed.

Therapy hints. The therapist should explain and demonstrate to the child that water will help him stay afloat if he relaxes and inhales as much air as possible.

Activity progressions

Jellyfish float. The child stands in waist-deep water with his feet shoulder-width apart. While bending forward at the waist, the child inhales deeply through his mouth. As the child places his face in the water, he slides his hands down his legs and grasps his ankles while keeping his legs fully extended.

Turtle float. The child starts by bending forward in waist-deep water and placing his hands on his thighs. After deep inhalation through the mouth he places his face in the water and at the same time brings his knees up to his chest and grasps his ankles.

Back float. The child assumes a supine position with the therapist supporting his head. This supportive position is advantageous for communication of confidence between the child and therapist. As the child begins to relax and gain confidence, the therapist can lower his shoulder, gradually reducing support and allowing the child to progressively float on his own. Necessary for an effective back float is the ability to relax while breathing easily, to keep the head well back in the water, to keep the arms underwater, and to hold the hips at the surface of the water.

Prone float. The child assumes a face-down position; as in the other float skills, the therapist supports the child according to his individual needs. Support is gradually reduced until the child has complete control.

Glide float. After the prone float has been learned a glide should be incorporated. To initiate the glide the child pushes both feet against the wall of the pool. Mechanics for a good glide include keeping the body straight by maintaining the head between the extended arms and the face down. After mastering the glide the child can explore and discover what happens when he moves his hands and arms and kicks his feet.

GAMES
Level VI

Purpose. The following games and activities can be used to develop motor fitness, movement skills, and a sense of security in the water environment.

Equipment and facilities. Retrieving rings, basketball goals, volleyball nets, and a variety of balls, including basketballs, volleyballs, balloons, and water polo balls.

Position of therapist and child. The therapist should position himself in such a way that he can direct activities and observe to see that safety precautions are being carried out.

Therapy hints. The following games are adaptable for children who are nonswimmers and have had very little exposure to water.

Activity progressions

Races. The children line up on one side of the shallow end of the pool. On the command "go" each child walks as fast as he can through the water; the first one to the opposite side is the winner. The following basic movements can be substituted for walking.
1. Walking backward
2. Walking sideward
3. Running
4. Skipping
5. Hopping
6. Galloping

Relay races can be run with each of the above-mentioned activities.

Underwater recognition
1. Counting fingers: The children divide into pairs. When one child ducks underwater, the other one extends any number of fingers underwater so that the submerged partner can see them. When the child is finished counting fingers, he stands up and checks with his partner to see if he is correct. Then the other child submerges to count fingers.
2. Body part identification: One child ducks underwater and the other points to a specific body part. The submerged child then stands up and identifies the designated body part.

Balloons. The child tries to keep his balloons in the air as long as possible by using:
1. Both hands and his head

2. His right hand
3. His left hand
4. His head

Variations include the following.

1. The children have contests to see who can keep his balloon in the air for the longest time.
2. The children get in a circle and try to keep one, two, or three balloons in the air.

Retrieving rings. The therapist tosses out a variety of weighted rings; the child is then shown a picture of one of the objects in the pool and then told to retrieve the object that is similar to the picture in both color and size. More than one object can be shown in the picture. For the child to successfully complete the task he must collect all the objects and present them to the instructor in the precise order in which they appeared in the picture. This type of task develops form, perception, color differentiation, and sequencing.

Forming shapes. This game can be played with a small group of children. The instructor calls out geometric forms such as lines, squares, circles, rectangles, and triangles; the children work together to form the designated configuration in the water.

Keep away. With selected teams and using balls of various sizes and shapes, one team tries to keep a ball away from the other team.

Dodge ball. Two teams are selected by the therapist. One team forms a circle

Fig. 21-4. Gaining eye-hand coordination in the water.

Fig. 21-5. The swimming pool provides an excellent opportunity for a wide variety of movement control activities.

around the other. The team on the outside has one or two low inflated rubber balls with which the children attempt to hit the members of the other team. When a player is hit, he joins the outer circle and helps retrieve the balls. When all the members of the team inside the circle have been hit, the two groups change places and the procedure is repeated. The winning team can be either the one using the smallest number of throws or the one using the shortest time to eliminate all the players.

Water basketball. The goals are placed on each side of the shallow end of the pool. Two teams are selected by the therapist and are given pinnies or water polo hats to designate one from another. Two points are scored each time a player throws the ball

into his basket. The player with the ball may not advance in the direction of his basket but may move laterally or backward. The ball can be passed in any direction to members of his team. A team may not use one specific player as a goaltender. The player with the ball may not be touched by members of the opposing team. If the violation occurs, the player is given a free throw from the spot of the violation.

As a lead-up activity to water basketball the children may practice throwing balls through targets such as Hula-Hoops (Fig. 21-4).

Water volleyball. Two teams are selected by the therapist and positioned on either side of a net placed so that the bottom is about 2 feet above the water. A water polo ball is most commonly used but any rubber ball of comparable size could be used. The side failing to return the ball over the net or batting it over the boundary lines loses the ball or the point. There is no restriction on the number of hits per side as long as the ball is kept out of the water. If the side that does not serve wins the play, it gains the serve; only the serving side can score points.

Swimming is an excellent activity for the clumsy child. According to the American Association of Health, Physical Education and Recreation, it is one of the best physical activities for developing and maintaining high levels of physical fitness, motor development, and physical proficiency (Fig. 21-5).

BIBLIOGRAPHY

Ajuriaguerra, J. In Wapner, S., and Werner, H.: The body percept, New York, 1965, Random House, Inc.

American Association of Health, Physical Education and Recreation: A practical guide for teaching the mentally retarded to swim, Washington, D. C., 1969, The Association.

American Association of Health, Physical Education and Recreation: Youth fitness test manual (revised), Washington, D. C., 1961, The Association.

American Association of Health, Physical Education and Recreation: Fitness youth statement, Prepared by the AAHPER Fitness Conference, Washington, D. C., September 1956.

Anderson, M. H., Elliot, M. E., and La Berge, J.: Play with a purpose, New York, 1966, Harper & Row, Publishers.

Annell, A. L.: The psychopathology of inflammatory brain diseases in childhood, Acta Paedopsychiatr. **29:**7, 1962.

Apgar, V.: A proposal for a new method of evaluation of the newborn infant, Curr. Res. Anesth. **32:**260, 1953.

Arnheim, D. D.: The relationship between skeletal dysplasia and incidence and recurrence of knee and ankle sprains among college sports participants, doctoral dissertation, Springfield College, Springfield, Mass., 1966.

Arnheim, D. D., and Pestolesi, R. A.: Developing motor behavior in children, St. Louis, 1973, The C. V. Mosby Co.

Arnheim, D. D., and Sinclair, W. A.: The effect of a motor development program on selected factors in motor ability, personality, self-awareness and vision, J. Am. Correct. Assoc. **28**(6):167-171, 1974.

Arnheim, D. D., Auxter, D., and Crowe, W. C.: Principles and methods of adapted physical education, ed. 2, St. Louis, 1973, The C. V. Mosby Co.

Ausubel, D. P., Scheff, H. M., and Goldman, M.: Qualitative characteristics in the learning process associated with anxiety, J. Abnorm. Psychol. **48:**538-547, 1953.

Ayres, A. J.: Sensory integration and learning disorders, Los Angeles, 1973, Western Psychological Services.

Ayres, A. J.: Manual: Southern California figure-ground visual perception test, Los Angeles, 1966, Western Psychological Services.

Ayres, A. J.: Manual: Southern California kinesthesia and tactile perception tests, Los Angeles, 1966, Western Psychological Services.

Ayres, A. J.: Manual: Southern California motor accuracy test, Los Angeles, 1964, Western Psychological Services.

Ayres, A. J.: Manual: Ayres space test, Los Angeles, 1962, Western Psychological Services.

Ballantine, F. A.: Age changes in measures of eye movements in silent reading. In Studies in the psychology of reading, Monographs in Education, No. 4, pp. 67-111, Ann Arbor, 1951, The University of Michigan Press.

Barrow, H. M., and McGee, R.: A practical approach to measurement in physical education, Philadelphia, 1971, Lea & Febiger.

Barsch, R. H.: Enriching perception and cognition, Seattle, 1968, Special Child Publications, vol. 2.

Barsch, R.: Achieving perceptual-motor efficiency, Seattle, 1968, Special Child Publications, vol. 2.

Barsch, R.: Six factors in learning. In Hellmuth, J., editor: Learning disorders, Seattle, 1965, Special Child Publications.

Bateman, B. D.: Temporal learning, San Rafael, Calif., 1968, Dimensions Publishing Co.

Bennett, R. L.: Principles of therapeutic exercise. In Licht, S., editor: Therapeutic exercise, ed. 2, New Haven, Conn., 1965, Elizabeth Licht, Publisher.

Bernstein, P. L.: Theory and methods in dance-movement therapy, Dubuque, Iowa, 1972, Kendall/Hunt Publishing Co.

Berscheid, E., Walster, E., and Bohrnstadt, G.: Body image, Psychol. Today **7**(6):119-131, 1973.

Bobath, B.: Treatment principles and planning in cerebral palsy, J. Physiother. **49**:122-124, 1963.

Bobath, K., and Bobath, B.: The facilitation of normal postural reactions and movements in the treatment of cerebral palsy, J. Physiother. **50**:246-262, 1964.

Bookwalter, K. W.: Physical education in the secondary schools, New York, 1964, The Center for Applied Research in Education, Inc.

Borovikov, M. O.: Motorik, Korperbau and Charaktog. Cited in Lassner, R.: Annotated bibliography of Oseretsky tests, J. Consult. Psychol. **12**:37-49, 1948.

Brace, D. K.: Measuring motor ability, New York, 1927, A. S. Barnes & Co., Inc.

Buswell, G. T.: Fundamental reading habits: a study of their development, Supplemental Education Monograph, vol. 21, Chicago, 1922, University of Chicago Press.

Chalfant, J. C., and Scheffelin, M. A.: Central processing dysfunctions in children, Ninds Monograph, No. 9, Washington, D. C., 1969, U. S. Department of Health, Education and Welfare.

Clarke, H. H.: Application of measurement to health and physical education, Englewood Cliffs, N. J., 1967, Prentice-Hall, Inc.

Coghill, G. E.: Anatomy and the problem of behavior, New York, 1929, Macmillan Publishing Co., Inc.

Conrad, C.: Exercising for physical fitness, Sacramento, 1971, California State Department of Education.

Cooper, K. H.: The new aerobics, New York, 1970, M. Evans & Co., Inc.

Cooper, K. H.: Aerobics, New York, 1968, M. Evans & Co., Inc.

Cratty, B: Movement behavior and motor learning, ed. 3, Philadelphia, 1973, Lea & Febiger.

Cratty, B.: Movement and spatial awareness in blind children and youth, Springfield, Ill., 1971, Charles C Thomas, Publisher.

Cratty, B. J.: Perceptual and motor development in infants and children, New York, 1970, Macmillan Publishing Co., Inc.

Cratty, B.: Perceptual-motor behavior and educational processes, Springfield, Ill., 1969, Charles C Thomas, Publisher.

Cratty, B., and Martin, Sister M. M.: Perceptual-motor efficiency in children, Philadelphia, 1969, Lea & Febiger.

Critchley, M.: Correlated disturbances: etiologic, associated, and secondary (part I). In Keeney, A. H. and Keeney, V. T., editors: Dyslexia, St. Louis, 1968, The C. V. Mosby Co.

Dauer, V. P.: Essential movement experiences for preschool and primary children, Minneapolis, 1972, Burgess Publishing Co.

Davis, R.: Writing behavioral objectives, J. Health Phys. Educ. Recr. **44**(4):47-49, 1973.

Delacato, C.: Neurological organization and reading, Springfield, Ill., 1967, Charles C Thomas, Publisher.

Dell, C.: A primer for movement description, New York, 1970, Dance Notation Bureau, Inc., Center for Movement Research and Analysis.

Denhoff, E.: Cerebral palsy: the preschool years, Springfield, Ill., 1967, Charles C Thomas, Publisher.

DePauw, K. P.: Investigation of the relationship between a sensory motor program and sensory integration of pre-school aphasic students, Master's thesis, California State University, Long Beach, 1974.

DeSantis, G. J., and Smith, L. V.: Physical education programmed activities for grades K-6, Columbus, Ohio, 1969, Charles E. Merrill Publishing Co.

deVries, H. A.: Physiology of exercise for physical education and athletics, Dubuque, Iowa, 1969, William C. Brown Co., Publishers.

Dimock, H. S.: A research in adolescence—pubescence and physical growth, Child Dev. **6**:176, 1935.

Doll, E. A.: The Oseretzky test, Ill. Training School Bull. **43**:1, 1946.

Doolittle, T. L., and Bigbee, R.: The twelve-minute run-walk: a test of cardiorespiratory fitness of adolescent boys, Res. Q. Am. Assoc. Health Phys. Educ. **39**:491-495, 1968.

Elliott, A. A.: Preschool delayed language children's human figure drawings, Master's thesis, California State University, Long Beach, 1974.

Fay, T.: Neuromuscular reflex therapy for spastic disorders, J. Fla. Med. Assoc. **44**:1234-1240, 1958.

Fay, T.: The origin of human movement, Am. J. Psychiatr. **3**:644-652, 1955.

Fiorentino, M. R.: Reflex testing methods for evaluating C.N.S. development, Springfield, Ill., 1963, Charles C Thomas, Publisher.

Ford, F. R.: Diseases of the nervous system in infancy, childhood and adolescence, Oxford, 1960, Blackwell Scientific Publications.

Frank, L. K.: On the importance of infancy, New York, 1966, Random House, Inc.

Frostig, M.: Developmental test of visual perception, Los Angeles, 1963, Consulting Psychologists' Press.

Furth, H. G.: Piaget for teachers, Englewood Cliffs, N. J., 1970, Prentice-Hall, Inc.

Garfield, E.: The measurement of motor ability, Arch. Psychol. **62**:1-47, 1923.

Gatz, A. J.: Essentials of clinical neuroanatomy and neurophysiology, ed. 3, Philadelphia, 1966, F. A. Davis Co.

Gearheart, B. R.: Learning disabilities: educational strategies, St. Louis, 1973, The C. V. Mosby Co.

Gellhorn, E.: Proprioception and the motor cortex, Brain **72**:35-62, 1949.

Gerald, N., Getman, K., Halgren, M., and McKee, G.: Developing learning readiness, New York, 1968, McGraw-Hill Book Co.

Gesell, A. L., and Amatruda, C. S.: Developmental diagnosis: normal and abnormal child development; clinical methods and pediatric applications, ed. 2, New York, 1947, Harper & Row, Publishers.

Gesell, A., and Amatruda, C. S.: The embryology of behavior, New York, 1945, Harper & Row, Publishers.

Getman, G.: The visuomotor complex in the acquisition of learning skills. In Hellmuth, J., editor: Learning disorders, Seattle, 1965, Special Child Publications, vol. 1.

Gibson, H. B.: The Gibson spiral maze test, J. Psychol. **60**(4):523-528, 1964.

Gilbert, L. C.: Reading before the eye-movement camera versus reading away from it, Elementary School J. **42**:443-447, 1966.

Ginott, H. G.: Between parent and child, New York, 1965, Avon Books.

Glasser, W.: Reality therapy, New York, 1965, Harper & Row, Publishers.

Goodenough, F. L.: Draw-a-man test, Chicago, 1934, World Book Co.

Gray, C. T.: Types of reading ability as exhibited through tests and laboratory experiments, Supplemental Education Monograph, No. 5, Chicago, 1917, University of Chicago Press.

Harris, D. B.: A revision and extension of the Goodenough Draw-A-Man test, New York, 1963, Harcourt Brace Jovanovich.

Harris, L., and Parker, W.: College studies in hygiene and physical education, Res. Q. Suppl. **9**:49-50, March 1938.

Harris, T. A.: I'm O.K.—you're O.K., New York, 1969, Harper & Row, Publishers.

Haynes, U.: A developmental approach to case finding, Washington, D. C., 1967, U. S. Department of Health, Education and Welfare, Social and Rehabilitation Service.

Hebb, D.: The organization of behavior, New York, 1949, John Wiley & Sons, Inc.

Hellabrandt, F. A., Houtz, S. J., and Eubank, R. N.: Influence of alternate and reciprocal exercise on work capacity, Arch. Phys. Med. **32**:766-776, 1951.

Hellmuth, J., editor: Exceptional infant: the normal infant, New York, 1967, Brunner/Mazel, Inc., vol. 1.

Hughes, J. G.: Synopsis of pediatrics, ed. 3, St. Louis, 1971, The C. V. Mosby Co.

Humphrey, J. H., Love, A. M., and Irwin, L. W.: Principles and techniques of supervision in physical education, Dubuque, Iowa, 1972, William C. Brown Co., Publishers.

Illingworth, R. S.: The clumsy child. In Bax, M., and MacKeith, R., editors: Clinics in developmental medicine, No. 10 (Spastics Society), London, 1963, William Heinemann, Ltd.

Jacobsen, E.: Progressive relaxation, Chicago, 1938, University of Chicago Press.

Johnson, B. L., and Nelson, J. K.: Practical measurements for evaluation in physical education, Dallas, 1970, Burgess Press.

Johnson, G. B.,: Physical skill test for sectioning classes into homogeneous units, Res. Q. Am. Assoc. Health Phys. Educ. **3**:128-136, March, 1932.

Jones, H. E. Motor performance and growth, Berkeley, 1949, University of California Press.

Kabot, H., and Knott, M.: Principles of neuromuscular re-education, Phys. Ther. Rev. **28**:107-111, 1948.

Keats, S.: Cerebral palsy, Springfield, Ill., 1965, Charles C Thomas, Publisher.

Keeney, A. H., and Keeney, V. T., editors: Dyslexia, St. Louis, 1968, The C. V. Mosby Co.

Kemal, C.: Contribution à l'étude des tests de développement moteur d'Oseretsky. Cited in Lassner, R.: Annotated bibliography of Oseretsky tests, J. Consult. Psychol. **12**:37-49, 1948.

Keogh, B. K.: The copying ability of young children, Educ. Res. **11**:43-7, Nov., 1968.

Kephart, N. C.: The slow learner in the classroom, Columbus, Ohio, 1960, Charles E. Merrill Publishing Co.

Kirchner, G.: Physical education for elementary school children, ed. 2, Dubuque, Iowa, 1970, William C. Brown Co., Publishers.

Knapp, B.: Skill in sport, London, 1964, Routledge & Kegan Paul.

Knickerbacker, B.: A central approach to the development of spatial and temporal concepts. In Hellmuth, J., editor: Learning disorders, Seattle, 1968, Special Child Publications, vol. 3.

Kopp, H.: The relationship of stuttering to motor disturbance, Nerv. Child **2**:107-116, 1943.

Laban, R., and Lawrence, F. C.: Effort, 1947, MacDonald & Evans.

Lerner, J. W.: Children with learning disabilities, Boston, 1971, Houghton Mifflin Co.

LeWinn, E. B., et al.: Neurological organization: the basis for learning. In Hellmuth, J., editor: Learning disorders. Seattle, 1966, Special Child Publications.

Louttit, C. M., and Browne, D. B.: Test performance of a selected group of part-Hawaiians, J. Appl. Psychol. **15**:43-52, 1946.

Lowen, A.: The language of the body, New York, 1958, Macmillan Publishing Co., Inc.

Maltz, M.: Psycho-cybernetics, Englewood Cliffs, N. J., 1960, Prentice-Hall, Inc.

McCloy, C. H.: An analytical study of the stunt type test as a measure of motor educability, Res. Q. Am. Assoc. Health Phys. Educ. **8**:46-55, Oct., 1937.

McCow, W. R.: Educational psychology, New York, 1964, Monarch Press.

McGraw, M. B.: The neuromuscular maturation of the human infant, New York, 1943, Columbia University Press.

McLennan, C. E., and Sandberg, E. C.: Synopsis of obstetrics, ed. 9, St. Louis, 1974, The C. V. Mosby Co.

Minnesota Rate of Manipulation Test, 1969 ed., New York, 1969, American Guidance Service, Inc.

Moore, J. C.: Neuroanatomy simplified, Dubuque, Iowa, 1969, Kendall/Hunt Publishing Co.

Morris, P. R., and Whiting, H. T. A.: Motor impairment and compensatory education, Philadelphia, 1971, Lea & Febiger.

Morse, W. C.: A comparison of the eye movements of fifth and seventh grade pupils reading materials of corresponding difficulty. In Studies in the psychology of reading, Monographs in Education, No. 4, pp. 3-64, Ann Arbor, 1951, The University of Michigan Press.

Mosston, M.: Teaching physical education: from command to discovery, Columbus, Ohio, 1966, Charles E. Merrill Publishing Co.

Mosston, M.: Developmental movement, Columbus, Ohio, 1965, Charles E. Merrill Publishing Co.

Mourouzis, A., et al.: Body management activities, Cedar Rapids, Iowa, 1970, Nissen Co.

Moyes, F. A.: A validational study of a test of motor

impairment, Master's thesis, University of Leicester, Leicester, England, 1969.

Mussen, P. H., Conger, J. J. and Kagan, J.: Child development and personality, New York, 1969, Harper & Row, Publishers.

Orem, R. C.: Montessori today, New York, 1971, G. P. Putnam's Sons.

Orpet, R. E.: Frostig movement skills test battery, Los Angeles, 1972, Marianne Frostig Center of Educational Therapy.

Oseretsky, N. A.: Metric scale for studying the motor capacity of children. In Lassner, R.: Annotated bibliography of the Oseretsky test of motor proficiency, J. Consult. Psychol. **12:**37-47, 1948.

Oxendine, J. B.: Psychology of motor learning, New York, 1968, Appleton-Century-Crofts.

Page, D.: Neuromuscular reflex therapy as an approach to patient care, Am. J. Phys. Med. **46:**816-837, 1967.

Pavlov, P.: Lectures on conditioned reflexes (Translated and edited by W. Horsley Gantt), New York, 1928, International Publishers Co., Inc.

Physical education framework for California public schools, kindergarten through grade twelve, Sacramento, 1973, The California State Board of Education.

Roach, E. G., and Kephart, N. C.: The Purdue perceptual-motor survey, Columbus, 1966, Charles E. Merrill Publishing Co.

Rood, M. S.: Neurophysiologic reactions as a basis for physical therapy, Phys. Ther. Rev. **34:**444-449, 1954.

Sage, G. H.: Introduction to motor behavior: a neuropsychological approach, Reading, Mass., 1971, Addison-Wesley Publishing Co.

Salkin, J.: The body ego technique, Springfield, Ill., 1973, Charles C Thomas, Publisher.

Schilling, F., and Kiphard, E. J.: Der Körperkoordinationstest für Kinder, 1967, Hünnekens, Kiphard, Kessellman.

Schoop, T.: The body is a blabbermouth, paper presented at the second national conference on programs and practice for the exceptional individual, Fullerton, Calif., 1974.

Selye, H.: The stress of life, New York, 1956, McGraw-Hill Book Co.

Semans, S.: The Bobath concept in treatment of neurological disorders, Am. J. Phys. Med. **46:**732-738, 1967.

Sheldon, W. H.: The varieties of human physique, New York, 1940, Harper & Row, Publishers.

Sherrington, C. S.: Selected writings (edited by D. Denny-Brown), New York, 1940, Harper & Row, Publishers.

Sinclair, W. A.: The effect of motor skill upon specific dyslexia, Doctoral dissertation, University of New Mexico, Albuquerque, 1970.

Sloan, W.: The Lincoln/Oseretsky motor development scale, Gen. Psychol. Monog. **51:**183-252, 1955.

Standin, E. M.: The Montessori revolution in education, New York, 1967, Schocken Books, Inc.

Stockmeyer, S. A.: An interpretation of the approach of Rood to the treatment of neuromuscular dysfunction, Am. J. Phys. Med. **46:**900-961, 1967.

Stott, D. H.: A general test of motor impairment for children, Dev. Med. Child Neuro. **8:**523-531, 1966.

Sundberg, N., and Ballinger, T.: Nepalese children's cognitive development as revealed by drawings of man, woman, and self, Child Dev. **39:**969-985, 1968.

Taylor, E. A.: Controlled reading, Chicago, 1957, University of Chicago Press.

Thorton, S.: Laban's theory of movement: a new perspective, Boston, 1971, Plays, Inc.

Tinker, M. A.: The reliability and validity of eye-movement measures of reading, J. Exp. Psychol. **19:**732-746, 1936.

Touwen, B. C. L., and Prechtl, H. F. R.: The neurological examination of the child with minor nervous dysfunction, Philadelphia, 1970, J. B. Lippincott Co.

Ulett, G. A.: A synopsis of contemporary psychiatry, ed. 5, St. Louis, 1972, The C. V. Mosby Co.

U. S. Department of Health, Education and Welfare, Social and Rehabilitation Service, Children's Bureau: The child with central nervous system deficit, report of two symposiums, Washington, D. C., 1965, U. S. Government Printing Office.

Voss, D. E.: Proprioceptive neuromuscular facilitation, Am. J. Phys. Med. **46:**838-899, 1967.

Walton, J. N.: Clumsy children. In Bax, M., and MacKeith, R., editors: Clinics in developmental medicine, No. 10 (Spastics Society), London, 1963, William Heinemann, Ltd.

Williams, E. T.: A comparison study of the behavioral changes between emotionally disturbed children and normal children participating in folk dance, Master's thesis, California State University, Long Beach, 1974.

Williams, M., and Worthingham, C.: Therapeutic exercise: for body alignment and function, Philadelphia, 1957, W. B. Saunders Co.

Wolf, J. M., and Anderson, R. M., editors: The multiply handicapped child, Springfield, Ill., 1969, Charles C Thomas, Publisher.

Yerkovich, K.: Employee manual for the Institute for Sensory Motor Development, California State University, Long Beach, 1972. (Unpublished.)

GLOSSARY

adiadochokinesia Inability to execute rapid and alternating movements.

agility Ability to move the body or any of its parts in any direction quickly, easily, and with control.

agnosia Inability to recognize a common object through one or more of the senses.

akinesia Motor dysfunction with resultant loss of movement.

aphasia Inability to understand spoken words due to cerebral dysfunction.

apraxia Inability to carry out plans to perform a complex movement.

asymmetry Position or movement of the body that is different on one side of the body when compared to the other.

ataxia Muscular incoordination primarily involving voluntary muscular movements.

athetotic movement Writhing, irregular, arrhythmical gross movement.

athetotiform movement Small, slow movement that is irregular and arrhythmical.

autism Childhood condition reflected in a withdrawing from reality.

balance Ability to assume and maintain any body position against the force of gravity.

body awareness Knowledge of the way the body parts move, for example, turn, twist, and stretch.

body image Perception of the body as derived from external and internal sensations.

body-space perception Ability to orient body movements in a integrated manner when confronted with specific obstacles.

cardiorespiratory endurance Ability of the heart and lungs to maintain efficient function during and after vigorous exercise.

cerebral dominance Tendency of one side of the brain to be more developed than the other. (For example, right-handedness is controlled by the left hemisphere of the brain.)

choreiform movement Small, jerky, irregular, and arrhythmical movement, usually of fingers and wrists.

choreotic movement Gross jerky movement expressed in irregular and arrythmical burst of activity.

circuit training Movement of the child among different stations at his own rate according to his level of fitness and skill.

convergence Medial rotation of the eyes to create focus on an object.

developmental retardation Maturational lag in basic neurological function such as locomotion.

diadochokinesia Ability to make rapid antagonistic movements such as in forearm supination and pronation.

directionality Awareness of space outside of the body. Involves (1) knowledge of directions in relation to right and left, in and out, and up and down; (2) the projection of one's self in space; and (3) the judging of distances between objects.

dynamic balance Ability to maintain a position while the individual is moving or the surface is moving.

dyskinesia Defect in voluntary movement.

dysmetria Inability to judge the range of movement (for example, too rapid or too forceful movement).

dyspraxia Difficulty in performing a motor act.

eye-foot coordination Ability to use eyes and feet together to accomplish a task.

eye-hand coordination Ability to use eyes and hands together to accomplish a task.

figure-ground discrimination Distinguishing objects from their background.

fine motor coordination Development of the muscles to the degree that they perform specific small movements.

flexibility Capacity to move a particular joint in the body through its range of motion.

force Mass times velocity.

gross motor coordination Development of the skeletal muscles to produce efficient total body movement.

haptic sense Integration of cutaneous and kinesthetic information.

hemisyndrome Syndrome indicating a unilateral lesion of the spinal cord.

heterophoria Tendency of an eye to move from its normal position when opposite eye is covered.

hyperkinetic behavior syndrome Behavior characterized by being uncontrolled and explosive in nature.

hypertonia Greater than normal muscle tension.

hypotonia Less than normal muscle tension.

interval training Training in which the child performs a series of activities at his own level or pace for a specified length of time.

ipsilateral Occurring on one side of the body.

laterality Internalizing the awareness of the difference between right and left.

locomotor movements Basic movements performed while moving the body on the feet from place to place.

manipulative skills Combinations of fine and gross motor skills, usually involving the hands.

maturational lag Growth and development patterns below typical standards.

motor aphasia Inability to express oneself in movement such as speech or writing.

motor pattern Select group of movement skills combined to produce purposeful motor behavior.

motor skill Specific set of movement responses requiring precision and accuracy for its accomplishment.

motor task Specific movement skill or pattern designed and directed by the therapist for performance by the student.

motor therapy Remediation of movement problems.

movement education Physical education approach utilizing basic movement patterns.

movement exploration Method of teaching physical education through nondirective methods in which the participant explores the environment using basic movement patterns.

movement flow Movement that is sequenced and conducted without hesitation.

muscular endurance Capacity of the muscles to continue activity requiring muscular strength without undue fatigue.

ocular regressions Right-to-left movements of the eye made in a reverse direction during the reading process.

perception Processing and utilizing information.

power Capacity of the muscles to move the entire body or any of its parts with explosive force.

reading eye camera Camera that records on film a detailed analysis of eye movements during the reading process.

reliability Ability of a test to produce the same results when repeated.

rhythm Conscious awareness or control of effort and time.

self-image Psychological concept of how an individual perceives himself as a person; it is his own appraisal of his personal worth and value and involves his body image.

sensory-motor Integrating the senses and movement responses.

space Surroundings of persons and objects.

static balance Balance in which the support is stable and the individual is not in locomotion.

stereognosis Ability to recognize solid objects by their touch.

strabismus Squinting.

synkinetic movements Associated or mirror movements.

tachistoscope Filmstrip projector that can present a series of timed exposures, generally ranging from 1 second to $1/1,000$ second.

time Movement speed (for example, quick, slow, sudden, sustained).

tremor Involuntary rhythmical alternating movements.

validity Degree to which a test measures what it was designed to measure.

APPENDIX
MEDICAL AND
DEVELOPMENTAL HISTORY

Dear Parents:

    To more fully understand and benefit your child in a program of motor therapy, please complete the following medical and developmental history.

    Where applicable, both parents should cooperate in reporting the requested information.

PLEASE PRINT

Child's full name _____ Nickname _____

Address _____ Telephone _____
          (street)   (city)   (zip)

Current date _____ Child's birthdate _____ Child's age _____
                                                             (yr)   (mo)

Grade _____ Name of school _____

Father's name _____ Age _____

Father's occupation _____ Education _____

Mother's name _____ Age _____

Mother's occupation _____ Education _____

Continued.

Brothers' and/or sisters' names and ages _____ , _____ ,

_____ , _____ , _____ ,

_____ , _____ , _____ ,

Indicate the primary reason for referral to the motor therapy program. _____

_____

_____

Referred to program by _____
(name)   (title)

_____
(address and city)   (telephone)

Birth and Health History

1. Full-term pregnancy?   Yes/No   If no, length of time _____

2. Normal pregnancy in every respect?   Yes/No   If no, explain _____

    _____

3. Apgar rating, if known _____

4. Normal birth in every respect?   Yes/No   If no, explain _____

    _____

5. Child's height at birth _____

6. Has child ever had a speech defect or problem with letters or sounds?   Yes/No   If

    yes, explain _____

7. Has child ever had a hearing problem?   Yes/No   If yes, explain _____

    _____

8. Has child ever had an orthopedic problem (condition of the muscle, joint, or bone)?

    If yes, explain _____

    _____

9. Has child ever worn braces or bars?   Yes/No   If yes, explain _____

    _____

10. Has child ever worn corrective shoes?   Yes/No   If yes, explain _____

    _____

11. Has child ever been in a cast for any reason?   Yes/No   If yes, explain _____

_____

12. Has child ever had problems with limbs (arms, hands, legs, feet)?   Yes/No   If yes,

explain _____

_____

13. Was child an active baby?   Yes/No _____

14. Is child active now?   Yes/No _____

15. When fatigued, does child sag?   Yes/No   Become irritable?   Yes/No   Become ex-

cited?   Yes/No

16. Has child been forced to spend long periods convalescing from illness?   Yes/No   If

yes, explain _____

_____

17. Has child ever had convulsions?   Yes/No   If yes, explain _____

_____

18. Has child ever had a very high fever?   Yes/No   If yes, explain _____

_____

19. Has child ever been unconscious?   Yes/No   If yes, explain _____

20. Has child ever been hospitalized?   Yes/No   If yes, explain and give dates _____

_____

21. Has child ever suffered a serious fall?   Yes/No   If yes, explain _____

_____

22. List all illnesses (other than minor colds) and their approximate dates _____

_____

_____

_____

23. Does child have any allergies?   Yes/No   If yes, explain _____

_____

24. Does child have difficulties in sleeping or have any unusual sleep habits? Yes/No

    If yes, explain _____

    _____

25. Is child currently under the care of a physician? Yes/No If yes, explain _____

    _____

26. Is child currently taking medication? Yes/No If yes, explain _____

    _____

27. Does child have a visual problem? Yes/No If yes, explain _____

    _____

28. Does child complain of one or more of the following problems: double vision, itching

    around the eyes, burning eyes, blurred vision, eye fatigue? Yes/No If yes, explain

    _____

    _____

29. Does child appear to have poor coordination? Yes/No If yes, explain _____

    _____

30. Is child careless with personal belongings? Yes/No If yes, explain _____

    _____

31. Is child clumsy or awkward in games? Yes/No If yes, explain _____

    _____

32. Does child get along well with other children of the same age? Yes/No If no,

    explain _____

    _____

33. Does child's coordination compare favorably with children of the same age? Yes/No

    If no, explain _____

    _____

Developmental Events

To the best of your ability, indicate at what age each of the following events occurred.

1. Rolled over   _____

2. Sat up without support   _____

3. Fed self   _____

4. Crawled   _____

5. Stood holding onto furniture   _____

6. Walked unassisted   _____

7. Threw ball   _____

8. Put shoes on (not tied)   _____

9. Pedaled tricycle   _____

10. Buttoned clothes   _____

11. Tied shoes   _____

School Progress

1. Did child attend a preschool program?   Yes/No   If yes, at what age and for how long?

_____

2. Age at entrance to kindergarten _____
                                                          (yr)   (mo)

3. Does child like school?   Yes/No   If no, explain _____

_____

4. Has child ever repeated a grade?   Yes/No   If yes, explain _____

_____

5. Any school difficulties?   Yes/No   If yes, explain _____

_____

6. What is child's weakest subject in school? _____

_____

Continued.

Family Relationships

1. Has there been a separation between parents or between parents and child during the child's lifetime?   Yes/No   If yes, explain _____

   _____

2. Is there a good relationship between father and child?   Yes/No   If no, explain _____

   _____

3. Is there a good relationship between mother and child?   Yes/No   If no, explain _____

   _____

4. Is there a good relationship between brothers and/or sisters?   Yes/No   If no, explain

   _____

   _____

5. Do you believe the family relationship with the child might be improved?   Yes/No   If yes, explain _____

   _____

6. Does any member of the family have problems similar to that of the child?   Yes/No If yes, explain _____

   _____

Child's Personality

1. Has your child ever been given a psychological evaluation?   Yes/No   If yes, indicate when, by whom, and the results _____

   _____

2. Does child revert to bad habits when under stress or pressure (for example, thumb-sucking or nail biting)?   Yes/No   If yes, explain _____

   _____

3. Is child a happy person?   Yes/No   If no, explain _____

   _____

4. Does child have abnormal fears?   Yes/No   If yes, explain _____

_____

5. Have any members of the immediate family required psychological counseling?

Yes/No   If yes, explain _____

_____

ADDITIONAL COMMENTS: _____

_____

_____

_____   _____
Date   Signature of father

                                                           _____
Signature of mother

INDEX